ARISTOTLE:
THE GROWTH AND STRUCTURE
OF HIS THOUGHT

ARISTOTLE:
THE GROWTH AND
STRUCTURE OF
HIS THOUGHT

BY

G. E. R. LLOYD

*Professor of Ancient Philosophy
and Science, and Master of
Darwin College, Cambridge*

CAMBRIDGE
UNIVERSITY PRESS

Published by the Press Syndicate of the University of Cambridge
The Pitt Building, Trumpington Street, Cambridge CB2 IRP
40 West 20th Street, New York, NY 10011–4211, USA
10 Stamford Road, Oakleigh, Melbourne 3166, Australia

© Cambridge University Press 1968

First published 1968
Reprinted 1973 1977 1980 1982 1988 1990 1993

Printed in Great Britain at the
University Press, Cambridge

Library of Congress catalogue card number: 68–21195

ISBN 0 521 07049 x hardback
ISBN 0 521 09456 9 paperback

To

JOHN RAVEN

CONTENTS

PREFACE

This book is intended to help the student to discover and explore Aristotle. Most people would agree that he is not an easy philosopher to approach. His treatises cannot be read for enjoyment purely as literature, as many of Plato's dialogues can, and the man behind the treatises has the reputation of being a dry, uninspiring, even rather inhuman, person. If in the popular view Plato is as much a poet as a philosopher, Aristotle is still generally thought of first and foremost as a dogmatist and systematiser. This account of him, which is largely the product of a tendency to confuse Aristotle with Aristotelianism, is grossly exaggerated. Like Plato, he conceived the business of philosophy to consist as much in the defining of problems, the examining of alternative views, and the exploring of difficulties, as in the propounding of solutions, and his thought, like Plato's again, underwent a gradual evolution, even though this is, in his case, much more difficult to reconstruct owing to the nature of our evidence.

But while Aristotle is neither as unimaginative nor as inflexible as he is sometimes represented, no one can deny that his thought is often opaque. The treatises make slow and difficult reading, although their difficulty arises as much from the complexity and subtlety of their ideas as from the obscurity of Aristotle's expression. Yet however daunting the texts appear, there is no substitute for a close study of Aristotle's own words to grasp his philosophy. The commentator's role is merely to mediate between Aristotle and his twentieth-century reader. Certainly nothing is to be gained from attempting to give him a spurious air of modernity, or from exaggerating the extent to which his ideas are relevant to current philosophical issues. To understand Aristotle one must place his philosophy in the context of the problems and controversies that interested him. But that is not to say that he is to be treated as a figure of purely antiquarian interest or that his thought is to be judged without regard to any philosophical or scientific idea that has been put forward since the fourth century B.C. On the contrary, to appreciate the originality and importance of his work it is essential to bear in mind subsequent developments in each of the fields that he investigated, and these include not only the various branches of philosophy and natural science but also what we should call sociology and even literary criticism.

The aim of the first part of this book is to tell the story of Aristotle's intellectual development in so far as it can be reconstructed, and of the second to present the fundamentals of his thought in the main fields of inquiry in which he was interested. The book is addressed to the beginner and the amateur, not to the experienced Aristotelian scholar. It is intended for the undergraduate who has reached a stage in his classical or philosophical studies when he can defer no longer the task of coming to grips with Aristotle, and for any reader who is interested enough in some aspect of Aristotle's work or influence to want to learn a little more about the philosopher and his thought. I have dealt only with essentials, but the reader should be warned that these involve some serious problems which cannot be ignored or glossed over. Aristotle is a difficult and profound thinker and his philosophy cannot, without distortion, be made to seem easy.

In writing this book my debt to scholars, teachers, friends and colleagues is incalculable. I have not striven for, nor would I claim, great originality in the account of Aristotle that I present. I owe much, first of all, to a long line of distinguished scholars who have written books and commentaries on Aristotle, and particularly to those who have worked, in recent years, on the question of his intellectual development. I have not attempted to acknowledge all such debts, since to have done so would have been to accumulate bibliographical references out of all proportion to the length and aims of the book. On a handful of occasions I have included such references in footnotes to the text to indicate a few of the most recent scholarly works in which important new suggestions and interpretations have been advanced. Then apart from what I owe to published works of scholarship, I have an enduring debt to all my teachers and colleagues in Cambridge. The extent to which my ideas on Aristotle and on Greek philosophy in general have been influenced by formal and informal discussions with them is hard to assess but is certainly very great indeed. Finally it is a duty and a pleasure to mention the help I have received from those who have commented on my work at various stages in its preparation, and particularly from Mr J. E. Raven, Mr J. D. G. Evans, Mr G. H. W. Rylands and Mr P. G. Burbidge. They have all devoted much precious time and trouble to reading and criticising the book in draft. Their cooperation has been a constant encouragement, and their advice has led to innumerable improvements in matters of both style and content. I consider myself particularly fortunate to have had such patient and painstaking critics, and I am happy to record my very special debt of gratitude to them. To Mr Raven, to whom the plan and execution of the work owe most of all, the book is respectfully and gratefully dedicated.

For the 1980 reprint I have brought the 'Suggestions for further reading' (pp. 316–17) up to date.

King's College   G.E.R.L.
Cambridge

ABBREVIATIONS

The abbreviations for the works of Aristotle and Plato that I have used are those in the Liddell–Scott–Jones Lexicon. Thus the main works of Aristotle appear as follows:

APo.	*Analytica Posteriora*	*Int.*	*de Interpretatione*
APr.	*Analytica Priora*	*Metaph.*	*Metaphysica*
Cael.	*de Caelo*	*Mete.*	*Meteorologica*
Cat.	*Categoriae*	*PA*	*de Partibus Animalium*
de An.	*de Anima*	*Ph.*	*Physica*
EE	*Ethica Eudemia*	*Po.*	*Poetica*
EN	*Ethica Nicomachea*	*Pol.*	*Politica*
GA	*de Generatione Animalium*	*Resp.*	*de Respiratione*
		Rh.	*Rhetorica*
GC	*de Generatione et Corruptione*	*SE*	*Sophistici Elenchi*
		Top.	*Topica*
HA	*Historia Animalium*		

Separate books are referred to by the corresponding Roman numerals in all cases except the *Metaphysics*, where the books are referred to by their Greek letters: this is to avoid the confusion caused by two different systems of Roman numeration, in one of which book α is treated as a separate book, while in the other it is not.

PART I

Intellectual Development

CHAPTER I

LIFE AND WRITINGS

Aristotle was born in 384 B.C. at Stagira, a small town in Chalcidice in northern Greece. His father Nicomachus was court physician to Amyntas, King of Macedon. A modern reader may be surprised that it was an otherwise quite undistinguished city-state, and not Athens or one of the other major cultural centres of Greece, that produced Aristotle. But many brilliant Greek philosophers and scientists came from cities which were of secondary economic importance. The atomist Democritus, for instance, came from Abdera, another small town in northern Greece not far from Stagira. Although Aristotle spent more than half his active life in Athens, he never became an Athenian citizen, and his connections with Macedonia were to prove an embarrassment to him, indeed after the death of Alexander the Great a danger to his life.

The fact that Aristotle's father was a medical man is not without importance, since it suggests that Aristotle was introduced to Greek medicine and biology at an early age. Although we have no information concerning the type of medicine that Nicomachus himself practised or professed, two of the most famous of the so-called Hippocratic treatises demonstrate that at least one notable representative of Greek scientific medicine was at work in northern Greece at the end of the fifth century B.C. These are the first and third books of the *Epidemics*, which contain case-histories collected from such places as Thasos and Abdera.

The Academy

In 367, at the age of seventeen, Aristotle was sent to the Academy, where for twenty years he was the pupil of Plato. This first stay in Athens is the first of the three main periods into which Aristotle's intellectual development may be divided. The question of his attitude towards the teaching of his master raises major problems which I shall discuss in due course, but it is certain that Plato was by far the most important formative influence on Aristotle's thought. In spite of the differences in the interests, methods and doctrines of Socrates, Plato and Aristotle, these, the three greatest Greek philosophers, form, as Renford Bambrough has nicely put it, a compact intellectual dynasty.

Plato died in 347 and the question of who should succeed him as head of the Academy arose. There were three possible candidates, Aristotle, Xenocrates and Plato's nephew, Speusippus. We do not know for certain what factors influenced the outcome, nor even whether the decision was Plato's own or one taken by the members of the Academy, but the facts themselves are clear. Speusippus was chosen, and both Aristotle and Xenocrates left Athens. Some scholars have supposed that the principal reason for the rejection of Aristotle was his doctrinal unorthodoxy. But this was evidently not a sufficient cause for his being passed over, since Speusippus too rejected the theory of Ideas in its original Platonic form. If faithfulness to the teaching of the master had been the criterion, we should have expected Xenocrates to have been made head, since he was the most conservative of Plato's three main pupils. One of the chief reasons why the succession passed to Speusippus may have been simply to keep Plato's property in the family, and there may also have been legal difficulties in making over the property of an Athenian citizen to a non-citizen such as Aristotle, although these were overcome when Xenocrates, another non-citizen, eventually succeeded Speusippus to become the third head of the Academy.

When Speusippus was elected, Aristotle's relations with him became so strained—as it is generally thought—that he decided to leave Athens. Here too, however, we lack proof of his motives. There is little reliable early evidence of any hostility between the two men, and we cannot discount the possibility that Aristotle acted in part, at least, for reasons unconnected with his relations with members of the Academy. It has, for example, been suggested that his departure should be linked with the current political situation, since there was an outbreak of anti-Macedonian feeling in Athens after Philip had sacked Olynthus in 348.[1] Nevertheless Aristotle's continued absence from Athens is proof enough that his connections with the Academy meant far less to him, after Plato's death, than the circle of friends who accompanied him on his travels, the chief of whom was his pupil, colleague and eventual successor as head of the Lyceum, Theophrastus of Eresus.

[1] This has been suggested by Ingemar Düring who has assembled the evidence concerning Aristotle's life in *Aristotle in the Ancient Biographical Tradition*, Acta Universitatis Gothoburgensis LXIII, 2, Göteborg, 1957.

Travels

When Aristotle left Athens he went first to Assos in Asia Minor at the invitation of Hermias, the ruler of Atarneus, who had on previous occasions befriended two other pupils of Plato, Erastus and Coriscus. This begins the second main period of Aristotle's philosophical activity, the so-called period of the travels, which he spent in various centres in Asia Minor and Macedonia and which was, as we shall see later, especially important for the development of his interests in natural science. He remained on excellent terms with Hermias and he eventually married Pythias who is variously described as Hermias' niece, his adopted daughter or his sister. But after three years at Assos he moved to Lesbos, and then another two years later, in 342, he accepted the invitation of Philip of Macedon to become tutor to the fourteen-year-old Alexander.

The idea of the greatest philosopher of the day instructing the boy who was to become the greatest general the Greeks ever produced is one that may fire the imagination. Yet the influence that Aristotle had on Alexander, either as his tutor or afterwards, was negligible. During his second period at Athens Aristotle enjoyed considerable Macedonian support, and this may well have included not merely political backing, but also assistance in, for example, the organisation of his biological researches. It is, however, hard to credit the suggestion that is sometimes made that Alexander collected and dispatched to Aristotle specimens of rare animals from Persia and India. Aristotle's nephew

Callisthenes certainly accompanied Alexander to Persia in the role of historian, but he was put to death on a charge of treason in 327, and this must have embittered the relations between Aristotle and his ex-pupil. On the rare occasions when Aristotle mentions authorities by name in the biological treatises, he usually refers to an earlier generation of travellers to the East, and especially to Ctesias, the Greek physician who attended Artaxerxes. And if specimens were sent back to Athens from India, one may assume that Aristotle's successors in the Lyceum benefited from this more than Aristotle himself, since he died within six years of Alexander's first penetration of the valley of the Indus. But in matters of political ideology a gulf separated the two men. Aristotle shows no awareness of the fundamental changes that Alexander's conquests were bringing about in the Greek world, and he would undoubtedly have considered any political development that led to a decline in the importance of the city-state as a change for the worse. If he knew of Alexander's policy of forging links between the Greek and the non-Greek peoples of his empire, he would certainly have regretted and opposed it.

The return to Athens

Aristotle remained in Macedonia until 335, the year when Alexander succeeded Philip. In that year he returned to Athens, but not to the Academy, where Xenocrates had by now succeeded Speusippus as head, but to teach on his own account in the Lyceum. The Lyceum itself was a grove just outside Athens frequented by other teachers—

Plato mentions it as one of Socrates' haunts—but the name came to be applied to Aristotle's school in particular. It was probably only after Aristotle's death, under Theophrastus, that the school acquired extensive property and had, like the Academy, the legal status of a θίασος or religious association. But however informal the school may have been under Aristotle, it was most important to him, since it enabled him to coordinate the work of a number of philosophers and scientists and to initiate an unprecedentedly ambitious programme of research in many different fields of inquiry. From 335 to 323 is the third and final main period of his philosophical activity, referred to as the period of the Lyceum or the second Athenian period. But when in 323 news of Alexander's death reached Athens, this sparked off an anti-Macedonian revolution and a charge of impiety was trumped up against Aristotle. Not waiting for a trial, he withdrew to Chalcis in Euboea, 'to save the Athenians', as our reports have it, 'from sinning twice against philosophy'. There he died the next year at the age of sixty-two.

We have little reliable information from which to try to reconstruct what sort of a man Aristotle was, but one valuable document has been preserved by Diogenes Laertius, his will. When his wife Pythias, who bore him a daughter, died, Aristotle lived with a woman named Herpyllis, and it was Herpyllis who according to our sources bore him his son Nicomachus. In his will we find Aristotle making provision for his family and household, for Herpyllis herself, of whom he speaks with gratitude

8

and affection, for his two children and for his slaves, to several of whom he promises freedom either immediately on his death or on his daughter's marriage. And he directs that his own bones be placed with those of Pythias, according to Pythias' instructions. The will shows Aristotle responsible, well-to-do, kindly and liberal, according to the standards of his day. Our other sources add little to this picture, but provide such snippets of information as that he lisped and dressed elegantly.

Writings

Aristotle's writings fall into two main groups, the treatises, which form by far the greater proportion of his extant work, and the literary or 'exoteric' works, which have survived only in the form of 'fragments', that is quotations preserved by other authors. The distinction between these two types of work is one to which Aristotle himself refers on several occasions in the treatises. In the *Nicomachean Ethics* (1102a18–28) for example, having pointed out that the student of human society needs to study the soul, he says that there is an adequate account of this subject in his 'exoteric' works. In this case he is referring principally to the dialogue known as the *Eudemus* or *On the Soul*.

The significance of this distinction between two main types of writing has been very variously interpreted. One suggestion that was already current in antiquity was that the treatises express the closely guarded true doctrines of Aristotle, while the literary works contain falsehoods for general consumption. But this is inconsistent with

Aristotle's own use of his 'exoteric' discussion of the soul in the passage of the *Nicomachean Ethics* that has just been mentioned. There the distinction is not one between a true and a false doctrine of the soul, but rather one between a specialised and a non-specialised treatment of the subject. 'The student of society', Aristotle says, 'must study the soul, but do so with his own subject in view, and only to the extent that his own inquiry demands. For to strive after greater exactness is more laborious, perhaps, than is necessary for our present purposes.'

Literary works

In most cases the 'exoteric' works differ from the treatises chiefly in being non-technical compositions written for wide dissemination. The force of the word 'exoteric' itself may be that they were more readily available to the general public outside the immediate circle of Aristotle's pupils. Many of these literary works were dialogues, some of them modelled on the dialogues of Plato, and their style was highly praised in antiquity. When Cicero, Quintilian and other ancient literary critics speak of the 'golden stream' of Aristotle's oratory, or of the 'grace' or 'sweetness' of his eloquence, they no doubt had the dialogues primarily in mind: such terms are certainly inappropriate to the treatises. But the importance of these literary works for us lies not in their aesthetic qualities, but in the insight they afford into Aristotle's intellectual development. Here, however, we enter difficult ground.

Some of the literary works appear to have been written

in Aristotle's youth while he was still very much under the influence of Plato. But the problems involved in using these works as evidence for the philosophical views that Aristotle held as a young man are considerable. To begin with, we have to establish what he wrote. In some cases we have what seem to be reasonably accurate quotations, but often our source is not a work that explicitly quotes Aristotle, so much as one that was written in imitation of him. In tackling a commonplace theme ancient authors frequently took models from earlier literature and followed them in a way we should regard as downright plagiarism. But even while most scholars accept that Iamblichus' *Protrepticus*, for example, is largely derived from Aristotle's lost work of the same name, there is still plenty of room for disagreement about whether any given passage in Iamblichus corresponds to one in his Aristotelian original.

Our second difficulty concerns the context of the fragments that have been preserved. With those of the lost literary works that are known to have been dialogues we are faced with the awkward, indeed in many cases unanswerable, question of who the speaker expounding any particular view may have been. Does the quotation represent Aristotle's own ideas, or views that were put forward at one point in the dialogue only to be challenged and refuted at some later stage in the work? The dangers of misinterpretation are obvious if one reflects how difficult it would be to gain an accurate picture of Plato's thought in the *Phaedo* or the *Republic* if those works had survived only in fragments.

Thirdly, the major problem that confronts any attempt to reconstruct Aristotle's intellectual development arises from the lack of reliable evidence by which to date the composition of different parts of his work. The treatises contain many cross-references to one another and to the 'exoteric' works. But these cross-references must be used with great caution as a guide to the relative dates of different works. The system as a whole contains inconsistencies, and in many cases, particularly where the passage containing the reference does not form an integral part of the argument, there is a distinct possibility that the cross-reference is an after-thought added either by Aristotle himself, or even by someone else, long after the bulk of the work in which it is embedded was written. Each such passage must, then, be considered on its own merits. But where the concrete evidence is insubstantial, the danger of arguing in a circle is increased. To take a crude example, if we believe that Aristotle's development can be represented as a steady progression away from 'Platonism', we naturally tend to think of different works as 'early', 'middle', or 'late' according to the amount of 'Platonism' they appear to contain. But it is then all too easy to assume this classification as a datum and to cite passages in the works thus classified as proof of the particular interpretation of Aristotle's development that we favour. This is admittedly an extreme case, but it serves to illustrate a common hazard in the discussion of the development of Aristotle's thought.

The literary works provide some valuable evidence on the difficult problem of Aristotle's early intellectual development, and I shall be discussing the relevant conclusions in my next chapter. But otherwise these works are only of minor interest and importance. Our chief source for Aristotle's ideas on each of the many subjects which engaged his attention is the collection of treatises that form the Aristotelian Corpus. Certain comments should now be made about the arrangement of the treatises in the Corpus itself, their authenticity and their style.

Treatises

We owe both the arrangement of the treatises and the text itself to the first editor of Aristotle, Andronicus of Rhodes. How he came by the manuscripts of the treatises is the subject of an astonishing, indeed barely credible, story. According to this, Aristotle's library passed, at his death, first to Theophrastus and then to Neleus of Scepsis. Neleus' heirs were apparently not interested themselves in the contents of the books, but to prevent them from being confiscated for the library of the Kings of Pergamum they hid them in a cellar in Scepsis. From there they were eventually recovered in a much damaged condition by a bibliophile named Apellicon, who brought them back to Athens. When Athens was conquered by Sulla in 86 B.C., he appropriated the books and sent them to Rome where, however, they suffered further maltreatment at the hands of copyists until Andronicus was put in charge of editing and publishing them in the second half of the first century B.C.

This story would imply that Aristotle's treatises were quite unknown from the beginning of the third to the middle of the first century B.C., but this is fairly clearly an exaggeration. It is hard to believe that the books that found their way to Scepsis represented the entire stock of his works in the Lyceum. Moreover a fragment of a letter of Epicurus that has been preserved refers to the *Analytics* and to certain unspecified physical works of Aristotle, and this shows that knowledge of the treatises was not confined to the school itself. Even so, Aristotle was generally known from his dialogues rather than from the treatises until after Andronicus had produced his great edition. Whether or not that edition incorporated newly rediscovered manuscripts, it certainly stimulated a rediscovery of Aristotle, and it formed the basis for all subsequent editions. Furthermore the traditional arrangement of the text, the divisions between books and the grouping of books into treatises, all ultimately derive from Andronicus, although in many cases this arrangement is supported by indications embedded in the text itself. Thus the rather heterogeneous collection of books which we know as the *Metaphysics* owes its title to its original position in Andronicus' edition. As the literal meaning of their Greek name indicates, this was simply the group of books that came after the physical works, and Aristotle's own general term for the subject-matter of most of these books is 'first philosophy'.

The two questions of authenticity and style are linked. Unlike the literary works, the treatises were not composed for publication as they stand, at least not for general publication. Some few passages excepted, they have no pretensions to literary polish. Their style is economical, sometimes to the point of obscurity. At times the text seems to contain little more than a series of headings jotted down for discussion or further development. The course of the argument is often interrupted by digressions as points arising from difficulties or possible objections are followed up, and there are many repetitions, the same problem being tackled from similar or slightly different angles on several occasions.

The suggestion that the treatises represent, for the most part, notes relating to the lecture courses that Aristotle gave in the Lyceum is plausible enough. Most scholars believe that they are the notes that Aristotle himself composed as the basis for his lectures, though the more sceptical would maintain that they are the work of a careful pupil who attended those courses. Granted that the issue cannot be settled for certain, the opinion that they are second-hand productions seems extremely unlikely in view of the unity and coherence of thought they exhibit. Nevertheless the way in which the treatises were composed allowed corrections and after-thoughts to be inserted, and some of these additions may well not be the work of Aristotle himself.

A second problem arises regarding the authenticity of whole books or groups of books. Here the attitude of scholars has changed a good deal since it has become accepted that Aristotle's thought is not a single dogmatic system but underwent a gradual evolution. When, for example, the first main collection of the fragments of the 'exoteric' works was made, the editor, Valentin Rose, considered those works spurious largely on the grounds that the doctrines they contained failed to tally exactly with what is found in the treatises. Similarly scholars no longer generally assume that such works as the *Categories* and the *Eudemian Ethics* should be treated as spurious, although there remain disagreements about whether they are more likely to be 'early' or 'late' productions. Nevertheless the Aristotelian Corpus undoubtedly contains certain works which were not written by Aristotle himself. One example is the treatise entitled *On Mechanics*, though in this and several other similar cases the author was probably a member of the Lyceum and a pupil of Aristotle. Another example is the collection of books of *Problems*, for although we know from references in other treatises that Aristotle wrote a work with that title, those references generally fail to correspond with any passage in the work that has come down to us under that name. It is more difficult to settle the claims of the fourth book of the *Meteorologica* and of large parts of the *Historia Animalium*: while book X can be confidently rejected, VII–IX are doubtfully authentic and extensive passages elsewhere in the treatise are suspect. Yet even if such books were not necessarily composed by Aristotle himself, they set out the results of programmes of research which he initiated, and on points of doctrine their position is in general fairly close to that which we find adopted in the more certainly authentic treatises. Similarly he is unlikely to have composed the whole of the collection of constitutional histories, of which there were 158 in all, although our sole surviving example, the *Constitution of Athens*, may well be authentic in the main. With Aristotle, as with most ancient authors, the scholar and the specialist must be on the lookout for corruptions and interpolations in the text. But the general reader may be assured that the great majority of what he finds in the main treatises of the Aristotelian Corpus is a faithful representation of Aristotle's thought.

Some of the negative qualities of the style of the treatises, such as the lack of literary polish, and the obscurity that sometimes arises from too great an economy of expression, have been mentioned. But the positive merits of that style should also be noted, especially as the treatises have often suffered unfavourably, and to some extent unjustly, from a direct comparison with the dialogues of Plato. Although there are faults such as over-compression, Aristotle's writing is often remarkably lucid and concise. There are few literary periods. But literary periods are, after all, quite out of place in the discussion of complex technical scientific and philosophical questions. The treatises reveal the philosopher at work, defining the problem he is to deal with, assessing the views of his predecessors, formulating his own preliminary opinion, considering whether this needs modifying in the light of difficulties and objections, rehearsing the arguments for different points of view, always searching, in short, for the most adequate solution or resolution of his problem. Obviously the style of the treatises would have been aesthetically more satisfying had some of the digressions and repetitions been cut out and other minor literary blemishes removed, but the reader who becomes well acquainted with these works is generally won round to the view that their style admirably fits their subject-matter and their purpose, their subject-matter being the major issues in the philosophy and science of Aristotle's day, and their purpose being not merely to propound theories, but to investigate and explore the issues fully.

CHAPTER 2

THE PUPIL OF PLATO

Until comparatively recently Aristotelian studies were dominated by the assumption that the doctrines the Corpus contains form a single perfected system. In this, as in many other respects, Aristotle was sharply contrasted with Plato. While Plato's thought was generally recognised—from the early nineteenth century, at any rate—as a complex entity that evolved throughout his life, Aristotle's philosophy was thought of as quite the opposite, a static, dogmatic, monolithic whole. When discrepancies were noted between the doctrines expressed in two different passages in the treatises, the tendency was to assume that one or other passage was corrupt and to emend the text accordingly. So long as Aristotle was treated, as he was throughout the Middle Ages, as a preeminent, if not infallible, authority on most philosophical issues, the possibility that this authority ever changed his mind was not seriously entertained. But even when a more critical attitude towards Aristotle became the rule, it was still generally assumed that his philosophy formed an unvarying dogmatic system, and this assumption was not challenged until well into the present century.

Jaeger's thesis

The major force in what may, without exaggeration, be called the revolution in Aristotelian studies was Werner

Jaeger. In 1912 Jaeger produced a study of the development of the *Metaphysics*, and then in 1923 appeared the first edition of his general work, *Aristotle: Fundamentals of the history of his development*. In this he argued that Aristotle's philosophy is not a 'static system of conceptions', but underwent a continual process of development which can be traced through the extant dialogues and treatises. Where the dialogues, in particular, appeared to express a different point of view from that which is put forward in the treatises, he did not simply dismiss the former as forgeries, as Rose had done, but attempted to fit the evidence they provided into the general pattern of Aristotle's development.

In very broad outline Jaeger suggested that Aristotle's philosophical evolution can be divided into three main stages, corresponding roughly to the three main periods in his life, the first Athenian period, the period of the travels, and the second Athenian period. There is a strong presumption that when Aristotle first entered the Academy he adhered for some time to the main doctrines of his master, Plato. But Jaeger claimed to find positive evidence of a Platonic period in Aristotle's career in such works as the *Eudemus* and the *Protrepticus*. As for Aristotle's departure from Athens on Plato's death, Jaeger described this as 'the expression of a crisis in his inner life'. 'The departure of Aristotle and Xenocrates', he wrote, 'was a secession. They went to Asia Minor in the conviction that Speusippus had inherited merely the office and not the spirit.' He held that it was during the period of the travels that Aristotle broke away from the philosophy of Plato and developed the central doctrines of his own metaphysics such as the theory of the four causes and the doctrine of substance.

But Jaeger believed that a second major change in interest or emphasis occurred after Aristotle had returned to Athens and had begun teaching in the Lyceum. Whereas both the first and the second periods of Aristotle's philosophical development were, he believed, marked by a preoccupation with metaphysical and epistemological problems, the third was principally devoted to what he called 'the organisation of research'. He assigned to the Lyceum period such works as the biological treatises and the collection of constitutional histories, productions which he described as representing 'a scientific type of exact research into the real world that was something absolutely new and pioneer in the Greek world of the time'. Broadly speaking, then, he represented Aristotle's development as one of *declining Platonism* and *growing empiricism*. Speaking of the collection of constitutions, for example, he put it that 'with this colossal compilation... Aristotle reached his point of greatest distance from the philosophy of Plato'. He not only drew a general distinction between the two strains of 'bold speculation' and 'extensive empirical investigation' in Aristotle's work, but also insisted that these two correspond, in the main, to different periods in Aristotle's life.

Jaeger's book stimulated a series of individual studies in which each of the main branches of Aristotle's thought, logic, metaphysics and theology, physics, psychology, biology, ethics and politics, was examined from the genetic or evolutionary point of view.[1] Both parts of his main thesis concerning Aristotle's development have been challenged and criticised. First on the question of Aristotle's disengaging himself from 'Platonism', the influence of Plato is apparent in several important doctrines which Aristotle seems to have neither abandoned nor modified. He held that a part of the soul, at least, is immortal, a doctrine which he shares not only with Plato but with many other Greek philosophers, and there is no evidence that he ever abandoned this belief even though it produces a discontinuity in his account of the soul. His doctrine of form is a second example where Platonic influences were never totally eliminated. Whereas in the sublunary region he insisted, against Plato, that form is inseparable from matter, he allowed exceptions to this rule in the celestial sphere where pure forms can and do exist, and we have no reason to doubt that he continued to hold this doctrine to the end of his life.

Secondly, parts of Jaeger's thesis concerning Aristotle's increasing empiricism also encountered objections. He

[1] Two of the more important earlier studies were H. D. P. Lee's article, 'Place-names and the date of Aristotle's biological works', *Classical Quarterly* XLII, 1948, pp. 61–7, and F. Nuyens' book, *L'Evolution de la psychologie d'Aristote* (trans. A. Mansion), Louvain, 1948. Marjorie Grene's *A Portrait of Aristotle*, London, 1963, contains a lively discussion of the problems facing developmental studies, and in the same year there appeared two articles taking stock of the progress of scholarship on the question: A.-H. Chroust's 'The first thirty years of modern Aristotelian scholarship', *Classica et Mediaevalia* XXIV, 1963, pp. 27–57, and F. Dirlmeier's 'Zum gegenwärtigen Stand der Aristoteles-Forschung', *Wiener Studien* LXXVI, 1963, pp. 52–67. These and I. Düring's *Aristoteles: Darstellung und Interpretation seines Denkens*, Heidelberg, 1966, contain extensive bibliographical references on the subject.

originally suggested that all the main biological works belong to the period of the Lyceum, the period of the 'organisation of research'. But H. D. P. Lee, developing a suggestion made by D'Arcy Thompson, pointed out that a high proportion of the place-names mentioned in the *Historia Animalium* relate to areas of Greece such as the Troad, Lesbos and Macedonia, which Aristotle is known to have frequented during the period of the travels. This does not mean to say that the *Historia Animalium* was already composed by the time he returned to Athens in 335. Indeed this is clearly not true of the treatise as a whole as we have it, since it contains a wealth of information accumulated over a long period of time and it includes extensive additions by other hands. Nevertheless the place-names do suggest that the research that formed the basis of the original treatise was begun in the period of the travels.

A final, more general, objection to Jaeger's interpretation is that his contrast between dogmatism and empiricism, or between metaphysics and research, is oversimplified. Scientific research is not conducted at random, but always in the light of certain more or less explicit theories or assumptions, and Aristotle is no exception. It is not too difficult to trace the influence of certain preconceived ideas on his empirical investigations both in the natural and in the social sciences. The organisation of research undoubtedly gathered momentum in the last period of Aristotle's life, and it was carried on and extended, after his death, by his successors in the Lyceum. But it is not necessary, and indeed it is quite implausible, to argue that his extensive empirical investigations entirely ousted his interest in theoretical problems in metaphysics and epistemology.

Although Jaeger's thesis is open to serious doubts, even his most severe critics have acknowledged their debt to him as the pioneer who led the way to a new appreciation of Aristotle's philosophy as something that gradually evolved. Despite the number of developmental studies that have been carried out the complex task of reassessing Aristotle has still only just begun, and so far other scholars have hardly been much more successful than Jaeger was in gaining acceptance for their interpretations of the way Aristotle's thought developed. The methodological problems involved in discussing this question are formidable. I have already mentioned one danger, that of arguing in a circle and of citing as evidence to confirm a particular thesis texts whose relative chronology has not been established on independent grounds. Moreover there is no compelling reason to assign two passages to two different periods of Aristotle's philosophical development unless the doctrines they contain are strictly incompatible, and this is very rarely the case. Often two theories that seem at first sight contradictory can be reconciled with one another when due allowances are made for the different points of view from which a complex problem may be tackled. To mention one example, Nuyens suggested that those passages that refer to the heart as the seat of certain vital functions represent a different stage in the development of Aristotle's psychology from the doctrine of the soul as 'the first actuality of the natural organic body'.

But here, as other scholars such as Block and Hardie have shown, there is no good reason why Aristotle could not have held both doctrines simultaneously, and indeed there are passages in the psychological treatises that strongly suggest that he did so, which would indicate that whatever we may think of the relationship between the two doctrines in question, Aristotle himself was unaware of any incompatibility between them.[1]

In view of the complexities of the problem it is hardly surprising that scholars now tend to be much less ambitious in their claims than Jaeger and some of his immediate successors. Furthermore it has recently been emphasised that chronological studies—the examination of the relative dates of composition of the dialogues and treatises—cannot and should not be expected to provide answers to questions concerning the predominant characteristics or preoccupations of Aristotle's philosophy. Many conflicting opinions have been expressed on this topic. One view has it that Aristotle is first and foremost a logician, whose work in biology and in other fields should be interpreted in the light of his logical theory. Another presents him as primarily a naturalist, whose metaphysics, logic and ethics all reflect, or indeed are based on, his biological interests and experience. This is an issue of the utmost importance. But as Marjorie Grene, for one, has

[1] Nuyens' book has been referred to above (p. 22, note). The other studies mentioned in this paragraph are I. Block's 'The order of Aristotle's psychological writings', *American Journal of Philology* LXXXII, 1961, pp. 50–77, and W. F. R. Hardie's 'Aristotle's treatment of the relation between the soul and the body', *Philosophical Quarterly* XIV, 1964, pp. 53–72.

rightly insisted, when we try to determine the fundamental ideas and interests in Aristotle's philosophy, the factors we must consider are not the relative chronology of the treatises in different fields, but the logical structure and interrelations of different aspects of his thought. The question is a philosophical one which would remain open even if we had precise information concerning the relative and absolute dates of composition of his various works.

I shall return to the major philosophical issue in my final chapter. But meanwhile our concern is with the historical question, the story of the formation of Aristotle's thought. How far has our understanding of this advanced since Jaeger? At first sight the progress that has been made seems distinctly disappointing when measured either against the effort expended on developmental studies or against the hopes that Jaeger's initial investigation raised. Although many detailed analyses have been undertaken, their authors have often differed sharply in the conclusions they have reached. Indeed so widespread have been the disagreements of scholars working on the problem that there has been, in recent years, a definite reaction against the tendency to try to explain the apparent discrepancies between different passages in Aristotle's writings by assigning them to different periods in his life. Yet this reaction, salutary though it is, should not obscure the positive results that have been achieved. First considerable progress has been made towards determining the relative order of books dealing with a single subject or set of problems. And secondly a good deal of the general picture of the growth of Aristotle's thought has become reasonably clear.

Under the first heading I may mention two examples. It is now generally held that the *Topics* represents an earlier stage in the development of Aristotle's logical theory than the *Prior* or the *Posterior Analytics*. One consideration that leads to this conclusion is that the theory of the syllogism is ignored in the *Topics*, and it appears to have been developed after that work, or at least the greater part of it, had been written. Here subsequent work has tended to confirm and elaborate one of Jaeger's suggestions. In my other example, however, Jaeger's conclusions have been modified. Of the works that deal with the problem of motion it now seems likely that the bulk of the *de Caelo* was composed before he had formulated the doctrine of the unmoved mover which is established in *Physics* VIII. Furthermore the *de Caelo* itself may, in the doctrine of aither, mark an advance on a still earlier position. In one of the fragments which probably comes from the lost work *On Philosophy* Aristotle is reported as denying both that the motion of the stars is enforced and also that it is natural, concluding that it is voluntary—they move because they are alive and have wills of their own—and this seems to reflect a stage in his thinking on this topic before he had arrived at the notion of a fifth element which moves naturally in a circle.

But we are less concerned here with matters of comparative detail than with the question of the overall interpretation of Aristotle's intellectual development. On this problem positive results are much more difficult to achieve, since they depend on establishing interrelations between his work in different fields. Certainly it now seems unlikely that the whole of his work in any one field, say ethics or logic or biology, is the product of one particular period in his life. The picture that emerges is, as we shall see, a complex one, of Aristotle's interests developing simultaneously over a wide range of topics. Any account of his general development must, however, begin with the question of his early relation to Plato.

On several occasions in the *Metaphysics* and elsewhere Aristotle uses the first person plural 'we' in referring to the Platonists, evidently including himself in the group even when criticising its doctrines. But Jaeger argued that there is concrete evidence in the dialogues of a Platonic period in Aristotle's career, and it is now time to examine this part of his thesis in detail. First it must be repeated that there is a strong presumption that, when Aristotle arrived in the Academy at the age of seventeen, he adhered for some time to the doctrines of his master. But how far do the dialogues provide evidence of a period in Aristotle's life when he was an orthodox Platonist? Did he, for example, maintain the Platonic theory of Forms or a Platonic doctrine of soul? How far had he already begun to react against Plato even in his early literary works?

The 'Eudemus'

The answers to these questions depend on a detailed analysis of the extant remains of two works, the *Eudemus* and the *Protrepticus*, particularly.[1] First the circumstances

[1] The literature dealing with the problems posed by these works is very extensive. Among the most useful recent discussions in English are O. Gigon's 'Prolegomena to an edition of the *Eudemus*', in *Aristotle and Plato in the mid-fourth century*, edited by I. Düring and

28

in which the *Eudemus* was composed have an important
bearing on its contents. We are told that Aristotle wrote
it for his friend Eudemus after the latter's death. The central themes of the dialogue are that the soul is immortal
and that the dead have a superior existence to the living.
The idea that 'it were best for men not to have been born
at all...but, once born, the next best thing is to die as soon
as possible' is a common topic of early Greek literature.
But three features of Aristotle's treatment of his subject
have particular philosophical significance. First the *Eudemus*, like the *Phaedo*, contained a series of arguments to
establish the doctrine of the immortality of the soul, and,
like the *Phaedo* again, it set out to refute the view that the
soul is an 'attunement' or 'harmony', a doctrine which
if it were correct would tell against the soul's being immortal. Secondly, Aristotle apparently argued that the
soul is in its true and natural state when it is separated from
the body, not when it is united with the body. Cicero
(Fr. 1, Ross) reports a story which implies that Aristotle
concurred in the view that when a man dies his soul returns to its true home, and a passage in Proclus (Fr. 5)
suggests that he compared the soul's existence without the

G. E. L. Owen, Göteborg, 1960, pp. 19–33, I. Düring's *Aristotle's
Protrepticus, an attempt at reconstruction*, Göteborg, 1961, and A.-H.
Chroust's '*Eudemus* or on the Soul: a lost dialogue of Aristotle on
the immortality of the soul', *Mnemosyne* 4th ser. XIX, 1966, pp. 17–30.
The discussion between C. de Vogel and Düring on the question
'Did Aristotle ever accept Plato's Theory of Transcendent Ideas' in
consecutive numbers of *Archiv für Geschichte der Philosophie* XLVII,
1965, pp. 261–98 and XLVIII, 1966, pp. 312–16, illustrates the extent
of disagreement that still exists on this issue. The most recent study
that is devoted to the exoteric writings as a whole is E. Berti, *La
Filosofia del primo Aristotele*, Padova, 1962.

body to health, and its life in the body to disease. Thirdly, two of our sources suggest that the soul has certain visions in its disembodied state. Unfortunately they are both very vague about the nature of those visions and their objects. Proclus (Fr. 5) mentions the idea in his commentary on Plato's *Republic*, and the visions in the passage in Plato that he is discussing, the myth of Er, are simply of the underworld. But our other admittedly much later source, the Arabic philosopher al-Kindi, speaks of the disembodied soul contemplating 'souls, forms and angels' (Fr. 11), and this suggests that whatever the visions referred to in the *Eudemus* owed to the myth of Er, they also derived something from other myths such as that of the *Phaedrus*, where what the soul sees is not the conventional apparatus of underworld mythology, but the true reality, that is, for Plato, the transcendental Forms.

The *Eudemus* is a consolation, not a systematic analysis of the nature of the soul, let alone of the problem of knowledge. The fragments we possess do not commit Aristotle to any definite ontological or epistemological doctrine: indeed, in view of the subject of the dialogue, it is doubtful whether any such doctrine was clearly stated in it. Our evidence does, however, suggest two rather striking conclusions about the contents of the *Eudemus*. First Aristotle advanced a doctrine of the soul existing naturally outside the body, which, as we shall see, contrasts strangely with the account of the soul presented in the treatises. And secondly the dialogue included a passage speaking particularly of the visions that the soul has when it leaves the body. This is another idea that cannot be paralleled in the treatises and it was evidently modelled on the eschatological myths in which Plato described the travels of the soul and the visions it has in its disembodied state. What we cannot say with any confidence, however, is how closely Aristotle may have followed any specific Platonic model: nor is it clear what weight should be attached to a passage which was obviously mythological in content. Our final remark is, then, a negative one: if we look for an explicit statement that the objects of knowledge are transcendental (Platonic) Forms, none is forthcoming in the extant fragments of the *Eudemus*.

Some of the reports relating to the *Eudemus* indicate that Aristotle's conception of the soul in that dialogue had much in common with Plato's. But one testimony may be taken to suggest that he already differed from Plato on this topic in certain respects. This is fragment 8, a passage in Simplicius' commentary on the *de Anima* in which he tells us, among other things, that 'in the *Eudemus* also' Aristotle declared the soul to be a 'form' and praised those who describe the soul as receptive of forms. The second sentence presents little difficulty, for Plato, among others, must surely be intended. In Plato, the soul is that which apprehends or grasps the Forms. Furthermore Aristotle himself continued to believe that the soul is 'receptive of forms', although in the passages in the *de Anima* which express this doctrine the 'forms' in question are not transcendental Platonic absolutes, but Aristotle's own 'perceptible' and 'intelligible' forms.

But the surprising feature of Simplicius' report is that

he says that in the *Eudemus* the soul was said to be 'a form'. Simplicius himself evidently believed that the doctrine of the *Eudemus* to which he refers is similar to that which is expressed in the passage in the *de Anima* on which he is commenting, since he says 'in the *Eudemus* also...he declares the soul to be a form'. And there are indeed several passages in both the psychological and the biological treatises where soul is contrasted to body as form to matter, although the technical definition of soul in Aristotle's developed doctrine is the 'first actuality' of the natural organic body. But assuming for the moment that Simplicius is correct, it is difficult to see how in the *Eudemus* Aristotle could have held at one and the same time both the doctrine that the soul is the form of the body in the Aristotelian sense of the term form, and the doctrine reported by Proclus that in its true and natural state the soul is separate from the body—and that when it is incorporated in the body it is, as it were, diseased. However it does not solve our problem to argue that Simplicius has simply misunderstood the meaning of the term 'form' as Aristotle used it in the *Eudemus*, and that it must have had a Platonic sense in the passage in question. Plato himself nowhere identified the soul as a transcendental Form, and indeed such a doctrine would be impossible to reconcile with the theory of Forms expressed in his dialogues. Our interpretation runs into difficulties, then, whichever sense we give to the term 'form': but on neither view is the doctrine reported by Simplicius a Platonic one. Whichever of the two rather unsatisfactory interpretations we prefer, it is clear that if Simplicius' report has any substance at all, Aristotle had already begun in the *Eudemus* to modify the teachings of Plato on the soul.

The 'Protrepticus'

The evidence from the *Protrepticus* points to a similar general conclusion. This work was an exhortation to study philosophy, but there are considerable difficulties in assessing its contents since we mainly depend not on direct quotations, but on passages in the *Protrepticus* of Iamblichus, which is generally held to have been largely modelled on Aristotle's work. First, however, it seems clear that as in the *Eudemus*, so also in the *Protrepticus*, Aristotle argued that the soul's existence in the body is unnatural and a penance. As suits the main theme of the work, great emphasis was laid on contemplation as the highest activity of man and on the attainment of knowledge and wisdom as his foremost goal. But the most interesting question that the evidence for the *Protrepticus* poses concerns the nature and objects of that knowledge. In one of the passages in Iamblichus (Fr. 11, Ross) which is thought to follow Aristotle fairly closely, the question is asked 'whether the object of this knowledge is the world, or something whose nature is different', but the question is raised at that point only to be deferred. Most of the terms used to describe the objects of the knowledge that the philosopher should try to attain are ambiguous. One of our texts (Iamblichus again, Fr. 10a) refers to the philosopher 'who has a sight of things eternal', but this might mean either the contemplation of eternal truths or merely the study of the eternal heavenly bodies, although admittedly the former sense is the more likely one. And elsewhere the objects of the philosopher's study are described simply as 'reality' or 'the truth'.

But one testimony does give us rather more to go on. This is the passage in Iamblichus (*Protr.* ch. 10, 54, 10 ff., Fr. 13) where it is argued that theoretical insight has practical advantages. First it is suggested that doctors, trainers and statesmen alike need 'experience of nature' to be good at their particular tasks, although the phrase 'experience of nature' is highly ambiguous, as the subsequent argument reveals. Craftsmen, it is claimed, have derived their best tools from 'nature', and this is explained by saying that such instruments as the ruler are derived from such natural phenomena as rays of light, and it is by reference to these instruments that we test what may seem to our senses to be sufficiently straight or smooth. But then the statesman too is said to need certain standards, ὅροι, by reference to which he will judge what is just or good or expedient, and these standards also are said to be derived from 'nature herself and the truth'. The law that most conforms to 'nature' is the best law. To be in a position to propose such laws the statesman must study philosophy.

However, having suggested this point of similarity between craftsmen and statesmen, that both get their 'standards' from 'nature', the argument goes on to draw a distinction between them, by considering the kind of 'imitation' they each practise. Craftsmen are said to derive both their tools and their most exact calculations not from 'the originals' or 'what is primary', αὐτὰ τὰ πρῶτα, but from copies at a first, second or further remove. The philosopher alone copies from 'those things that are exact themselves', ἀπ' αὐτῶν τῶν ἀκριβῶν. He alone 'contemplates them and not their imitations'. Just as a builder should use a ruler rather than an already existing building as his standard for straightness, so the philosopher-statesman cannot expect to create good laws if he uses as his standard the existing laws of some state, for an imitation of what is itself neither divine nor stable cannot be stable either. The philosopher alone, however, can achieve stable rules because 'he alone lives his life contemplating nature and the divine'.

It must be repeated that we do not know how far this whole passage reproduces Aristotle. Moreover the argument is admittedly confused and difficult to interpret. First the sense of the term 'nature' fluctuates. When the craftsman is said to derive his tools from 'nature', it stands for certain physical phenomena. But when the statesman is recommended to take the standards by which he will judge what is just and good and expedient from 'nature herself and the truth', 'nature' here does not stand for any data of experience, but rather for an abstract ideal, and the statesman's experience of actual laws or existing constitutions is explicitly excluded. Secondly the 'standards' mentioned in this fragment must evidently be distinguished from those referred to elsewhere in our evidence for the *Protrepticus*. Thus in Fr. 5 we find the common Aristotelian idea that the good or the wise man acts as a standard of what is good for other men—what he judges to be good or evil is good or evil: 'what measure, κανών, or standard, ὅρος, more exact than the wise man, ὁ φρόνιμος, do we have for what is good?' But if both Fr. 5 and Fr. 13 are genuine, it seems that Aristotle not only set up the wise man as a standard of good and evil for mankind in general, but also argued that the statesman himself needs certain standards to refer to. These latter are not supplied by 'the good man', nor by any aspect of experience. Rather they come from 'the truth', and to grasp these standards the statesman must study philosophy, here conceived as a theoretical inquiry which contemplates objects that are described as 'primary' and 'exact'.

If Fr. 13 is based on the *Protrepticus* and does not completely misrepresent it, then in that work Aristotle distinguished between different types of activity—philosophy and artistic production—according to the status of the objects they imitate, contrasting the imitation of exact originals on the part of the philosopher with the imitation of copies on the part of ordinary craftsmen. Moreover philosophy thus conceived is assumed to be directly relevant to the work of the political scientist, for without doing philosophy he will not be able to grasp the true standards of right and wrong. This second doctrine, especially, contrasts with the point of view expressed in the ethical treatises. There the doctrine of *Protrepticus* Fr. 5, that the good man provides a standard of good and evil, is elaborated, for example at *EN* 1113 a 25 ff. But we hear no more of the dependence of political science on any exact inquiry: indeed the inexactness of ethics and politics themselves is emphasised in the strongest possible terms. 'The same degree of precision—τὸ ἀκριβές', he says at *EN* 1094 b 12 ff., 'should not be demanded in all

36

inquiries...Fine and just actions, which are the subject-matter of politics, admit of plenty of differences and variations...It is as inappropriate to demand demonstration in ethics as it is to allow a mathematician to use merely probable arguments.' Again he argues at *EN* 1095 a 30 ff. that the starting-point in ethical discussions is what is better known to us, that is the particulars, not what is better known absolutely, the universals. Yet the *Protrepticus*, by contrast, depreciates consideration of particular existing laws and constitutions, and advocates that the legislator should keep his gaze fixed on what is stable and divine and eternal.

Our extant texts do not make clear the ontological status of the originals that the philosopher contemplates, except to say that they are 'primary' and 'exact'. There is no explicit evidence that they are transcendental Platonic Forms. Yet the Platonic overtones of Fr. 13 are obvious. Where it is usual for Aristotle simply to distinguish between universals and particulars, he apparently drew a distinction between originals and copies, and this idea clearly owes a great deal to the way in which Plato described the relation between the Forms and the particulars. Equally the account of the dependence of the practical science of the statesman on the exact, theoretical inquiry of the philosopher has more in common with the ethical theses that Plato attempted to establish with the help of the theory of Forms than with the view that Aristotle was later to put forward on the nature of ethical inquiry in the *Nicomachean Ethics*.

Like the *Eudemus*, however, the *Protrepticus* shows signs

of Aristotle diverging from Platonic theses at certain points. While the distinction drawn in Iamblichus between original and copy is strongly reminiscent of the discussion of different types of creation in the tenth book of Plato's *Republic*, there is at least one important point of disagreement between the two doctrines. Both in the *Republic* and the *Cratylus*, for example, Plato is prepared to concede that the craftsman who makes a bed or a shuttle imitates the Form of the artefact directly. In the *Republic* it is only the painter or sculptor or poet who imitates copies. Yet in Iamblichus, at least, all craftsmen appear to be on a level with the painters and sculptors and poets of *Republic* x. According to the text we considered, when the instrument-maker makes his tools, he does not take the 'originals' themselves as models: on the contrary, these tools are said to be taken from copies that are at a first, second or further remove from what is exact. It is difficult to be certain exactly what is meant by this, unless the idea is that the ruler, for instance, is not taken from absolute straightness itself, but rather from such natural phenomena as rays of light—as had been suggested earlier in the passage. Nevertheless, if Iamblichus is to be trusted, the doctrine of the *Protrepticus* differed from Plato's in interposing a stage in the creation of instruments which is not mentioned in Plato's own discussions of the matter, and in allotting a correspondingly lower status to most craftsmen.

Thus two of Aristotle's early literary works contain doctrines which have obvious affinities to Platonic theses and which contrast with the views which we find expressed in Aristotle's own treatises. The notion that the soul in its true and natural state is separate from the body and that its stay in the body is an affliction and a penance was held by other early Greek thinkers, and in particular by the Pythagoreans, before it found its most dramatic expression in Plato. It reappears, unexpectedly, in the *Eudemus* and the *Protrepticus*, in striking contrast to the definition of the soul as the 'first actuality of the natural organic body' which Aristotle was later to propose in the *de Anima*. Again, some of the *Protrepticus'* views on the nature of ethical and political discussion differ sharply from those that are advanced in the *Nicomachean Ethics*.

The evidence concerning Aristotle's attitude towards the theory of Forms itself is less certain. Neither dialogue refers explicitly to the transcendental Platonic Forms. Yet the *Eudemus* seems to have contained a passage concerning the visions of the disembodied soul modelled, in part, on the myth of the *Phaedrus*. And the distinction drawn in the *Protrepticus* between the 'primary' and 'exact' originals that the philosopher contemplates, and mere imitations or copies, obviously derives from, while it modifies, the distinction between model and copy that played such an important part in Plato's account of the relationship between Forms and particulars. In both cases the evidence falls short of a proof that Aristotle accepted the theory of Forms as such at the time. All that it shows is that he was prepared to take over and use, for his own purposes, ideas and images that originate in Plato's expositions of that theory. And while his readiness to do this might suggest that he was, if not an adherent of the theory, at least sympathetic towards it, the extent of his sympathy or support remains very much a matter of conjecture.

The influence of Plato on the *Eudemus* and the *Protrepticus* is strong. But there is definite evidence in both works that Aristotle had begun to diverge from the teachings of his master. Moreover these are the *only* two works where there is substantial evidence of his maintaining important Platonic theses that he was later to reject. The treatises themselves contain no hint that at any stage in his career Aristotle tolerated, let alone upheld, Plato's theory of Forms. The tone of some passages where he considers that theory is milder than that of others, but even in those parts of the *Metaphysics* where he brackets himself with the Platonists, he rejects the transcendental Forms in unequivocal terms. Furthermore several of the lost works too, both literary and technical, contained fundamental criticisms of the Forms, and while we cannot be sure of their dates, they include some that may well have been produced during the first Athenian period—that is while Plato was still alive.[1] Two of our sources, Plutarch and Proclus, report that the dialogues contained refutations of the Forms, and Alexander supplies extensive and detailed information concerning the work entitled *On Forms*, in particular, in which Aristotle set out the arguments by

[1] Some scholars would argue that certain such works, including *On Forms* and *On Philosophy*, were composed even before the *Eudemus* and the *Protrepticus*. While this view is possible, it seems to me more likely that the last two works were written before Aristotle had formulated his main objections to the central doctrine of Plato's ontology.

which the Platonists hoped to establish their theory together with his own criticisms and objections.

We may reasonably assume that at the very outset of his philosophical career Aristotle accepted much of the teaching of Plato. Two of his early works, the *Eudemus* and the *Protrepticus*, provide us with a glimpse of an Aristotle whose doctrine of the soul, for example, and whose conception of ethical inquiry are closer to Plato than to the views expressed in the treatises. The concrete evidence of his acceptance of the theory of Forms itself is tenuous, and in any case his adherence to that theory can only have been shortlived, since it was rejected not merely in such treatises as *Metaphysics* A, but also in some of the early dialogues and in the work *On Forms*. Yet even after he had formulated his principal objections to the doctrine of Forms, Aristotle still remained deeply influenced by other aspects of Plato's teaching. Not only did he inherit many of his problems from Plato, but his criticisms of Plato often provide the starting-point and foundation of his own theories. His ideas are often developed, in fact, in deliberate contrast to those of Plato. The evidence for a period in Aristotle's life when he may be considered in some respects, at least, an orthodox Platonist has been reviewed: it is, as we have seen, very limited. There remains the far more intricate and important issue of the more fundamental influences that Plato had on his pupil. The next step is to consider the nature of the principal criticisms that Aristotle brought against the philosophy of his master.

CHAPTER 3

THE CRITIC OF PLATO

Jaeger saw Aristotle's departure from Athens in 347 as the expression of a crisis in his inner life and described that departure as a secession. Although we may readily believe that leaving Athens marked an important development in his relationship with the Academy, we know that he began to criticise the Platonists while still considering himself a member of their circle. He regularly uses the first person plural in referring to the Platonists in his critical review of their philosophy in *Metaphysics* A ch. 9, and even before that he had set out his objections to the theory of Forms at length in the lost work *On Forms*. His rejection of this central doctrine of Platonism may well date from a period when Plato was still alive. Ultimately Aristotle's criticisms of his master's theories extended over a very wide range of topics, including physics, cosmology, psychology and ethics. But the key to his reaction against the philosophy of Plato is undoubtedly his rejection of the theory of Forms. This was the corner-stone of his master's teaching and from the rejection of this doctrine many of his other minor objections stem.

Aristotle's arguments are directed not so much against the Plato we know from the *Phaedo* and the *Republic*, as against the Platonism current in the Academy in his own day. Indeed both the positions he attacked, and the arguments he used to attack them, owe a great deal to the discussions of the Academy. Several of his points strike one immediately as captious and unfair as criticisms of Plato himself. Sometimes the explanation of this may be that they are aimed at other members of the school. On the other hand some of his objections are certainly exaggerated, especially when he has a thesis of his own to defend on the problem under discussion. For our present purposes we need not enter too far into the fascinating, but complex, questions of the extent to which Aristotle may have misrepresented Plato or Platonism or the reasons for his doing so. The problem that chiefly concerns us is rather to discover the points of real disagreement between Plato and Aristotle on issues of philosophical importance. What are the main philosophical grounds for Aristotle's rejection of the theory of Forms? And how much do Aristotle's own ideas on substance and causation still owe to Plato?

Criticisms of the Forms

The chief criticisms brought against the theory of Forms can be grouped under three main heads, (1) criticisms of the arguments used to establish the Forms, (2) criticisms of aspects of the theory itself, and (3) criticisms of its usefulness, that is of its ability to provide solutions to the problems it was intended to resolve.

Under the first head, Aristotle claims that either (a) the arguments that the Platonists used to establish the theory of Forms are inconclusive and do not prove anything at all, or (b) if they prove anything, they prove too much, in that they prove the existence of Forms of things of which the Platonists denied there were Forms (*Metaph.*

990b8ff.). He goes on to refer to the main arguments used to establish the Forms by the short and rather cryptic titles by which they were known in the school, such as 'the one over the many', and the argument 'from thinking of something that is no more'. However with the help of Alexander's commentary, which draws on the work *On Forms*, it is possible to reconstruct the arguments in question and Aristotle's objections to them.

Thus the 'one over the many' argument, for instance, may be summarised as follows: if for every class such as that of men there is something, the general predicate 'man', which is predicated of each of the members of the class but which is identical with none of them, this will be separate from the particulars and eternal; but that which is separate from the particulars and eternal is the Form; and so there are Forms. But to this Aristotle objected first that the argument involves the Platonists in setting up Forms of negations, for even a negative term, 'not-man', for example, is predicated as a single identical term of many subjects; and secondly that this argument does not prove that there are Forms. All that it tends to show is that that which is predicated in common is different from the particulars of which it is predicated: it does not establish that the common predicate is a real object with a separate and independent existence. Aristotle's objections to other arguments take a similar form. It is, however, rather surprising to discover that he criticised certain arguments on the grounds that they implied Forms of artefacts and of relative terms. Plato himself had not hesitated to speak of the Form of a bed or of the Form of largeness, and yet Aristotle now represents it as an unwelcome consequence of certain arguments that they implied these Forms. Evidently he believed that to postulate such Forms ran counter to general principles that the Platonists had to accept. And in the case of Forms of relatives the principle in question may well have been derived from the distinction that Plato himself had drawn between self-subsistent, καθ' αὐτά, and relative, πρὸς ἄλλα, entities in the *Sophist* (255c).

Aristotle concludes that none of the arguments used to establish the Forms is convincing. But then he also criticises certain aspects of the theory itself. He objects especially to the account that was given of the relationship between Forms and particulars. He protests at *Metaph.* 991a20ff. that to say that the Forms are patterns, παραδείγματα, and that the other things share in them, μετέχειν, is empty talk and mere metaphor. The Platonists, he says, held that the Forms are separate and apart from the particulars of which they are the Forms: his terms are χωρίς and χωριστά. But that being so, neither resemblance nor participation can give an adequate account of the relationship between the two. Here he may be represented as enlarging upon a difficulty of which Plato himself was aware and which he discussed in the *Parmenides*, although whether Plato modified his attitude on this question in the light of the objections he considers in that dialogue is a highly controversial subject. But as far as Aristotle is concerned, his criticism of the terms used to describe that relationship reflects his own rejection of the assumption that the Forms are separate entities.

But the third and most important type of criticism that Aristotle has to make of the Forms is that they provide no solution either to the problems of change and coming-to-be or to the problem of knowledge. What the Platonists had done, he remarks acidly at one point (*Metaph.* 990a34ff.), was to postulate entities equal in number to the objects that had to be explained, as if doubling the number of things they had to consider provided a solution to the problem of their causes. But what do these Forms contribute, he asks (*Metaph.* 991a8ff.), to sensible objects? They cause neither movement nor change. Moreover, arguing once more from the point of view of his own conception of immanent form, he denies that the Forms help towards either the knowledge of particulars or their being.

To the first point, that the Forms cause neither movement nor change, Plato himself would no doubt have answered that what originated movement, in his cosmological system, was the world-soul or the Craftsman who is described in the *Timaeus* as bringing the world out of disorder into order and as creating things after the pattern of the eternal Forms. It may be that there were Platonists who kept the theory of Forms while abandoning the doctrines of the world-soul and the Craftsman. But even against Plato himself Aristotle's objection has this much point that the Forms themselves provide no answer to the question of the origin of movement. Indeed Plato had emphasised the immutability of the Forms and had opposed them in this respect to the particulars which he described as always changing.

On the second point, that the Forms contribute neither towards the knowledge of particulars nor towards their being, Plato certainly intended his theory to help to resolve both epistemological and ontological questions, as we should call them. Aristotle could not validly object that Plato provided no answers to the questions of what is knowable and what is real, but he believed the answers Plato gave to be mistaken in that his Forms are separated from the many particulars of which they are the Forms. And even granted the existence of the Platonic Forms, it is only the Forms themselves that are the objects of knowledge, and that can be said to be, in the strictest senses of those terms: the many particulars are merely the objects of opinion and they belong to the world of becoming, not of being.

The major grounds on which Aristotle rejected the Forms can be represented as being that they provided an inadequate solution to the physical problem of change, and to the metaphysical and logical problems of what is real and what is knowable. But to say this is simply to identify the areas of his disagreement with Plato, not to explain that disagreement or clarify its basis. To do this we have to go into Aristotle's own views on the questions of substance and of causation.

Substance

We may begin with the doctrine of substance, the central topic of what Aristotle calls 'first philosophy', but one of the most opaque and difficult parts of his thought. The term in Aristotle that is generally translated 'substance' is οὐσία, literally 'being'. But he also uses some strange circumlocutions, particularly τὸ τί ἦν εἶναι or 'the what it is to be a thing'. This expression seems very obscure, but what Aristotle means by the 'what it is to be an X' is, in each case, the answer to the question 'what is it to be an X?'—'what is it to be a table?', for example, or, as we might put it, 'what is it that makes a table a table rather than anything else?' But what is the problem that Aristotle uses these terms to deal with? Indeed is there, one might ask, a recognisable problem here at all? Certainly Aristotle believed so. In fact, the central problem, as he understood it, is one whose origins can be traced in much earlier philosophy.

The original and primary sense of οὐσία in Greek is property or wealth: the English 'substance' is used in an equivalent sense in such phrases as 'a man of substance'. But even though there is no certain pre-Platonic use of the term οὐσία in the philosophical sense 'being', the question of what really exists was already the subject of keen dispute by the time of Plato. In the fifth century there was a complex and protracted debate between the Eleatics and their opponents concerning both the validity of the senses and the nature of 'what is': can the changing world of phenomena be said to exist, or is reality one and unchanging? Can we accept the evidence of the senses, or must we trust reason and argument alone? Parmenides' *Way of Truth*, in particular, is an exploration of what may be said to follow from the single statement ἔστι, 'it is': in it he denied the reality of change and plurality and concluded that what is is one and indivisible, and subject neither to coming-to-be nor to destruction.

Plato's ontology is a good deal more subtle than that of the Eleatics. It has often been remarked that his Forms share certain of the characteristics of Eleatic being: they are unchanging and eternal and the objects of true knowledge. But he does not deny all reality to the changing particulars. It is true that there are texts where he appears to do this in describing the Forms alone as real; but more often and more accurately he speaks of two kinds of being, one of which is ὄντως ὄν, 'really real', and the other ὄν πως, real only in a secondary sense. Thus in the *Phaedo* 79 a ff. he speaks of two sorts of things that are, the visible kind and the invisible kind, and in the *Republic* 479 d he describes the many particulars as being 'tossed about' between being and not-being.

To illustrate Plato's distinction between different levels of being we may consider one of the most important topics to which it is applied, that of moral and aesthetic values. Here he was, of course, following and developing the teachings of Socrates. In the early dialogues he represents Socrates demanding what beauty, or justice, or courage, or piety, is, and very often the reply that Socrates is given consists of an example of whatever quality or virtue they are discussing. When that happens Socrates points out the distinction between beauty itself and a particular instance of it, and he insists that to give an example is an inadequate answer to a question of the form 'what is beauty?' Whether Socrates himself formulated any clear idea of what sort of objects beauty, justice and courage might be, is extremely doubtful, but Plato evidently began to do so in his writings from the *Phaedo* and the *Symposium* onwards. From pointing out the distinction between beauty itself and beautiful particulars, Plato often goes on to contrast the two. Beauty itself is nothing but beauty, and it is always, and everywhere, and to everyone, what it is. But the many particular beautiful objects have other qualities besides beauty itself: a beautiful woman, for instance, is tall or short, fair-haired or dark, young or old. Moreover she may appear beautiful to one person, but ugly to another, beautiful in one respect, but not in another, beautiful at one moment, but not at another, and so on. Most important, while particular beautiful objects come to be and are destroyed, beauty itself remains unaffected by their fate. From distinguishing beauty itself from beautiful particulars, it is a short step, but an important one, to contrasting the two in respect of their stability or permanence or reality.

The theory of Forms commits Plato to a view of what deserves to be called 'real' in the fullest sense and to a view of the highest type of knowledge. Particulars have a share in reality in so far as they have a share in the Forms, but it is the latter, separable from, and independent of, the particulars, that are 'really real', and the highest type of knowledge is knowledge of these transcendent entities, to obtain which, it is repeatedly stressed, the soul must act as far as possible on its own, divorced from the body. Aristotle's doctrine of substance can be seen as a rival to Plato's theory of Forms, and in particular it suggests that we should adopt a different tactic in our pursuit of knowledge. It is true that there is more to his doctrine than simply a riposte to Plato, and indeed, as we shall see later, it is doubtful whether Aristotle means to propose a single, clear-cut and definitive conception of substance. But what concerns us for the moment is the light that his discussion of substance throws on his reaction against the central thesis of Plato's philosophy.

Aristotle's answers to the questions 'what really exists?' and 'what can be known?' take him far away from the Platonic theory of Forms. Yet in at least two respects he follows Plato quite closely. (1) For both philosophers it is form that is knowable. Aristotle is more explicit than Plato in that he contrasts the form of each object with its matter. He distinguishes between the wood a table is made of, and the form the table has, that is what differentiates a table from some other object made of wood such as a chair. But like Plato he considers that it is the form that makes a thing knowable. We distinguish a table from a chair by their forms. Two identical tables are conceptually indistinguishable: the mere fact that twice the amount of material has been used in their construction does not help us to distinguish them except in number. (2) Like Plato, again, Aristotle tends to associate 'substance' or 'being' with that which is permanent or that which persists through change. Both philosophers require that 'being' should be intelligible and definable. These are important points of resemblance which indicate that Aristotle continued to have a good deal in common with Plato even in a part of his philosophy where he rejected the main core of Plato's teaching. But while there are these general similarities between the two philosophers' ideas of being, elsewhere their points of view are fundamentally opposed.

For Plato, the particular objects of the world of everyday experience certainly 'share in' the Forms and are not totally non-existent: but what is 'really real' is the Form in its pure state. For Aristotle, at least according to the doctrine of the *Categories*, 'substance' is a term applied primarily to the concrete individual object, the complex of form and matter, this table, this chair, Socrates, this specimen of a dogfish and so on. In his view form and matter are certainly distinguishable logically, but in the sublunary region at least they are not distinguishable in fact. The form of a table does not have a separate existence: it does not exist except in conjunction with matter of some sort, wood or metal or marble. The addition of the qualifying words 'in the sublunary region' is necessary because Aristotle does speak of pure form and pure substances in the heavenly region, where there is, in any case, no terrestrial matter, no earth, water, air or fire, at all. But if this introduces a complication into his theory, so far as the sublunary region is concerned the theory itself is quite clear. The doctrine of the *Categories* states that it is the individual complex of form plus matter, for example Socrates or Callias, that is substance in the primary sense, while the genus, animal, and the species, man, are substance in a secondary sense. In the *Categories* Aristotle may, in effect, be said to have reversed the order of priorities that Plato set up when he distinguished between two sorts of being in the *Phaedo* and insisted that the invisible Forms—which are comparable with the genera and species of Aristotle's *Categories*—are both prior and superior to the visible particulars such as Socrates or Callias or this table.

We can point to a major contrast between the two philosophers in their accounts of being, but how far can we go towards explaining or elucidating it? Perhaps not very far. But it does seem possible to associate their different conceptions of form, to some extent, with their different interests. Why Plato 'separated' the Forms is, admittedly, not the sort of question to which we could ever give, or should ever expect, a full and definitive answer. The known influences on the development of Plato's thought are extremely complex, and there are no doubt others of which we remain ignorant. But one major factor, certainly, was the need to find an answer to those who argued that morality is purely a matter of convention and has no natural, objective basis—the point of view that Plato himself associates with the sophist Protagoras in the *Theaetetus*, for example. That the theory of Forms is not the only possible counter to sophistic moral relativism may be seen from the fact that Aristotle himself chose a different line of defence. As we shall discover when we discuss his ethics, he rejected both the thesis that right and wrong are merely relative, and the thesis that there is in each case a single Form corresponding to Justice, the Good and so on. But for Plato to insist that Justice is not only distinct from particular just acts, but quite different in kind from them, a separate and independent entity, was one way, and certainly a most dramatic way, of expressing his conviction that, whatever may be conceded to the argument that a particular just act may appear just to one person but unjust to another, Justice itself must nevertheless exist, and there must be objective moral standards.

In his rejection of the independent 'hypostasised' Forms Aristotle was partly motivated, on his own evidence, by logical considerations. Many of the arguments that he brought against the Platonists in the work *On Forms* are based on his analysis of predication. He insisted that all that such arguments as 'the one over the many' established was that a common predicate is distinct from the many particulars of which it is predicated. But while we may and should distinguish the universal from the concrete particulars, it was, in his view, both unnecessary and superfluous to attribute separate existence to the universals.

Secondly, he disagreed with Plato on the epistemological question of how we should set about acquiring knowledge of the Form. Although Plato believed that particulars can, under certain circumstances, stimulate the soul to recollect the Form, he repeatedly emphasised the contrast between on the one hand true opinion, which is derived from sense-perception, and which is the best state of cognition we can attain with regard to particulars, and on the other knowledge, which has as its objects the Forms and which the soul acquires through reasoning and recollection. But if Plato's view was that we should direct the soul's gaze away from the particulars to contemplate the Forms, Aristotle on the contrary insists that we should investigate the general form by first studying the particular instances of it. We should proceed from the particular to the general, for it is the particular that is ' better known to us'.

Here we might say that Aristotle's view is what common-sense might suggest. But it seems possible to be more specific than that. His doctrine that the particular provides the starting-point of our investigation of the general form is not merely a theoretical solution to a logical problem. It provides the basis of a practical policy in his actual researches both in the social and in the natural sciences. For the naturalist, in particular, the individual specimen is the embodiment of the species, that is the form: the word in Greek is the same, εἶδος. The species consists of its individual members, and it is through them that it is perpetuated. This in turn allows boundaries to be drawn between the various species of animals and plants where, by contrast, in ethics or politics, just or courageous acts, or democratic or oligarchic constitutions, do not form clearly delimitable, let alone self-perpetuating, species at all. The naturalist may and indeed must discount the peculiarities of any particular specimen. But the individual specimens taken together evidently provide his total source of direct information on the species. The properties and characteristics of a particular species of animal or plant cannot, in practice, be deduced by *a priori* methods of reasoning. The naturalist has no option but to proceed in the way in which Aristotle suggests the philosopher in general should proceed.

Some aspects of the ontology and epistemology that

Aristotle developed in opposition to the theory of Forms may be associated with his interests in the natural sciences. The need for an alternative epistemological policy must have made itself felt in that field especially. But two cautions are necessary. First his rejection of the Forms should not be seen as the direct consequence of his detailed investigations in physics and biology. While the effect of those investigations was undoubtedly to confirm him in his rejection of Plato's epistemology, the principal objections he had to make against that theory are general ones and they must have occurred to him long before the bulk of his extensive researches in such fields as zoology had been carried out.

Secondly, the difference between the two philosophers should not be construed as an absolute contrast between on the one hand a disinterested seeker after facts and on the other a dogmatic moralist. For one thing, Aristotle is ready enough to exhort and persuade in parts of his ethical and political works. For another, his science, unlike modern science, is permeated with a teleology that has strong ethical overtones, and one of his main motives for investigating nature is to reveal the order and finality of natural changes. Moreover Plato for his part often demonstrates his skill as an observer, particularly as an observer of human nature, and he shows a nascent interest in the natural sciences, especially in the *Timaeus*. But although the contrast between Plato and Aristotle is far from an absolute one, there is a clear distinction, in their methods, in the relative importance they attach to the particulars and to the concrete example. Aristotle insists that the starting-point of the inquiry, both in the investigation of nature and in the study of ethics and politics, is the particulars and what he calls τὰ φαινόμενα. The interpretation of this term provides an important insight into his method: although in certain contexts the translation 'phenomena' is not inappropriate, the Greek term is both vaguer and more general than the English. It comprises a good deal besides what we should call the observed facts: it can and often does include the commonly held opinions, ἔνδοξα, and what is said or thought about a subject, λεγόμενα, and even the implications of the way in which terms are used. The recommendation to consult the φαινόμενα occurs in several passages in Aristotle, in both physical and ethical treatises, and this certainly enables us to distinguish his method from Plato's. Yet the extent to which the method Aristotle recommends is what we should call an empirical one should not be exaggerated, for under τὰ φαινόμενα he includes not only the results of his own extensive researches in the biological and social sciences, but also the accepted opinions on whatever subject is under discussion.[1]

Causation

Aristotle's doctrine of substance is one topic that throws light on the main grounds of his reaction against the philosophy of Plato. Another is his doctrine of causation. We have already noted Aristotle's explicit objection, in

---

[1] The meaning of the term φαινόμενα in Aristotle has been examined by G. E. L. Owen in his recent illuminating discussion of the dictum τιθέναι τὰ φαινόμενα in *Aristote et les problèmes de méthode*, Louvain and Paris, 1961, pp. 83–103.

the *Metaphysics*, that the Platonic Forms cause neither movement nor change, but one of the striking features of this charge is that it relates specifically to the field of physics. It is interesting, then, to compare the role Aristotle himself assigns to form in his account of natural change. But first we have to outline the principles on which that account is based, and in particular the two famous doctrines of the four causes, and of actuality and potentiality. The texts here come mostly from the first two books of the *Physics*.

In *Physics* I Aristotle's own doctrine of causation is developed, typically, against the background of a discussion of his predecessors' ideas. He notes the persistence, in earlier thought, of the view that change takes place between opposites of one kind or another, and this provides the basis of his own general theory of form, εἶδος, and privation, στέρησις. Change takes place between a pair of opposites, such as hot and cold, one of which represents the 'form', the other the 'privation'. But a further factor is necessary besides the opposites, namely that which is subject to, or undergoes, the change, τὸ ὑποκείμενον or 'substratum'. Boiling a kettle involves not only a change from cold to hot, but also something that changes, the water that is first cold and then hot. Water, then, may be called the 'substratum' of change in this example. But while it is not too misleading to say that it is water that changes in the example of the boiling kettle, water itself naturally possesses certain qualities, and we may, if we wish, carry our logical analysis further. If we do so, we find that what is the 'substratum' in the strictest sense is an abstraction, quality-less matter. So far, then, we have identified two types of cause, (1) form—change being either from the form to the privation or *vice versa*—and (2) matter or the substratum. But then, building once more on ideas whose origins can be traced in earlier philosophy, Aristotle adds two further types of cause, the moving or efficient cause, and the final cause.

The four causes are, then, form, matter, moving cause and final cause. What Aristotle means by these can best be seen from some examples. Take first an example of artificial production, the making of a table. To give an account of this four factors must be mentioned. First matter, for the table is made out of something, usually wood. Secondly form, for the table is not just any lump of wood, but wood with a certain shape. Thirdly moving cause, for the table was made by someone, the carpenter. Fourthly final cause, for when the carpenter made the table he made it for a purpose, to provide a raised flat surface which could be used to write upon or eat at. Similarly, in a slightly more complicated example, the building of a house, the four causes are: (1) the bricks, mortar, wood and stone that are used in its construction; (2) the arrangement of those material components in a certain manner; (3) the builder, or as Aristotle sometimes puts it, the building art; and (4) the purpose the builder had in mind, to provide a shelter capable of being used for human habitation. If we consider an example from nature, a similar analysis applies. Take the reproduction of a species of animals, say man. The matter, Aristotle believes, is supplied by the female parent, the mother. The form is the specific character of man and what makes him different from other animals: the stock Academic definition, which Aristotle still uses quite often, was rational two-legged animal. The moving cause is supplied by the father: according to Aristotle, the semen does not contribute to the matter of the embryo, which all comes from the mother, but serves only to activate or inform that matter. Lastly the final cause is the end towards which the process is directed, the perfect, fully-grown man.

Aristotle believes that these four factors should be taken into account when considering change of any sort. The four are always logically distinguishable. But it is easy to see that while logically distinguishable, they are not always distinguishable in fact. In particular, matter is often contrasted with the other three causes taken together. In the reproduction of animals, for instance, the matter stands apart, but the formal cause, the moving cause and the final cause are all embodied in different ways by the mature male animal. It is the fully grown man that possesses the form of man, that—as the father—provides the moving cause in the process of reproduction, and that —as the mature man into whom the young boy grows— is the end towards which the process is directed.

The relation between these three causes is particularly important if we are to understand Aristotle's criticisms of Plato's doctrine of Form. In such cases of artificial production as the making of a table the carpenter is obviously external to the object he makes: and the final cause, the use the table serves, may be thought of as the product of the craftsman's conscious deliberation. In natural coming-to-be, however, the final cause or end is immanent in the object itself, the living and growing animal or plant. The subject of Aristotle's teleology will be taken up again later, but three points are relevant here. First, he was well aware that there is no *conscious* purpose in nature. In an important passage in the *Physics* (199 b 26 ff.) he considers an objection that might be made to his conception of the final cause in nature, namely that nature does not deliberate. Here he concedes that nature does not, in fact, deliberate, but maintains nevertheless that one can speak of 'ends' in nature, or 'that for the sake of which' natural processes take place. Secondly, he does not hold that nature fulfils its ends as an absolute rule without exception, only as a general rule: natural processes, as he often says, take place 'always or for the most part'. Thirdly, if one asks why he continued to believe in final causes in nature, despite the fact that nature does not deliberate, his main ground for doing so is simply the regularity of natural changes. First the movements of the heavenly bodies provide a model of regularity and uniformity; there is a uniformity, too, in the reproduction of natural species, in that each kind produces its own kind, man generating man and horse horse; and regularity is also to be found in the natural movements of the four elements, earth always falling and fire rising when nothing impedes their movement. These, then, were some of the main grounds for his belief that nature as a whole is not random and haphazard, but exhibits order and regularity, and if order and regularity, then 'ends', although not conscious ends.

The contrast with Plato becomes apparent when we compare Aristotle's final and efficient causes with Plato's δημιουργός or Craftsman. Although Aristotle points out that nature does not deliberate, he often compares nature's activity with that of ordinary craftsmen, and many of the metaphors and comparisons he uses in this context are strongly reminiscent of those found in the *Timaeus*. However there is an important difference between the two philosophers in that Aristotle goes much further than Plato towards making his literal meaning explicit. We cannot be sure of the force of many of Plato's technological metaphors. Obviously we should not press the literal interpretation of his descriptions of the Craftsman: for to do so would be to convict Plato of a vulgar anthropomorphism of which he was certainly not guilty. Nevertheless it is far from clear how we should understand the images he uses to convey his idea of the creative force at work in cosmology, or what account we should give of the relationship between the Craftsman and the world-soul. Aristotle, on the other hand, explicitly denies that nature consciously deliberates, and he clearly recognises that his metaphors are metaphors. He repeatedly says that nature does not act without a goal, and even, on occasions, graphically compares nature with a painter, a modeller or some other type of craftsman. But he makes it plain that he does not postulate a divine mind controlling natural changes from outside. On the contrary, natural objects have their 'ends' within themselves. Earth naturally seeks its own place, and the young boy naturally grows into the mature man.

Potentiality and Actuality

The example of natural growth provides the stepping-stone to the next important aspect of Aristotle's analysis of change, the doctrine of potentiality, δύναμις, and actuality, ἐνέργεια. The doctrine of the four causes, one may say, provides a résumé of the factors that Aristotle believes have to be taken into account in describing natural or artificial change. But he also analyses change in another way which puts far more emphasis on the dynamic aspects of the process of change. If the clearest examples to illustrate the distinctions between the four causes come from artificial production, the notions of potentiality and actuality are best seen in the case of natural growth. The seed of a tree is 'potentially' the mature tree: it is 'potentially', as Aristotle says, what the mature tree is 'actually'. This doctrine draws attention to the continuity of natural change. The goals towards which natural changes are directed are the ends of continuous processes. But while the ideas of potentiality and actuality are obviously relevant in this way to natural growth, Aristotle generalises the doctrine and applies it to other types of change as well. A hunk of wood in a carpenter's shop is potentially a table or a chair or a desk. A piece of marble in a sculptor's studio is potentially the Apollo Belvedere or the Venus de Milo. In each instance it is the relatively formless matter, the shapeless wood or marble, that may be said to possess potentiality. Quality-less matter, the abstraction, is pure potentiality. But relatively formless matter possesses potentialities in different senses and to different degrees. We may note, for instance, the different senses in which a seed is potentially a tree and a piece of wood is potentially a table, or again those in which a young man is potentially a man, and earth, water, air and fire are potentially a man, and indeed Aristotle himself calls attention to the differences in the meaning of potentiality in such cases. Form and the final cause are found in the end-product of natural and artificial changes. But the doctrine of potentiality allows Aristotle to suggest that even the relatively formless matter is potentially what the end-product is actually. Form is not something transcendent and separate, as it had been for Plato, but something that is gradually acquired and brought into actuality during the process of change.

Before leaving the doctrine of potentiality and actuality I may note that besides providing an interesting example of the contrast between Plato's notion of Form and Aristotle's, this doctrine was the basis of Aristotle's solution to the problem posed much earlier by Parmenides when he denied the existence of change. Parmenides' argument is sometimes represented in our secondary sources, although not in his poem itself, in the form of a dilemma. How can anything be said to come to be? It cannot be said to come to be either (1) from what is not, since that is totally non-existent, or (2) from what is, for then it does not come to be, but is already. The first step towards the clarification of this problem was taken by Plato in the *Sophist* (255 e ff.) when he explicated the meaning of 'that which is not' and showed that one can say of something that 'it is not X', meaning that it is different from *X*, without denying that the thing exists. Yet the problem of how to account for change and coming-to-be still remained a problem even after Plato had drawn certain distinctions between the uses of the verb 'to be'. It was Aristotle, in fact, who first came to terms with it. He held, just as much as Parmenides and most other Greek philosophers had done, that coming-to-be in the absolute sense is impossible. Nothing comes to be from what is totally non-existent. But things can nevertheless come to be in a relative sense, as when a seed becomes a tree or a piece of wood is made into a table. In these instances the tree and the table may be said to come into being, but they come to be not from nothing, the totally non-existent, but from something—the seed, the wood—that is potentially what the end-product is actually. In each case the substratum acquires a new form. If an Eleatic asked, then, whether a tree came to be from what is, or from what is not, a tree, the answer would be that in a sense the seed is the tree—that is, it is *potentially* a tree —but in a sense it is not—it is not *actually* a tree.

The focal point of Aristotle's reaction against the philosophy of Plato is his rejection of the theory of Forms. This theory is criticised from several different points of view. As a logician Aristotle offers a different analysis of predication. As an ontologist and an epistemologist he argues in the *Categories* that it is the concrete particular, not the universal, that is substance in the primary sense, and that provides the starting-point in our investigation of the form. Thirdly as a physicist he points out that the separate and transcendent Forms are useless in accounting for change and coming-to-be. The Platonic Forms belong to the world of unchanging being. But the study of change, Aristotle holds, involves the investigation of form in the changing objects of the world of becoming. Where Plato directed the philosopher's attention primarily, if not exclusively, to the study of immutable being, Aristotle's view redeemed physics as a fit object of the philosopher's inquiries.

Aristotle's reaction against Platonism reflects, above all, his interest in, and his estimate of the importance of, the world of nature, including not only the unchanging heavenly bodies but also the changing objects in the sublunary world. Eventually he was to criticise Plato's theories in a great many different contexts. In the *Ethics* he rejects the relevance of the Form of the Good in particular, besides disagreeing with Plato on many points of ethical theory, as for example on the nature of virtue or that of pleasure. In the *Politics* he criticises the political recommendations of the *Republic* and the *Laws* in some detail. In the physical, psychological and biological treatises he frequently comments—not always unfavourably, of course—on aspects of Plato's cosmology or the natural science of the *Timaeus*. Yet for all his disagreements with Plato and his often pungent and sometimes rather unfair criticisms of both Plato and the Platonists, he continues to share certain important ideas with his master. He believes that it is the universal form that is knowable —and this notion, when combined with his belief that concrete particulars are substance in the primary sense, leaves a major problem in his philosophy. And secondly he believes, like Plato, that the world as a whole, and natural changes in particular, exhibit order and finality. Despite his rejection of the key doctrine of transcendental Forms he remained in certain respects deeply indebted to Plato, not only on particular points of detail but also on certain fundamental issues. He emerged from his training in the Academy as a critical and independent thinker with interests that ranged over a far wider variety of subjects than had engaged Plato's attention. But as we shall see when we consider his theories subject by subject, the similarities between the two philosophers are often as remarkable as the differences between them.

CHAPTER 4

THE PHILOSOPHER OF NATURE

Our analysis of Aristotle's main criticisms of Plato has already suggested that his reaction against Platonism owes a good deal to his interest in natural science. The realisation of the need to begin the investigation of natural species with the concrete particulars must have deepened, even if it was not the sole cause of, his dissatisfaction with the theory of knowledge advocated by Plato in connection with the Forms. In attempting to document the growth of Aristotle's interests in natural science we have two precious pieces of evidence. First there is the connection which I have already noted between many of the place-names mentioned in the *Historia Animalium* and the areas of Greece where we know Aristotle lived during the so-called period of the travels from 347 to 335 B.C. The *Historia Animalium* contains some detailed information about the peculiarities of the animals, especially of the marine animals, found in and around the island of Lesbos, and particularly in the straits and lagoon of Pyrrha on that island, and Pyrrha figures again in the documentation of the two other main biological treatises, the *de Partibus Animalium* and the *de Generatione Animalium*. Aristotle's interest in biology no doubt dates from before the time he went to Asia Minor. His father was a medical man, and the problems of classification, particularly of the classification of natural species, were a much discussed topic in the Academy. But we may be fairly confident that during his stay in Asia Minor he initiated some intensive research in zoology, the results of which were eventually to be set out, along with other work, in the *Historia Animalium*. It was, in all probability, during this period of his life that he began the detailed empirical studies that we now recognise as marking the beginnings of biology as a scientific discipline.

Secondly, there is evidence within the biological works themselves which shows that Aristotle saw his role as that of a pioneer in biology and felt the need to justify his study of the subject. The most important passage is a famous chapter in the first book of the *de Partibus Animalium* which is so remarkable that it must be quoted at length.

The programme of the 'de Partibus Animalium'

Of natural substances, some are ungenerated and indestructible throughout eternity, others share in generation and destruction. The former [that is, the heavenly bodies] are precious and divine, but we have less opportunity to investigate them since the evidence available to the senses, by means of which one might study them and the things that we long to know about, is very scanty. But concerning the things that perish, that is plants and animals, we have much better means of obtaining information, since we live among them. For anyone who is willing to take sufficient trouble can learn a great deal concerning each one of their kinds. But each of these two groups has its own attraction. For even though our comprehension of the heavenly bodies is small, yet because they are so precious it brings us more pleasure than knowing everything in our region, just as a partial glimpse we chance to get of those we love brings us more pleasure than an accurate vision of other things, however many or great they are. On the other hand our knowledge of the things that perish has the advantage in that we can obtain more and better information about them; and again since they are nearer to us and more closely related to our own nature, this restores the balance to some extent as against the study of the things that are divine.

Since we have already discussed the things that are divine and set out our opinion about them, it remains to speak of animals without, as far as possible, omitting any one of them, but dealing with noble and ignoble alike. For even in those that are not attractive to the senses, yet to the intellect the craftsmanship of nature provides extraordinary pleasures for those who can recognise the causes in things and who are naturally inclined to philosophy. For if we derive enjoyment from looking at imitations of these things because we are then contemplating the art of the craftsman—whether painter or sculptor—who made them, it would be strange and absurd not to delight far more in studying the natural objects themselves, provided at least that we can perceive their causes. And so we must not feel a childish disgust at the investigation of the meaner animals. For there is something of the marvellous in all natural things. The story goes that when some strangers who came to visit Heraclitus entered and saw him warming himself at the kitchen stove, they hesitated: but Heraclitus said, 'Do not be afraid. Come in. For there are gods even here.' Similarly we should approach the investigation of every kind of animal without being ashamed, since in each one of them there is something natural and something beautiful.

The absence of chance and the serving of ends are found in the works of nature especially. And the end for the sake of which a thing has been constructed or has come to be belongs to what is beautiful.

Aristotle then points out that if anyone is squeamish about examining animals, he ought to be so about man also:

But if anyone considers that the investigation of the other animals is beneath his dignity, then he ought to hold a similar view about the study of himself. For it is not possible to look at the constituent parts of human beings, such as blood, flesh, bones, blood-vessels and the like, without considerable distaste. But when we discuss any one of the parts or structures, we must not suppose that what we are talking about—and the object for which our inquiry is undertaken—is their material, but rather the whole form, just as in discussing a house, it is the whole form, not the bricks and mortar and timber in themselves, that is our concern. So too the student of nature investigates the composition and the substance as a whole, and not the materials which are not found apart from the substance of which they are the materials (*PA* I, ch. 5, 644b22–645a36).

This chapter provides a fascinating insight into the resistance that Aristotle had to overcome among some of his contemporaries in order to get biology accepted as a worthy subject of the philosopher's investigations. He acknowledges that research in anatomy cannot be carried out without considerable distaste. But he insists that 'anyone who is willing to take sufficient trouble' can learn a great deal concerning all the different kinds of animals, and he justifies studying them on the grounds that 'there is something of the marvellous in all natural things' and that in every kind of animal 'there is something natural and something beautiful'.

He does not recommend that the study of biology should in any way replace astronomy or other inquiries. Jaeger, who appreciated the importance of this passage, admitted as much, but held nevertheless that the chapter was composed at a time when 'the metaphysical and conceptual attitude of his early decades, though still forming the constructive framework of his general view, no longer held any place in his creative activity'. This is dubious, to say the least. Aristotle's own words in no way suggest that he was no longer actively engaged on the study of such metaphysical problems as those of substance and form. The passage does not imply any diminution or contraction of his interests. On the contrary, its message is that a new field of inquiry, biology, should take its place alongside those more generally accepted as fit studies for the philosopher. He concedes that astronomy has nobler objects as its subject-matter, and he emphasises that the study of the heavenly bodies must be taken as far as it can. But what is new in our passage is that it draws attention to the vast possibilities of research in the field of biology. Even so, the point of view from which Aristotle suggests that biology should be studied is strictly in accordance with his general physical principles. He is careful to point out that the object of their study is not matter alone, but the substance as a whole, and especially its form. Their aim is not merely to discover facts (that things are so), but to reveal causes (how and why they are so), and in particular to reveal the final causes and the absence of chance in the works of nature.

Whenever the passage itself was composed, the idea it expresses represents an important turning-point both for Aristotle and for the history of Greek science in general. It marks an entirely new appreciation of the value of detailed, empirical investigations in natural science. But if the programme of biological research outlined in the *de Partibus Animalium* is both admirable and revolutionary, how much did Aristotle actually achieve in practice in this field? The biological treatises amount to more than a fifth of the total extant works in the Aristotelian Corpus, and they contain a wealth of interesting material to which it is impossible to do justice here. I may, however, illustrate some aspects of his work in biology and draw attention to those features of it that are particularly important for an understanding of the development of his thought.[1]

The first point to remark is simply the range of his researches. Well over 500 different species of animals are referred to in the biological treatises, even if many of these are no more than mentioned. A precise estimate of the number of species he had dissected is impossible. References to the method are frequent, but not all of these can be taken to relate to dissections that he had carried out personally. Nevertheless the detailed and specific reports, in our texts, that give information that could only have been obtained from dissections, establish beyond a doubt that he was familiar with the method and used it regularly, even though the number of different species on which he did so may not have been as high as

[1] There is no single work in English that deals at all comprehensively with Aristotle's biology, but the reader interested in following up the subject may supplement the chapter in Ross' general work by consulting T. E. Lones, *Aristotle's Researches in Natural Science*, London, 1912. The notes in D'Arcy Thompson's Oxford Translation of the *Historia Animalium* are invaluable, and his two Glossaries, *Greek Birds*, 2nd ed. 1936 and *Greek Fishes*, 1947, are the chief authorities on the problem of the identification of the species to which Aristotle refers. The classic work on his taxonomy remains J. B. Meyer's *Aristoteles Thierkunde*, Berlin, 1855.

the fifty that is sometimes suggested, and even though it is extremely unlikely that he ever dissected a human being. To illustrate his methods and the quality of his observations I may take two examples, one from anatomy and the other from zoology.

Methods in biology: researches on the vascular system

My first example is the description of the heart and the system of the blood-vessels. There are several texts which outline the structure of the heart and the main blood-vessels in the body, and the minor discrepancies between these various accounts suggest that his views on the subject may have undergone certain modifications. But the fullest description is that in the *Historia Animalium* III, chh. 3 and 4, on which I can do no better than repeat the excellent comments of D'Arcy Thompson: 'The Aristotelian account of the vascular system is remarkable for its wealth of detail, for its great accuracy in many particulars, and for its extreme obscurity in others. It is so far true to nature that it is clear evidence of minute inquiry, but here and there so remote from fact as to suggest that things once seen had been half-forgotten, or that superstition was in conflict with the results of observation.' Where his main predecessors had been content with largely schematic accounts, Aristotle provides a recognisable description of the principal blood-vessels, including, for example, a quite detailed account of the superior Vena Cava and its branches. It is often said that he failed to distinguish between the arteries and the veins, and he certainly uses the same term, φλέψ, indiscriminately of both. Yet he

74

recognises that the blood-vessels deriving from the Aorta form a parallel system to those connected with—and in his view deriving from—the Vena Cava. All the other blood-vessels, he remarks at *PA* 667b17, are but offshoots of these two. And on several occasions he calls attention to the differences in texture between the Aorta and the Vena Cava as also between their respective branches. But under the heading of superstitious beliefs we may include his uncritical acceptance of the idea that there is a blood-vessel connecting the liver with the right arm (*HA* 514 a 37, b 8). He also considers, oddly, that the heart has three chambers, apparently treating the fourth, the right auricle, either as part of the right ventricle or as the dilated junction of the superior and inferior Venae Cavae. And this doctrine may well owe something to mystical beliefs concerning the number three.

His account of the vascular system is a strange mixture of careful observation and folk-belief. But we may find this less surprising when we recognise the difficulties he faced in his inquiry. He prefaces his own account in *Historia Animalium* III with a summary of the opinions of earlier investigators, whom he criticises for giving inaccurate descriptions. At 511 b 13 ff. he points out that:

The reason for their ignorance is the difficulty of carrying out observations. For in dead animals the nature of the most important blood-vessels is unclear because they especially collapse immediately the blood leaves them...And in living animals it is impossible to investigate the nature of the blood-vessels because they are internal. And so those who have examined dead bodies by dissection have not observed the principal sources of the blood-vessels, while those who have examined very emaciated living men have inferred the sources of the blood-vessels from what could then be seen externally.

Having recorded the views of three earlier investigators, Aristotle offers his own suggestion about the correct method, which consists in a combination of both of those that had been used before:

The inquiry, as I remarked before, is a difficult one, but if any-one concerns himself with such things, it is only in animals that have been first starved to emaciation and then strangled that the facts can be discovered sufficiently (513a12ff.).

He then proceeds to his description, noting, in the course of it, that there are differences in the structure of the heart in different animals and remarking that the courses of the blood-vessels are especially difficult to trace in some of the smaller species. This and his other des-criptions of the heart and the blood-vessels vividly illustrate the difficulties that Aristotle encountered in con-ducting his anatomical investigations and his persistence in attempting to overcome them.

Methods in biology: the generation of bees

My second example to illustrate his methods is a zoologi-cal one, his account of the generation of bees in *de Generatione Animalium* III, ch. 10. Here we find him adopt-ing a highly theoretical approach to the problem. He be-gins with a passage summarising the possible methods of generation of the three kinds of bees, the workers, whom he calls simply 'bees', the drones, and the Queens, whom he refers to either as 'kings' or 'leaders'.

They must either (1) fetch the young [that is, the larvae] from elsewhere, as some think—the young having either come into

76

being spontaneously or been produced by some other animal; or (2) generate them themselves, or (3) fetch some and generate some—for this view too is held by some people who say that it is only the young of the drones that are brought from elsewhere [that is, into the hive]. If they generate the young, this must be either with or without copulation; if with copulation, then either (a) each kind generates its own kind, or (b) one of the three kinds generates the others, or (c) one kind unites with another kind. I mean, for instance, either (a) 'bees' are generated from the union of 'bees', drones from the union of drones, 'kings' from the union of 'kings', or (b) all the rest are generated by one kind only, for example by the so-called 'kings' or 'leaders', or (c) by the union of drones and 'bees', for some think that the drones are male and the 'bees' female, others that the 'bees' are male and the drones female.

But all of these theories are impossible, if one reasons first from the particular facts concerning bees, and then from those that apply more generally to other animals.

First he adduces evidence and arguments to refute the idea that the bees are produced spontaneously or from the seed of some other animal. But then he argues, incorrectly, that all three kinds are produced without copulation, that is parthenogenetically. He denies that the workers are either male or female in a passage where he is unhappily misled by some bizarre general principles.

Nor is it reasonable to suppose that the 'bees' are female and the drones male. For nature does not give defensive weapons to any female creature, and while the drones are stingless, all the 'bees' have a sting. Nor is the opposite view reasonable, that the 'bees' are male and the drones female: for no male creatures are in the habit of taking trouble over their young, whereas in fact the 'bees' do (GA 759 b 1 ff.).

77

He concludes that the workers are neither male nor female. So far as the ability to generate is concerned, they are female, for they produce the drones, doing so parthenogenetically. But since they possess a sting, 'they have the male as well as the female principle, just as plants do'.

Having established that the drones are produced parthenogenetically by the workers, he argues that the Queens and the workers themselves are also produced without copulation. The Queens cannot be produced by either the drones or the workers. So they must generate themselves and indeed the workers also.

Thus what happens is this: the 'leaders' generate their own kind, and also another kind, that of the 'bees'; the 'bees' generate another kind, the drones, but do not also generate their own kind, since that has been denied them. And since what is according to nature is always orderly, therefore necessarily it is denied to the drones even to generate some other kind...And so well has this been arranged by nature that the three kinds always continue in existence and none of them fails, although not all of them generate (760a27ff.).

Many of his conclusions are quite mistaken. It is true that the workers do rarely produce eggs which, being unfertilised, turn into drones, but Aristotle believes that this is the only way in which the drones are produced. And arguing by analogy he infers wrongly that the other two kinds of bees, the Queens and the workers, are also produced parthenogenetically. But although his discussion of this problem is in many respects an unfortunate one, he ends it with a passage that lays down an extremely important methodological principle.

This, then, seems to be what happens with regard to the generation of bees, judging from theory and from what are thought to be the facts about them. However, the facts— τὰ συμβαίνοντα—have not been sufficiently ascertained. And if they ever are ascertained, then we must trust the evidence of the senses rather than theories, and theories as well, so long as their results agree with τοῖς φαινομένοις [—that is, as the context makes clear, with what is observed] (760 b 27 ff.).

In spite of the abstract nature of his discussion of this and many other problems in the biological treatises, Aristotle clearly recognised that theories must wait on evidence and he reversed Plato's view that abstract argument is more trustworthy than observation.

Despite his many lapses, Aristotle's skill as an observer is demonstrated by passage after passage in the biological works. He carried out, for example, a detailed investigation of the growth of the embryo chick, noticing that the heart appeared 'like a speck of blood on the white of the egg' on the fourth day after laying: 'and this point beats and moves as though alive' (*HA* VI, ch. 3, 561 a 11 ff.). Naturalists have also remarked on the fineness of his descriptions of the internal and external parts of the various kinds of Crustacea, particularly of the crawfish (*HA* IV, ch. 2), and they have drawn attention to his accounts of the fishing-frog and the torpedo in *HA* IX, ch. 37, where he describes how the fishing-frog uses the filaments that project in front of its eye as bait to catch small fish, and how the torpedo lies in wait, hidden in the sand or mud, to narcotise its victims.

In the *Historia Animalium* VI, ch. 10, 565 b 1 ff., he describes a species of dog-fish, the 'so-called smooth shark', and this passage is deservedly famous. The species in question, *Mustelus laevis*, is externally viviparous, as indeed are several of the cartilaginous fishes, but it is exceptional in that the embryo is attached by a navel-string to a placenta-like structure in the womb of the female parent. Aristotle's description runs, in part, in D'Arcy Thompson's translation:

And the young develop with the navel-string attached to the womb, so that, as the egg-substance gets used up, the embryo is sustained to all appearance just as in the case of quadrupeds. The navel-string is long and adheres to the under part of the womb (each navel-string being attached as it were by a sucker), and also to the centre of the embryo in the place where the liver is situated...Each embryo, as in the case of quadrupeds, is provided with a chorion and separate membranes.

For a long time this account was generally disbelieved. Although there were occasional references to similar observations in the sixteenth and seventeenth centuries, it was not until 1842 that Johannes Müller published the results of his investigations of *Mustelus laevis* and related species and established that Aristotle's account is in all essentials correct.

Two other similar cases where it has proved unprofitable to dismiss the observations recorded in the *Historia Animalium* may also be mentioned. In *HA* IX, ch. 37, 621 a 20 ff., there is an account of the way in which the male of a species of river-fish called *Glanis* protects its young. It stands guard over the spawn or fry for forty or fifty days, until the young are big enough to be able to get away from the other fish, and it wards off intruders by darting at them and by emitting a kind of muttering noise. This too was long treated as fictitious as it conflicted with the observed behaviour of *Silurus glanis* or sheat-fish common in European rivers. But in the nineteenth century an American naturalist, Louis Agassiz, noted that some North American cat-fishes behave in a way very similar to that described by Aristotle, and this led him to establish (in 1856) that the species Aristotle was referring to was not *Silurus glanis*, but a distinct species of siluroid which is found in the rivers of Greece, and which he named *Glanis Aristotelis*.

Finally Aristotle described a most strange phenomenon, which is still not fully understood, the 'hectocotylization' of one of the tentacles of certain Cephalopods, where the tentacle of the male is modified to form a generative organ and is used to transmit the spermatophores into the funnel of the female. Aristotle refers to the use of the tentacle in copulation on several occasions, although interestingly enough in one of the passages in which he does so (*GA* 720b32ff.) he argues against the supposition that the tentacle does in fact act as a generative organ, preferring to believe that its function is only to link the male and female together.

Theoretical issues in biology

Aristotle's skill as a descriptive, observational biologist needs no further illustration. But the purpose of studying animals is not merely description, but explanation. What were the chief problems that he was investigating, and how far did he go towards resolving them? This too is an

immense topic, but his treatment of the main problems in embryology in particular provides some good
examples to illustrate the strengths and weaknesses of his
discussion of theoretical issues.

Problems in embryology

There were two main controversies connected with the
problem of reproduction. The first was on the question
of whether the seed is drawn from the whole of the body
or not. The former view, known as the 'pangenesis' doctrine after Darwin's term for a similar, though not completely identical, theory, had been stated and defended by
some of the Hippocratic writers, and it probably goes
back to Democritus. In the *de Generatione Animalium* I,
chh. 17 and 18 Aristotle quotes and criticises the evidence
that had been adduced for this view. Thus it was commonly supposed that not only congenital but also acquired
characteristics are inherited—Aristotle's terms are σύμφυτος
and ἐπίκτητος—and that mutilated parents, for example,
have mutilated offspring. But to this Aristotle replied
simply by denying that this is always the case (724a4ff.).
Against the pangenesis theory he brings indeed a mass of
counter-arguments. One aims to show the incoherence of
the theory by posing a dilemma (722a16ff.). The seed
must be drawn either (1) from all the uniform parts, such
as flesh, bone, sinew; or (2) from all the non-uniform
ones—by which he means the hand, the face etc.; or (3)
from both. But against (1) he objects that the resemblances
that children show to their parents lie rather in such
features as their faces and hands than in their flesh and

bones as such. And against (2) he points out that the non-uniform parts are actually made up of the uniform ones. A hand is composed of flesh, bone, blood, nail and so on. Against (3) he uses the same consideration. Resemblances in the non-uniform parts must be due either to the material—but *that* is simply the uniform parts—or to the way the material is arranged. But if to the latter, nothing can be said to be 'drawn' from the *arrangement* to the seed, for the arrangement is not itself a material factor. In either case the seed cannot be drawn from such parts as the hands or face, but only from what those parts are made of. But then the theory loses its point, which was that all the individual parts of the body, and not merely all the constituent substances, supply material to the seed. Among his other more empirical arguments are analogies drawn from what happens in the case of plants. He notes at 722 a 11 ff. that certain parts of plants can be torn off, and yet the seed thereafter produces a new plant that is identical with the old, and he points out at 723 b 16 ff. that plant cuttings bear seed and this would suggest that even when the cutting belonged to the parent plant the seed it bore did not come from the *whole* of the plant. He rejects the pangenesis doctrine, then, and in the main he was certainly right to do so, although his own solution to the problem was equally in error in that he believed, for instance, that the semen of the male contributes no material to the embryo, but merely supplies the form and the efficient cause of generation.

Then the second great debate in embryology was that between the theories we know as 'preformation' and 'epigenesis'. Does the embryo contain all its parts in miniature from the beginning, as the preformationists held? Or is there a true formation of new structures as the embryo grows—an 'epigenesis'? Aristotle states the alternative views in the *de Generatione Animalium* II, ch. 1. His own theory was that what happens in both generation and growth is that something that exists potentially is brought into actuality by the agency of something that is itself already actual, and in thus favouring epigenesis he was largely right. While the controversy remained a live issue until well into the nineteenth century, the epigenesis view eventually prevailed, thanks largely to the work first of Caspar Friedrich Wolff and then of K. E. von Baer.[1]

In both these cases Aristotle's discussion has the great merit that it provides a clear statement of the opposing theories and sets out the main arguments and evidence *pro* and *contra*. Most of the evidence referred to consisted in well-known facts, or what were taken to be facts, but Aristotle shows considerable ingenuity in drawing out the implications of the available evidence. Yet we should observe how his own theoretical preconceptions influenced his solutions to both problems. The form/matter dichotomy provides the basis of his account of the roles of male and female in generation, and his answer to the question

[1] Wolff's *Theoria Generationis* appeared in 1759, parts one and two of von Baer's *Über Entwickelungsgeschichte der Thiere* in 1828 and 1837. The history of the controversies mentioned in this and the preceding paragraph may be followed up in A. W. Meyer's *The Rise of Embryology*, Stanford, 1939, and J. Needham's *A History of Embryology*, 2nd ed. Cambridge, 1959.

of preformation or epigenesis is founded on his distinction between potentiality and actuality.

Physiology

Aristotle's analysis of the main problems in embryology is eminently lucid and it contains several fruitful suggestions. Elsewhere, in his physiology for example, his theories are, as one might expect, often very oversimplified. He looks in each case for the final cause of the physiological process. He believes that respiration, for instance, serves to cool the excessive heat in the region round the heart. The higher the animal, as a general rule, the hotter it is. So it is not only necessary, but also good, for the larger animals to have lungs, for this enables them to counteract their greater heat. Yet his interest in final causes in no way prevents him from investigating the manner in which physiological processes take place and in particular their efficient causes. He discusses in some detail the question of which animals breathe and which do not. He denies that fish do, imagining that they effect the cooling of their hearts not by means of air, but by means of the water drawn in through their gills. And he describes the way in which the lungs draw in and expel the air, comparing them at *Resp.* 480a 20 ff. to a bellows, although he believes that it is the heat of the heart that controls the expansion and contraction of the lungs, and he has no conception of the part played by the diaphragm and the muscles in the thorax. Similarly in his account of digestion, for instance, he makes suggestions both about the vital functions that digestion serves and about how it takes place, comparing the 'concoction' of the nourishment in the body with the boiling or cooking of food in its preparation in the kitchen (*Mete.* 381 b6 f.).

Taxonomy

But one of the main problems, if not *the* main problem, which he was concerned with in his biological researches, is that of the classification of animals. Generally speaking, the aim of the *Historia Animalium* would seem to be to collect data concerning the similarities and differences of animals as a preliminary to classification. It is, however, only a preliminary. Aristotle nowhere attempts to set out a definitive, systematic classification of animals. Several aspects of his approach to this problem are worth noting. First he firmly refutes any attempt to classify animals by using the method of dichotomous division which had been favoured by the Platonists and which Plato himself had employed in his definitions of the sophist and the statesman in the *Sophist* and the *Politicus*. In the first book of the *de Partibus Animalium* Aristotle devotes a long discussion to showing how the attempt to classify animals by dividing and sub-dividing groups into pairs of opposites, such as 'winged' and 'wingless' or 'footed' and 'footless', is, as he puts it, 'in one respect impossible, in another futile'. While he brings many other arguments against the method, the chief of them is that it breaks up the natural groups, such as birds and fish. Dichotomy provides a neat schema of classes and sub-classes, but it is arbitrary and artificial and it obviously conflicts at certain points with the data.

Among the important passages in which Aristotle conveys some of his own ideas on this problem is *de Generatione Animalium* ii, ch. i where he discusses it from the point of view of the methods of reproduction of the various kinds of animals. He remarks on the overlapping of the main natural groups.

Bipeds are not all viviparous (for birds are oviparous), nor all oviparous (for man is viviparous). Quadrupeds are not all oviparous (for the horse and the ox and a great many others are viviparous), nor all viviparous (for lizards and crocodiles and many others are oviparous). Nor does the difference lie in having or not having feet: for some footless animals are viviparous, such as vipers and the cartilaginous fishes, while others are oviparous, as are the other fishes and the rest of the snakes. And of the animals with feet, many are oviparous, many viviparous, such as the quadrupeds just mentioned. There are animals with feet that are internally viviparous, such as man, and animals without feet too, such as the whale and the dolphin (*GA* 732 b 15–26).

Having shown that division cannot be carried out according to the organs of locomotion, he goes on to distinguish animals according to their modes of reproduction and embryonic development. According to this criterion there are five main groups, ranging from the most perfect animals, which are viviparous, through those animals that produce either a perfect or an imperfect egg, down to the insects, which do not produce an egg at all, but only a larva which becomes, he believes, 'egg-like' as it develops.

In *GA* ii, ch. i Aristotle demonstrates the lack of correlation between the organs of locomotion and the methods of reproduction of animals. Elsewhere he points out how difficult it is to draw a hard and fast line between living and lifeless things or between animals and plants. One such passage is *PA* 681 a 9 ff., where he remarks on the difficulty of classifying such intermediate kinds as the ascidians, the sponges and the sea-anemones, and again at *HA* 588 b 4 ff. he says:

Thus nature proceeds little by little from inanimate things to living creatures, in such a way that we are unable, in the continuous sequence, to determine the boundary line between them or to say on which side an intermediate kind falls. Next after inanimate things come the plants: and among the plants there are differences between one kind and another in the extent to which they seem to share in life, and the whole genus of plants appears to be alive when compared with other objects, but seems lifeless when compared with animals. The transition from them to the animals is a continuous one, as remarked before. For with some kinds of things found in the sea one would be at a loss to tell whether they are animals or plants.

These and other passages from the biological treatises show that much of his thinking on the question of the classification of animals is tentative and undogmatic. Certain definite assumptions do, however, underlie not only his treatment of this problem, but also his attitude towards the animal kingdom as a whole. First there is his belief that natural species are fixed and unchanging. Long before Aristotle, Anaximander had raised the problem of how the earliest human beings to appear on earth could have survived, and, noticing how vulnerable the young of the human species is, he had suggested that man in his original form must have had some other mechanism of survival. But even those theorists who held that changes must have taken place in natural species in the past generally had no clear idea of continuous natural evolution in the present and future. Aristotle himself, like most other Greek naturalists, firmly believed in the permanence of natural species as we know them. Yet interestingly enough there is one passage in which he mentions the belief in 'earth-born', that is spontaneously generated, men and considers the possibility of man and the higher animals growing either from larvae or from eggs (GA 762b28ff.). His discussion of these two suggestions is, however, purely hypothetical, for he would have denied the premiss on which the discussion was based, namely that man evolved from another species.

Secondly his remarks on the classification of animals are permeated by the notions of finality and fulfilment which influence so much of his biology. Man differs from the other animals, and the animals in turn differ from the plants, in the vital faculties they possess. And within the animal kingdom he often draws distinctions between higher and lower species. In GA II, ch. 1, for instance, the main groups are arranged in a hierarchy according to their methods of reproduction. The Vivipara are said to be the most perfect animals, for their young are perfectly formed when they are born. And within the oviparous animals he distinguishes between higher and lower kinds according to whether they lay perfect eggs, as birds do, or imperfect ones, as do the fish, whose eggs gain in size after they have been laid. All living creatures are arranged, if only very roughly, in a scale of perfection, comparable with, if less systematic than, what later came to be known as the Scala Naturae. Man is the most perfect animal, for he alone is rational, and by comparison with him the other animals are all imperfect: and yet each species achieves its own proper form and actuality.

Biological research and Aristotle's development

These two features of Aristotle's conception of the animal kingdom, the idea of the permanence of natural species, and the scale of perfection, take us back to the question of the relevance of his work in biology to the development of his philosophy as a whole. Undoubtedly the most important single effect of his biological researches was to establish a method of procedure for the natural sciences. It was in biology far more than in any other branch of natural science that the possibility of carrying out detailed empirical investigations was most clearly appreciated and the value of doing so was most amply demonstrated. The first book of the *de Partibus Animalium* describes the opportunities and indicates the method, and the claims it makes for the inquiry are fully vindicated by the actual results set out in the biological treatises as a whole.

But granted that his field-work in biology helped to establish a method, how were his investigations related to the theoretical assumptions on which his philosophy of nature was based? The part played by such doctrines as those of form and matter, and potentiality and actuality, in his biology has been noted on several occasions. Both doctrines figure prominently in, for example, his account of reproduction and growth. But it is quite clear that these general theories were not originally suggested by, but were rather brought to bear on, these specific biological problems. The major doctrines of substance, the four causes, actuality and potentiality, were the outcome of critical reflection on problems of a high order of generality that he had inherited from Plato and earlier philosophy: what has the best claim to be said to exist? How can anything be said to come to be? What factors must be mentioned in giving an account of change of any sort? And while at several points the particular answers he gave to those questions show that he paid special attention to the conditions that apply to change in the natural sphere, these major doctrines do not presuppose his detailed investigations in natural science, but provide, rather, the framework in which they were carried out. His field-work in biology led, so far as we can tell, to no major modifications or amendments in his general account of causation, but supplied a wealth of further examples to which his main theses could be applied.

Moreover the effect of his detailed empirical work was not merely to confirm him in his rejection of certain aspects of Plato's epistemology. This it certainly did do. But it also provided evidences endorsing, or appearing to endorse, certain features of his general doctrines in which he stayed close to Plato. Two examples of this may be given. The first is his doctrine of form. Here his work in biology no doubt seemed to him to corroborate the chief aspect of his theory in which he agreed with Plato, namely that it is form that is knowable. Aristotle, as much as any naturalist, appreciated that while it is the individual specimen that the biologist investigates, he does so from the point of view of the species as a whole and of what is common to all or most of its members, not from the point of view of the peculiarities of the individual specimen itself. Again the notion that forms or species—εἴδη—are real, and not merely matters of convention or figments of the human imagination, would have seemed to him to have been dramatically and overwhelmingly endorsed by the regularity with which natural kinds normally reproduce themselves. While he knew that hybrids can be formed by crossing species that are close to one another, these, like monstrous births and other abnormalities, were treated as exceptions to a rule which nevertheless holds good in the vast majority of instances throughout the animal kingdom.

My second example is Aristotle's teleology. Here too the similarities between his position and Plato's are more striking than the differences, important though these are. But where Plato in the *Timaeus* had cited a mere handful of examples to illustrate the rational design of living creatures and the adaptation of their parts to fulfil certain ends, Aristotle's biological researches provided him with a mass of data which could be taken to support his similar thesis of the role of the final cause in nature. Indeed he expressed the view that one of the main purposes of the study of animals is to reveal in them the order and the beauty of nature. Physiological processes, the parts of animals, even the problem of the classification of animals, are all studied with this in mind. Although the phenomena and processes of biology fall short of the regularity and uniformity of the movements of the heavenly bodies, the animal kingdom provides, nevertheless, evidence in abundance of 'the absence of chance and the serving of ends' of nature.

The passage I quoted from the first book of the *de Partibus Animalium* shows Aristotle attempting to overcome the prejudices of some of his contemporaries against biological research. As a statement of how much could be learnt from painstaking, empirical investigations in this field, it marks a turning-point in the history of biology and of natural science as a whole, and at the same time a reversal of Plato's attitude towards the study of particulars. In reaction against Plato, whom he represents as the philosopher of transcendent or disembodied form, Aristotle became more and more the philosopher of nature and of living form. Yet for all his application of new methods, and for all his many specific discoveries, in physics and biology, his conception of nature is still in some ways remarkably Platonic. Paradoxical though it may at first sight appear, the effect of some of his work in biology—a field in which he was so much the pioneer—was to reinforce certain theses concerning form and the role of the final cause which, while they are not identical with those of Plato himself, certainly owe a great deal to his ideas.

CHAPTER 5

THE FOUNDER OF
SYSTEMATIC RESEARCH

So far I have discussed three main features of Aristotle's intellectual development, the influence that Plato had on the young Aristotle, his reaction against the principal tenets of his master's philosophy, and the development of his interests in natural science, particularly in biology. But in concentrating on the main lines of his intellectual development during the earlier part of his life many other aspects of his work have necessarily been neglected. Yet from the beginning the range of problems that engaged his attention was wide, and it is now time to do more justice to this fact before turning to consider the chief characteristics of his work during the final period of his life.

As a young man in the Academy Aristotle would have discussed not only the ontological and epistemological questions connected with the theory of Forms, but also a large number of other subjects which certainly included logic or dialectic, ethics, politics and psychology. In each of these fields criticisms of Platonic theses are the starting-point of some of Aristotle's own theories, and in some cases these criticisms may well have begun to take shape while he was still Plato's pupil. In logic, for example, the nature of dialectic and the difference between the dialectician and the sophist are discussed at some length by Plato in the later dialogues. Academic debates on these topics undoubtedly provide the background against which Aristotle developed his own complex classification of the different main branches of reasoning, demonstrative, dialectical, rhetorical and eristic, and it is natural to suppose, in this instance, that this analysis is, in the main, a product of the period of his first residence in Athens.

Political science had an important place not only in the curriculum of the Academy, as a theoretical study, but also in the practical activities of many of its members, and Aristotle's interest in ethics and politics, as also in the question of the nature of the soul, certainly goes back to the first Athenian period. In each case we can trace certain developments in his theories from the internal evidence of his own writings. In ethics, for instance, a comparison between the two main treatises, the *Eudemian* and the *Nicomachean Ethics*, reveals some differences in his conception of φρόνησις, and it is likely that, as Jaeger already argued, the *Eudemian Ethics* represents a stage in Aristotle's thinking before he had fully worked out his doctrine of the relation between practical intelligence and moral virtue. Both treatises, however, specifically criticise the Platonic Form of the Good, and in doing so they incorporate some of his general philosophical objections to the theory of Forms: and both reject the idea that ethics is based on an exact inquiry which is suggested in one of our sources for the *Protrepticus*.

Psychology provides another good example where a development in his thought can be traced from the internal evidence. As we saw in ch. 2, the evidence for the *Eudemus* and the *Protrepticus* suggests that he originally adopted an other-worldly conception of the soul, in which the soul's residence in the body was considered unnatural. But the chief doctrine that he put forward in the treatises was that the soul is the form or actuality of the living body. The date of this remarkable change in emphasis cannot be fixed precisely, but by the time he embarked on his extensive investigations into the animal kingdom he must have held that the soul belongs naturally to the living body—and those investigations no doubt appeared to confirm, if indeed they did not suggest, another feature of his mature psychology, his belief that the heart is the seat of certain vital functions. Yet he continued to criticise the doctrines of Plato in the treatise in which he set out his definitive theory of the soul, namely the *de Anima*, and this may well be one of his latest productions. In it he explicitly refuted the Platonic conception of a tripartite soul, for example, when presenting his own more complex theory of its various faculties.

Although we cannot go far towards defining the precise contribution of each of the three main periods of his philosophical activity to his physics, to his ethics and to his logic, we can at least be sure that his interest in each of these three fields extended throughout his life. Several of his major ontological and epistemological theories, including the doctrine of substance put forward in the *Categories*, the theory of the four causes, and the doctrine of actuality and potentiality, had been worked out either before he left Athens in 347, or very shortly afterwards. And by the time he came back to Athens in 335 the foundations of his work in each of the main fields of inquiry in which he was interested had probably been laid. Granted that any attempt to identify the specific theories that he had formulated by this time involves a good deal of pure conjecture, they are likely to have included the following: in logic, the theory of the syllogism, and the doctrine of scientific method set out in the *Posterior Analytics* (see ch. 6). In physics (chh. 7 and 8), the theory of the four terrestrial elements with their natural upward or downward movement, the doctrine of the fifth element, aither, that moves naturally in a circle, and the idea of an unmoved first mover, as well as many of his detailed theories, such as his conception of the earth as a spherical mass at rest at the centre of the universe. In psychology (ch. 9), the view that the soul belongs naturally to the living body, although not necessarily the final definition of soul as the 'first actuality of a natural body that potentially has life': also his conception of the heart as the central seat of sensation and life, and his doctrine of a plurality of faculties of soul—which in turn provides the basis of his conception of the scale of perfection of living beings ranging from plants to gods. In ethics and politics (chh. 10 and 11), the rejection of Plato's theories of the Good and of the ideal state, the positive doctrines that he put in their place, and probably much else besides. Indeed the earlier of the two main ethical treatises, the *Eudemian Ethics*, in which the doctrine of moral virtue as a mean is already worked out in detail, might be taken to correspond fairly closely to the stage of development that Aristotle's moral philosophy had reached during the period of the travels.

The Lyceum period

But if the foundations of his principal logical, physical and ethical theories were laid by the end of the period of the travels, a great deal was added to his original ideas in the period of his second residence in Athens. This is clear if only from the fact that many of the treatises represent, in the form in which they have come down to us, the notes for the lecture-courses in the Lyceum. In most cases they show signs of having undergone editorial revisions and additions which, where they are authentic, must have dated from the Lyceum period. Moreover Aristotle left certain work uncompleted, particularly in his researches in the natural and social sciences, and this too provides some clues about the nature of his interests in the last period of his philosophical activity.

Aristotle's school

It would be hard to exaggerate the importance of the Lyceum not only in Aristotle's intellectual development, but also from the point of view of the history of western European philosophy and science as a whole. He began teaching there shortly after his return to Athens in 335. By this time Xenocrates was head of the Academy, and Aristotle's school was no doubt to some extent modelled on the older institution of Plato: it certainly came increasingly to act as its rival. Both schools may be seen as the natural development of the informal associations between the master and his friends and pupils which were such a feature of the intellectual activity not only of Plato and Aristotle, but also of many other Greek philosophers and scientists.

Like the Academy, the Lyceum had two main functions, those of teaching and research. As the tutor of Alexander, Aristotle had already been obliged to be something of a schoolmaster, and in the Lyceum he offered popular, as well as specialist, courses. But if in its educational role the Lyceum rivalled but did not outshine the Academy, as a centre of research it far outstripped any earlier institution. Indeed in the whole of antiquity only the Museum at Alexandria was to surpass it. Here again the school at Athens represented a natural development of some of Aristotle's earlier interests, or rather the culmination of his earlier ambitions. Apart from the evidence from the biological treatises which has already been reviewed, there are indications that he started detailed investigations in other fields as well during the period of the travels. One of the minor tasks of historical research that he undertook was to establish a complete list of the winners of the Pythian games. But as his collaborator in this work was Callisthenes, it must have been started before 334, when Callisthenes left to accompany Alexander on his expedition to the East. And other lost books also, such as the researches into the competitions at the Dionysiac and the Lenaean festivals, and the study of barbarian customs, probably incorporated work done during the period of the travels.

There is good evidence to show that Aristotle had begun a number of investigations both in the natural sciences and in the field of historical and social studies before his return to Athens. But the Lyceum enabled him to embark on a far more ambitious programme of inquiries. First of all it was, or came to be, equipped with a number of important instruments of research, a library, maps, a collection of anatomical diagrams, and perhaps also a collection of biological specimens. And even more important than the material equipment which Aristotle and the successive heads of the school collected was the presence of a number of like-minded friends and pupils who could share in the work of research. The Lyceum concentrated together under a common leadership a body of individuals who were to carry out more extensive investigations over a wider range of scientific, historical and social subjects than had even been imagined, let alone attempted, ever before.

Most of this work was not completed until after Aristotle's death, but much of it was planned and organised by him, and all of it was stimulated by his example. First there was a series of histories of different branches of speculative thought. These may be seen as developing the brief outlines of the views of his predecessors that Aristotle often gives before setting out his own ideas in the treatises. The histories of the main physical doctrines and of the theories of sense-perception were undertaken by Theophrastus, for example, and fragments of both these works have come down to us. To another pupil, Meno, was delegated the task of writing the history of Greek medicine, of which again we possess some rather meagre excerpts. Secondly, there was the vast collection of histories of political constitutions, and here too the project as a whole was organised by Aristotle who was probably himself responsible for the *Constitution of Athens* which served as a model for the other studies. Thirdly, in the domain of the natural sciences, Aristotle's own zoological works were complemented by the equally full and admirable botanical treatises of Theophrastus. In what we should call chemistry, the fourth book of the *Meteorologica*, which attempts among other things to classify the compounds of earth and water according to certain of their physical properties, was followed up by a detailed study of minerals, again by Theophrastus, the treatise *On Stones*. And in statics and dynamics Aristotle's own rather unsystematic discussion of movement and weight in the *Physics* and the *de Caelo* was complemented and extended by the treatise *On Mechanics* and by the work of the third head of the Lyceum, Strato of Lampsacus. *On Mechanics* includes a study of the lever and of three other simple machines, the pulley, the wedge and the windlass, and Strato seems to have been the first person to attempt to carry out a series of empirical investigations in dynamics, doing so in connection with the phenomena of acceleration in particular.

Although the Pythagoreans, the medical schools and the Academy each contributed something to the growth of the idea of undertaking scientific investigations as a cooperative effort, the Lyceum was the first centre of systematic research organised on a considerable scale. Its importance as the prototype of all research institutions in the West is easy to grasp. But the school was also important in Aristotle's personal intellectual development, and this needs some elucidation. Once again Plato may serve as a point of reference. One of the most important features of Aristotle's reaction against his master was his rejection of Plato's epistemology and especially of his evaluation of particulars. The organised historical, social and scientific researches of the Lyceum represent, one may say, the full fruit of Aristotle's own methodology, and especially of his insistence that the starting-point of any investigation is what is 'better known to us'—the concrete particulars. Aristotle is also undoubtedly a great systematiser. Certain fundamental ideas pervade large areas of his work, the notions of form and finality being particularly important examples. But the fundamental ideas that provide the connecting links between different branches of his work did not impede the independent development of those various branches. The key methodological doctrine that stimulated and guided Aristotle's own researches and those of the Lyceum after him was that in dealing with a problem one must first examine both the particular data and the common opinions before attempting to resolve the issues. It was this that provided the incentive to study each field of inquiry in detail and in depth, and with reference to the history of previous thought on the topic. And it was this that ensured a measure of objectivity in the investigations that were carried out, a willingness to let theory wait on evidence, to consider alternative solutions to a problem and to criticise each of them in the light of both reason and the findings of research.

The range of Aristotle's interests

The researches of the Lyceum period represent the full exploitation of a methodology the origins of which probably date from early on in Aristotle's reaction against the philosophy of Plato. But we must not assume that his more empirical investigations completely ousted his other interests towards the end of his life. Both the natural and the social sciences lent themselves particularly well to the technique of detailed research which he practised with increasing vigour and success. But to do justice to the range of his intellectual activities, we must also acknowledge his achievements in more purely abstract inquiries, in ontology and theology, and in the philosophy of mind, for these too formed an important part of his interests in the latter part of his life.

This can be illustrated by referring to a set of theories that spans a number of different inquiries. His doctrines of the source of movement, of god, of substance and of reason are evidently closely interconnected and form a carefully worked out whole. Very briefly, the ultimate source of movement is a mover that acts as a final cause and is itself unmoved. It is pure substance and actuality, for while in the sublunary sphere form exists only in conjunction with matter, in the celestial sphere, which is constituted not by the four elements but by aither, pure substance can and does exist. But the activity of this divine unmoved mover is defined as reason or contemplation, and this provides a link both with Aristotle's psychology and with his ethics. In his final psychological theory the only part of the soul that can be immortal is reason, and even then only a part of it, the so-called active reason. And in the ethics the highest life for man is said to be the life 'according to reason'. In this activity man resembles the gods, although unlike the gods he cannot practise it continually.

This total theory, in which Aristotle's theology, his doctrine of causation and movement, his psychology and his ethics all meet, obviously forms a most important part of his vision of the universe, and the descriptions of the unmoved mover in *Metaphysics* Λ and of the life according to reason in the tenth book of the *Nicomachean Ethics* provide the occasions for some of his most deeply moving, indeed poetic, writing. There can be no doubt that he continued to subscribe to these beliefs. The ethical doctrine of the superiority of the life according to reason, for example, clearly remained a part of his personal credo to the end of his days, for he continued to practise and exemplify this life in every branch of his philosophical and scientific studies.

This would suggest at the very least that he did not abandon this set of doctrines. But we can be more positive than this. There is concrete evidence that they formed part of his active interests in the period of the Lyceum. The doctrine of the unmoved mover, for example, was the outcome of successive attempts to give a satisfactory account of the movements of the heavenly bodies. I have noted before (p. 27) that there are passages in the *de Caelo* that were probably composed before he had formulated the theory of a transcendent unmoved mover, for in them he appears to assume that the doctrine of aither, the fifth element that moves naturally in a circle, provides by itself a sufficient explanation of the motions of the heavenly bodies. But once he had propounded the theory that the

ultimate source of movement is an unmoved mover acting as a final cause, he continued to be actively engaged
on working out the details of how it operates. Thus when
he raises, in *Metaphysics* Λ, ch. 8, the question of how many
of these unmoved movers are necessary in order to account
for all the observed movements of the stars, the planets,
the sun and the moon, his own theory represents a modifi-
cation of those of Eudoxus and Callippus, and while the
evidence we possess concerning the date of Callippus is
scanty and imprecise, it remains extremely improbable
that Aristotle knew his theory or had worked out his own
reply to it before the period of his second residence in
Athens.

While the pursuit of detailed empirical researches undoubtedly intensified in the last period of Aristotle's
activity, there is no reason to believe that this was bought
at the price of an abandonment of, or even a serious
slackening in, his other interests. On the contrary, his
studies in such fields as theology and the philosophy of
mind continued to develop in the Lyceum, and the same
is also true of his conception of substance and his ethics.
Among the important treatises that probably incorporate
a great deal of work done during the final period of his
life are the *de Anima, Metaphysics* Z and H, and the *Nicomachean Ethics*. In some respects his biological researches,
so far from undermining such fundamental ideas as his
teleology and his doctrine of form, tended to reinforce
them. His investigations into the similarities and the
differences of the various kinds of animals, for instance,
served to confirm him in his belief in a scale of perfection

of living creatures, and this was not merely a biological doctrine, but one that extended into other disciplines as well. In the ethical works, his account of man's proper function and of his proper virtue or excellence is based on the idea that man is a rational animal, different from the other animals in possessing reason, but an animal nevertheless. And the scale can be extended upwards, for the gods also possess the faculty of reason, although they do not have the lower faculties of soul that men share with the animals. There is, then, an important sense in which what are for us the independent disciplines of biology, psychology, ethics and theology were, for Aristotle, linked together, forming parts of a single whole. The Lyceum period may be seen as the climax not only of his empirical, but also of some at least of his more purely abstract, inquiries. While these two terms, empirical and abstract, enable us to draw a rough and ready distinction between, for example, the detailed description of the parts of animals, and the investigation of substance, it is quite clear that these two different types of inquiry in no way exclude one another, and that both form complementary parts of Aristotle's mature interests.

The history of Aristotle's intellectual development is one of a continuous expansion of interests and widening of horizons. In the Academy, he was no doubt, to begin with, very much in Plato's shadow. We have only a dim picture of this stage in his thought, but to judge from the scanty remains of some of his earlier literary productions, these were generally modelled fairly closely on Plato's dialogues, and they incorporated many Platonic theses, even if they show signs of Aristotle already diverging from his master's views. In his subsequent development, some of the main landmarks are clear. First there is his reaction against the teaching of Plato. Here the focal point is his rejection of the theory of Forms, which evidently took place while he still considered himself a member of the circle of Platonists. But not only did he criticise the fundamental doctrines of Platonism: he also developed interests in many fields of inquiry, particularly in natural science, that went far beyond Plato's. While the essentials of his own theory of causation seem to have been already developed by the time he left Athens on Plato's death, the next period probably saw him undertaking, among other things, the first detailed empirical investigations in biology. And here we have in the first book of the *de Partibus Animalium* a text which, whenever it was composed, testifies eloquently to the fact that Aristotle himself recognised that he was pioneering a new field of study. Then when he returned to Athens, he planned and organised, in the Lyceum, a truly remarkable series of researches in the natural sciences and in the field of historical and social studies.

Whether any of these developments, including the initial break away from Platonism, involved any drastic revolution in his thought seems doubtful. Naturally he changed his mind on many points of doctrine, as he looked for the best solution to the problems that presented themselves. But there is an important continuity in his intellectual development. First in such fields as physics proper and ethics his interests remained fairly constant, and his ideas developed quite gradually, throughout his life. And then many of the new studies that he pioneered may be seen as natural extensions of earlier interests, in which he applied certain basic methodological principles to new subject-matter or investigated in depth problems that had only been touched on by previous writers. Even his formal logic owes something to Academic discussions of the nature of dialectic, and in his biology he is at pains to criticise the Academic method of division as applied to the classification of animals. Finally the development of new interests did nothing to undermine the old. His achievements are extraordinarily far-ranging. Yet certain fundamental notions, and a common method, are exhibited in a great deal of his thought. My next task is to review his contribution to each of the most important fields of inquiry that he investigated, after which I shall return to the question of the unity and coherence of his thought.

PART II

Fundamentals of Aristotle's Thought

CHAPTER 6

LOGIC AND METAPHYSICS

The first part of this study has been devoted to giving the outlines of Aristotle's intellectual development. In the second I shall take the main branches of his work in turn and attempt to describe and elucidate the fundamentals of his thought, locating his principal ideas in the context of the philosophical and scientific discussions of the time, and assessing their value and importance. The first general field I shall consider is logic. Here his work is particularly comprehensive, very largely original and for the most part eminently lucid. It is, moreover, highly professional, and the specialist will find a great deal that is of interest in the logical treatises apart from those sections of them that contain what still remains an excellent introduction to the study of elementary logic. For the sake of illustrating his work in this field, however, it will be enough to select three topics for particular comment, his doctrine of categories, his syllogistic and his conception of so-called 'scientific' knowledge.

The logical treatises, known collectively as the Organon or 'tool' of thought, begin with two short works, the *Categories* and the *de Interpretatione*, dealing with terms and with propositions respectively. The first chapter of the *Categories*, for example, begins by drawing distinctions between things named (1) 'homonymously', (2) 'synony-mously' and (3) 'paronymously'. Things are named 'homonymously', first, when they have only the name in common and the definition corresponding to the name is different in each case. In English, 'box' is the name of both a container and a shrub, but the definition corresponding to the name is different in each case. Secondly, things are named 'synonymously' when both name and the corresponding definition are the same. A man and an ox are both said to be 'animals', and the definition corresponding to the term 'animal' is the same in both cases. Thirdly, a thing is named 'paronymously' when it derives its name from some other word, as a grammarian derives his name from grammar.

In the *de Interpretatione*, ch. 4, for example, he distinguishes between a sentence and a statement or proposition. A sentence is any significant combination of words. A proposition is a sentence that affirms or denies something—a predicate—of something else—the subject. Propositions are either true or false, but this is not true of every sentence. A prayer, for instance, is a sentence but is neither true nor false (*Int.* 17 a 4 f.). And later in the same work, ch. 10, 19 b 5 ff., he discusses various pairs of affirmations and negations, where he points out, for example, that the contradictory of 'every man is just' is not 'every man is not-just', but rather 'not every man is just'.

These are all simple distinctions that seem obvious enough to us, but it is worth bearing in mind that for the most part they had not been stated clearly and explicitly before Aristotle. The doctrine of the categories itself is at once better known and more obscure than these useful but elementary logical points. In ch. 4 of the *Categories* he classifies the things that are signified by simple expressions under ten heads, giving examples of each:

> substance (man, horse)
> quantity (two cubits long, three cubits long)
> quality (white, grammatical)
> relation (double, half, greater)
> place (in the Lyceum, in the market)
> time (yesterday, last year)
> position (lies, sits)
> state (has shoes on, has armour on)
> action (cuts, burns)
> affection (is cut, is burnt).

Elsewhere there are slightly different classifications, and the number of categories mentioned varies. In the *Topics* (I, ch. 9) there are again ten, although when the list is introduced at 103 b 22 the first category is referred to as 'what it is', τί ἐστι, rather than as οὐσία, substance or being. In other passages there are shorter lists, of eight or six or five categories, but substance, quantity and quality are always included. Such differences are not particularly important, but we should beware of assuming that Aristotle intended any of his lists to be definitive and exhaustive.

The first question that might be raised is whether the classification is one of things or of terms, an ontological, or a logical, classification. To this the answer must be that the categories are primarily intended as a classification of reality, of the things signified by terms, rather than of the signifying terms themselves. This, at least, is how the classification is introduced at the beginning of ch. 4

(1b25ff.): 'of things said without combination, *each signifies* either substance or quantity...' Yet he evidently arrived at his classification mainly from a consideration of linguistic facts, that is of what kinds of things may be said, and of what kinds of questions may be asked, about anything, and this is natural enough, for he assumes that the logical distinctions that these data suggest will reflect and reveal the real distinctions between the things signified in which he is interested. The original logical meaning of the word κατηγορία itself is 'predicate', although in the first category primary substances, that is individuals such as Callias or Socrates, are not logical predicates, but subjects of which other things are predicated: the term for subject is ὑποκείμενον, literally what underlies, the same term that he uses in a different context for the 'substratum'. In part, the categories may be derived from considering what may be predicated of a subject and examining what sorts of things these predicates signify. Callias is six foot tall, white, larger than Socrates and so on. If we ask what whiteness, for example, is, we shall answer first that it is a colour, but then we can ask the same question about colour, answering in turn that it is a quality: when we arrive at the category, the process stops.

The categories are the ultimate classes into which whatever exists or is real may be said to fall. But what is the use or value of this doctrine? When in ch. 5 he develops the distinction between 'primary' and 'secondary' substance, he is evidently combatting Plato. For Aristotle, 'what is called a substance most strictly, primarily and most of all' is the individual man, the individual horse and so on (2a11ff.). The species and genera—man, horse, animal—are secondary substances. Even though the Platonic Forms are not mentioned, he is clearly joining issue, in this passage, with Plato's view that the Forms are ontologically prior to the particulars. Against the Platonic doctrine Aristotle argues that individuals are substances in the strictest sense, for they are the subjects for all other things, and all other things are either predicated of them or are in them (2b15ff., 37ff.). If the primary substances did not exist, he says at 2b5f., it would be impossible for any of the other things to exist: qualities, for example, cannot exist by themselves, that is apart from the individual substances that have the qualities.

The distinction between primary and secondary substance, and the doctrine that the other categories presuppose substance, are important points that Aristotle brings out in the course of developing his doctrine. But in general he does not spell out in the *Categories* itself how his doctrine is to be used. Its usefulness and value only become apparent when we turn to passages in other treatises where Aristotle puts the doctrine to work to draw distinctions either between classes of things or between the meanings of terms. Thus in the *Physics* (I, chh. 7 and 8 and V, chh. 1 and 2) and in the *de Generatione et Corruptione* (I, ch. 3) he points out that change differs according to the category in which the change takes place, and this is particularly relevant to earlier physical speculation, since it helps him to emphasise that to deny that there is unqualified coming-to-be in the category of substance is not to deny that other types of change may take place, for example locomotion in the category of place. To deny that anything can come to be from what is totally non-existent is not to deny that a hot thing may become cold, or that a young animal may grow into a mature one, or that an arrow may be shot from a bow. Again at several points in the *Metaphysics*, for example at 1017a22 ff., he brings the doctrine of categories to bear on the vexed question of the ambiguities of the verb 'to be', and in the *Topics*, 107a3 ff., he recommends examining the categories in which a predicate is used as a general method of detecting ambiguities in reasoning.

The syllogism

By far the best known, and the most typical, product of Aristotle's work in logic is the theory of the syllogism. In its usual form the syllogism consists of two premisses and a conclusion. Very occasionally the conclusion is stated in the form of an *inference: A* belongs to all *B; B* belongs to all *C; therefore A* belongs to all *C*. But as a general rule the syllogism is expressed as a form of *implication: if A* belongs to all *B*, and *B* belongs to all *C*, *then A* belongs to all *C*.

The premisses and conclusions of syllogisms are differentiated according to three criteria, quantity, quality and modality. Under quantity, first, he distinguishes universal, particular and indefinite statements. In a universal statement something is said to belong to all or none of X, and in a particular one something is said to belong, or not to belong, to some of X. These are usually illustrated by such examples as 'all men are animals' and 'some men are wise', but Aristotle's premisses are generally stated in a slightly different form, which is rather less natural in English, thus: 'animal belongs to, ὑπάρχει, or is predicated of, κατηγορεῖται, every man'; 'wisdom belongs to some men'. Finally an indefinite statement says that something belongs or does not belong to X without specifying whether it is to all or to some of it: one of Aristotle's examples is 'pleasure is not good'.

Secondly under quality he distinguishes affirmative and negative statements. If we leave aside indefinite statements, these first two differentiae may be combined to give a fourfold division of statements:

universal affirmative: A belongs to all B
universal negative: A belongs to no B
particular affirmative: A belongs to some B
particular negative: A does not belong to some B.

These four types, which form the traditional schedule of propositions, are referred to, for the sake of convenience, by the letters A, E, I and O respectively, these letters being derived from the vowels in the two verbs *affirmo* and *nego*.

Thirdly under modality he distinguishes between the three types of statements (i) 'A belongs to B', (ii) 'A necessarily belongs to B' and (iii) 'A may belong to B', or put more simply (i) 'B is A', (ii) 'B must be A' and (iii) 'B may be A'. These three kinds are generally referred to as 'assertoric', 'apodeictic' and 'problematic' statements respectively.

Passing from his consideration of different types of premiss in the opening chapters of the first book of the

Prior Analytics Aristotle turns in ch. 4 to examine how syllogisms are produced, for not every combination of a pair of premisses enables a conclusion to be drawn. Here he distinguishes between three different *figures* of the syllogism according to the relationships between the terms in the premisses. These terms themselves are known as major, middle and minor. Take the stock Aristotelian example, 'if A belongs to all B, and B belongs to all C, then A belongs to all C'. The *middle term* is that which appears in both premisses—B. The *major term* is that which is predicated of something else in the conclusion—A. And the *minor term* is that of which something else is predicated in the conclusion—C. The major and minor terms each appear in only one of the two premisses, and the premiss in which each appears is named after it. Thus the *major premiss* is the one in which the major term appears—'A belongs to all B' in my example—and the *minor premiss* is that in which the minor term appears—'B belongs to all C'.

Syllogisms in the first figure may be described as those in which something is predicated of the middle term in the major premiss, and the middle term is predicated of something else in the minor premiss. The stock example is the one I have been using: 'if A belongs to all B, and B belongs to all C, then A belongs to all C'.

Syllogisms in the second figure are those in which the middle term is predicated of something else in both the major and the minor premiss, as in 'if M belongs to no N, and M belongs to all O, then N belongs to no O'.

Syllogisms in the third figure are those in which something is predicated of the middle term in both the major and the minor premiss, as in 'if P belongs to all S, and R belongs to all S, then P belongs to some R'.

The three figures are, as it were, the genera of the syllogism that Aristotle recognises. But in each figure there are different *moods*, depending on the quantity and the quality of the premisses. Take syllogisms in the first figure. In the stock example, 'if A belongs to all B, and B belongs to all C, then A belongs to all C', both premisses are universal affirmatives. But a combination of a universal affirmative major premiss and a particular affirmative minor one also yields a syllogism, this time with a particular affirmative conclusion: for if A belongs to all B, and B belongs to some C, then A belongs to some C. On the other hand, if one combines a universal affirmative major premiss with a particular negative minor one no conclusion follows: if we are given that animal is predicated of all men, and that man is not predicated of some white things, this does not allow us to establish any relation between animals and white things. Equally in the second and third figures there are various valid moods besides the examples I have already given. At *APr.* 27 a 36 ff., for instance, Aristotle shows that a combination of a universal affirmative major premiss and a particular negative minor one, which was found to produce no syllogism in the first figure, yields a particular negative conclusion in the second: if M belongs to all N, and M does not belong to some O, then N does not belong to some O.

Book I of the *Prior Analytics* contains a detailed exposition of the three figures of the syllogism not only with 'assertoric', but also with 'apodeictic' and 'problematic' premisses and with the various combinations of these, such as one assertoric with one apodeictic and so on. In the course of his discussion he draws some general conclusions, as for example that it is only in the first figure, and only in one mood of that figure, that a universal affirmative conclusion can be established: this alone yields what he calls 'perfect' syllogisms, and all the other valid moods of the syllogism can be reduced to universal syllogisms in the first figure. Again in the second figure only negative conclusions can be established, and in the third only particular ones. He gives general rules for syllogisms in any figure, pointing out that a syllogism contains three and only three terms, for even if intermediate terms are introduced, there is still only one term that acts as a middle term in each syllogism. And for a syllogism to be formed one or other premiss must be universal, and one or other premiss must be affirmative.

The most remarkable feature of the theory as a whole is undoubtedly its originality. Concrete arguments that have a syllogistic form are occasionally found in earlier texts, and there are several passages in fifth and fourth century writers where the logic of individual arguments is challenged. Moreover Plato drew attention to several important general points connected with different types of argument, as for instance when he emphasised the distinction between demonstrative and merely probable arguments in passages in the *Phaedo* (92 c d) and *Theaetetus* (162 e). But none of this alters the fact that it was Aristotle who conducted the first systematic analysis of the forms of argument as such. It was he who took the important step of introducing the use of symbols that can stand for *any* term, and he was the first to investigate the conditions of the validity of arguments and to draw up rules of implication.

His theory of the syllogism is, as far as it goes, admirably lucid, thorough and economical. But as is hardly surprising when we remember that it was Aristotle himself who invented the science of formal logic, it does not go far enough, and he was mistaken in his claim that all other forms of reasoning can be reduced to the syllogism. That he did not recognise the so-called fourth figure of the syllogism is a point of small importance. The fourth figure is that in which the middle term is the predicate in the major premiss and has something else predicated of it in the minor, reversing the positions it has in these premisses in the first figure, but most of the syllogisms that occur in the fourth figure are more naturally dealt with under the other three, and indeed he implicitly recognises each of the valid moods of this figure during the course of his discussion. But a more serious criticism of his syllogistic is that while his discussion of the four types of propositions, *A*, *E*, *I* and *O*, is very full, there are other types that he discusses much less fully or indeed scarcely at all. In his analysis of syllogistic argument he is chiefly interested in propositions that express relations of class-inclusion and class-exclusion between two terms. But he only rarely mentions, and certainly never deals systematically with, propositions expressing such transitive relations as, for example, 'greater than', 'equal to' or 'simultaneous with', although these too form syllogisms, such as 'if A is greater than B and B is greater than C, then A is greater than C'. And while he introduced symbols to stand for *terms*, he failed to appreciate the value of employing symbols to stand for *propositions*. Had he done so, he might have drawn attention to other relations of inference and types of implication besides those that have a pure syllogistic form, as for instance compound arguments formed from the combination of a composite premiss and a simple one such as the following: either p or q; not p; therefore q (where p and q stand for propositions). Or again: not both p and q; q; therefore not p. As it is, while he uses certain arguments of these forms in practice quite often, he does not analyse them systematically, and it was left to later logicians to classify their types.

'Scientific' knowledge

Having given his theory of the syllogism in the *Prior Analytics*, Aristotle turns in the *Posterior Analytics* to discuss demonstration, for demonstration, he says, is a form of syllogism, specifically a syllogism that is capable of producing ἐπιστήμη. ἐπιστήμη itself is defined as the sort of knowledge 'when we know the cause on which the fact depends as the cause of the fact, and that the fact could not be otherwise' (*APo.* 71 b 10 ff.). This knowledge comes from a demonstration that has a syllogistic, that is deductive, form. But being syllogistic, demonstration must proceed from premisses. These premisses must have certain intrinsic characteristics. They must be true, and they must be primary, indemonstrable and immediate, in the sense that the predicate attaches to the subject directly, not through a middle term. Aristotle denies both that all propositions are demonstrable, and that no proposition is demonstrable, maintaining that certain conclusions can be demonstrated from premisses that are themselves indemonstrable but known to be true. The premisses must, moreover, contain the causes of the conclusions, for it is only when we know the cause that we have ἐπιστήμη.

All teaching and learning that take place by means of reasoning proceed, Aristotle says, from already existing knowledge, and he distinguishes three kinds of starting-points or primary premisses that 'scientific' demonstration requires, namely (1) 'axioms', (2) 'definitions' and (3) 'hypotheses'. The 'axioms' are the principles without which no reasoning is possible, as for example the law of excluded middle that states that any predicate must be either truly affirmed or truly denied of any subject, provided, of course, that neither the subject nor the predicate is used equivocally. 'Definitions' are the assumptions of the meanings of terms, 'hypotheses' the assumptions of the existence of certain things corresponding to the terms: the geometer, in one of Aristotle's examples, assumes both the meaning and the existence of points and lines.

'Scientific' knowledge is of things that cannot be otherwise than they are. It demonstrates connections that are 'universal', καθόλου, in a special sense that Aristotle elucidates in *Posterior Analytics* I, ch. 4 (73 b 26 ff.). First the attribute must belong to every instance of the subject without exception. Secondly it must belong to the subject *per se*, that is it must be essentially, not merely accidentally, true of it. Thirdly it must belong to the subject precisely *qua* itself. There is, then, a 'universal' connection between subject and attribute when (1) the attribute is proved true of any instance of the subject, and (2) the subject is the widest class of which it is proved true. Thus possession of angles equal to two right angles is a universal attribute of 'triangle', but not of 'figure', nor of 'isosceles triangle'. It is not a universal attribute of figure, obviously, since while it can be proved true of some figures, it cannot be proved true of any chance figure. But it is not a universal attribute of 'isosceles triangle' either, for although it satisfies the first requirement, it does not satisfy the second. It can be proved true of all isosceles triangles, but it is true of them not *qua* isosceles, but *qua* triangle, and 'triangle' is in fact the widest class of which the attribute is proved true.

The *Posterior Analytics* is a detailed investigation of the conditions of certain knowledge and proof. In the strict sense of the terms, knowledge and demonstration are concerned with necessary, eternal, 'universal' connections, and almost all of Aristotle's examples in the first book are drawn either from mathematics itself or from such mathematical sciences as optics, harmonics and astronomy. Yet while the mathematical sciences serve as his chief model throughout the *Posterior Analytics*, his study is not solely directed to mathematics and to the deductive element in proof. In the second book, where he discusses definition and other related topics, a broader selection of examples is used, including several drawn from the biological sciences. Thus in II, ch. 17, 99a23ff., he uses as an example of a strict demonstration a syllogism in which the conclusion is that all broad-leaved trees are deciduous. It is clear that while mathematics provides the paradigm of knowledge throughout the treatise, he believes that his analysis of the conditions of knowledge applies in other fields as well.

Induction

Moreover while most of his attention is devoted to the deductive element in demonstration, he also recognises the importance of induction. In particular it is by induction that we get to know the universal, and it is again by induction that we apprehend the immediate primary premisses—axioms, definitions and hypotheses—on which demonstrations are based. It is true that this is only discussed at length in a single chapter (II, ch. 19) of the *Posterior Analytics*, and his scattered remarks on induction elsewhere in the Organon are in several respects unsatisfactory. Thus in the *Prior Analytics* (II, ch. 23) he attempts to reduce induction to a deductive form, primarily, one suspects, in order to establish the priority and superiority of his favourite type of argument, the syllogism. He shows that when the induction is perfect or complete, that is when all the particulars of a class are passed under review, an inductive argument can be expressed in the form of a syllogism. His example is: if man, horse, mule, etc. (*C*) are long-lived (*A*), and man, horse, mule, etc. (*C*) are bileless (*B*), then—provided *B* is no wider than *C*—it follows that all bileless animals (*B*) are long-lived (*A*).

His remarks on induction in the *Posterior Analytics* indicate that it has a much more important role than the analysis in *APr.* II, ch. 23 would lead us to expect, but at the same time they leave unresolved certain questions about its nature. Thus he stresses that we cannot *know* the particular, only the universal: this is stated explicitly at 81 b 6 f., for instance, and again in the *Metaphysics*, for example at B, ch. 4, 999 a 26 ff. And yet he also recognises on four separate occasions that we arrive at knowledge of the universal only from an examination of particulars. Thus at *APo.* 81 b 2 ff. he says that it is impossible to get a view of (θεωρῆσαι) universals except by induction, and that this is true even when the universals are abstractions: an example might be when a student learns from inspecting a diagram that a mathematical figure has certain properties. At 88 a 4 f. he says that the universal becomes clear from the several particulars. At 97 b 7 ff. he suggests that in defining we must start by trying to see what is common to a set of similars, that is the similar individuals. And finally in II, ch. 19 he considers how we know the primary premisses of demonstrations, and he argues that this knowledge is not innate but acquired by means of induction. He does not justify this process, but merely describes its origin and development. Typically he traces its ultimate origin to a faculty that is common to both men and animals, namely sense-perception. But only a few animals have memory, the power of retaining what they have perceived. From memory comes experience, and from experience in turn both τέχνη, 'art', and ἐπιστήμη, 'scientific knowledge'.

The *Posterior Analytics* investigates the conditions of knowledge and proof as exhibited particularly in mathematics. But while most of Aristotle's discussion is devoted to deductive reasoning, his brief remarks on induction make it clear that it plays a fundamental role in his theory of knowledge, since it is by induction that we know universals and the primary premisses on which demonstrations are based. He has, however, little to contribute on that favourite problem of later philosophy, the validity of induction, for he does not attempt to justify the process whereby we come to know the universal, but merely asserts and assumes, as well he may, that it does take place.

Metaphysics

The philosopher as logician investigates the tools of thought. As 'first philosopher' or metaphysician he is chiefly engaged in a study of cause and substance, not as attached to particular events and objects, but in themselves, that is of cause *qua* cause, and of substance *qua* substance. I have already discussed in ch. 3 Aristotle's theory of causes and his doctrine of substance from the point of view of his reaction against Plato and his rejection of Plato's theory of Forms. It now remains to comment in rather more detail on his subtle, complex and important discussions of substance.

On many occasions in the course of the *Metaphysics* Aristotle points out that 'being' has many senses: τὸ ὂν λέγεται πολλαχῶς. It is not, however, a merely equivocal term, one used 'homonymously' like 'box' applied to a container and to a shrub. Rather, as he puts it in one of the most important discussions of the problem, in *Metaph.* Γ, ch. 2, 'being' is used with reference to one thing and to a single nature. He illustrates what he means by comparing the way in which the term 'healthy' is used. Various things may be described as 'healthy'. One thing is called healthy because it preserves or produces health—for example when we say that regular exercise is healthy; another in that it is a symptom of health—for example a blooming complexion; and another in that it is capable of being healthy—for example a living body. But everything that is said to be healthy is related in some way to one thing, health itself. So too, he suggests, 'being' is used with reference to a single thing.

Some things are said to be because they are substances, others because they are the attributes of substances, others again because they are a process towards substance [i.e. a coming-to-be] or destructions or privations or qualities, or productive or generative of substance or of things related to substance, or negations of one of these things or of substance: for we say even of not-being that it *is* not-being (1003 b6 ff.).

Elsewhere when he offers a definition of 'being' in *Metaph.* Δ, ch. 7 he draws attention to further distinctions. First there is the distinction between its being used 'accidentally'—κατὰ συμβεβηκός—and 'essentially'—καθ' αὐτό. It is used *per accidens* in such an example as 'the man is musical'—he happens to be musical—which is like saying that the musician builds: the builder happens to be musical, or the musician happens to be a builder. With this one may contrast the 'essential' or *per se* use in such a case as 'man is an animal'. Secondly, he shows that 'being' is used differently in each of the categories. 'Some predicates indicate what the subject is, others quality, others quantity, others relation, others action or affection, others place, others time', and 'being' has as many senses as there are categories (1017a24 ff.). It is, however, used primarily of the category of substance itself, as he points out later, for example at 1028a13 ff. Substance, indeed, may be said to be the single thing or root idea with reference to which 'being' is used, in the way in which health is that with reference to which the term healthy is used. Yet this does not get us very far, for unlike 'health' the term 'substance' is not easy to grasp: it too is used in different senses, and we need to have a clearer idea of what it is. Like the discussion of the various meanings of 'being', this is a problem that is approached from slightly different points of view in different passages in the *Metaphysics*. But the chief discussion of it is in books Z and H.

There after some preliminaries Aristotle notes that substance is applied to four main objects: (1) the essence or 'the what it is to be a thing'; (2) the universal; (3) the genus, and (4) the substratum, and he distinguishes three different aspects of the substratum, (i) matter, (ii) form and (iii) the combination of the two (the concrete individual). The discussion that follows in the rest of books Z and H is far-ranging, obscure and controversial. Its obscurity arises largely because each of the four chief objects under consideration is examined from many different points of view, and the criteria by which substance is to be recognised are complex. Moreover each of his four main candidates is found to fulfil *some* of these criteria, and in view of this it seems unlikely that his sole, or even his main, aim is to eliminate all but one of his candidates and to identify substance with the one that is left.

It is true that he is fairly confident in rejecting the claims of (2) the universal, and (3) the genus: at least he states that 'neither the universal nor the genus is substance' when he recapitulates the findings of Z in the opening chapter of H (1042 a 21 f.). Yet even in these two cases, he sees fit to repeat, in the same chapter, that there are arguments that point to the conclusion that the genus has more of a claim to be considered substance than the species, and the universal than the particulars (1042 a 13 ff.), and he is probably not thinking solely of discredited Platonic theses when he expresses this view. He may, for example, have in mind his own earlier discussion of a genuine difficulty, how if universals are not substances there can be definition, when (1) it is mainly substance that is definable, and (2) definition is of universal marks—and particulars are not definable (especially 1039 a 14 ff.).

His examination of the claims of matter takes a similar form. There is an explicit statement, at 1029 a 26 f., to the effect that it is impossible for matter to be substance. Here the grounds given are that 'separability' and 'thisness' seem to belong especially to substance, 'and so form and the concrete individual would seem to be more substance than matter', and elsewhere he shows that matter fails to fulfil the criterion of knowability, for 'matter *per se* is unknowable' (1036 a 8 f.). Yet again in summarising his conclusions in book H he says 'clearly matter also is substance' (1042 a 32), and while this statement comes in a passage where he is discussing what he calls the 'generally agreed' substances, the argument he adduces is not a popular one, but one based on his own theory of causation: matter is substance because it is matter that underlies change.

Certainly when he considers 'essence' and 'form' he shows that these have special claims to the title of substance, for while substance is applied in one sense to the individual complex of form and matter, in another it is used of the form alone. He suggests at 1028a32 f. that two of the marks of substance are that it is first in definition and in order of knowledge. But we know a thing, he says at 1031b20f., for example, when we know its 'essence', or what it is to be that thing. Again he says at 1042a17, for instance, that the definition of a thing is the formula of what it is to be that thing. In Z, ch. 17, especially, when he makes a fresh start in his inquiry, he argues that the object of their investigation is the cause of a thing, and that this is the 'essence', that which makes a thing what it is, or the form. And finally in H, chh. 2 and 3, where he considers substance as actuality, he shows that this is the form.

According to the criteria of definability, knowability, permanence and actuality, the root idea of substance is 'the what it is to be a thing' or the form. Nevertheless Aristotle's treatment is an exploration of the different meanings and aspects of substance, and a discussion of difficulties connected with the idea, rather than a dogmatic statement of a single clear-cut doctrine. But might not the criticism be made that his discussion of οὐσία only goes to show that, despite his claims to the contrary, the term is hopelessly ambiguous? We might feel inclined to say this. Yet it is far from self-evident that the problem can be dismissed in this way as a pseudo-problem. Indeed whether or not we do so will obviously reflect, and depend upon, our own philosophical assumptions. Certainly Aristotle tends to assume more readily than we might that there is a reality corresponding to the Greek term οὐσία. Yet he can hardly be criticised for taking language as the starting-point of his discussion: in a sense this is what any philosopher always and inevitably does, although different philosophers may take different views about how reliable a guide to reality linguistic data are, and some philosophers at least would be more prepared than Aristotle was to consider the evidence of other languages besides their own. But given that his study is confined to the Greek language, his discussion of being and substance is an ingenious and subtle one which remains valuable as an exploration of the complexities of the question, whether or not one agrees with the particular conclusions that Aristotle proposes.

CHAPTER 7

THE PHYSICS OF THE
HEAVENLY REGION

The range of 'physics'

As φύσις is simply the Greek word for nature, φυσική is much wider than our 'physics', for it is the science of nature as a whole. Natural objects are those that have a capacity for change or movement within themselves, and φυσική is the science (1) of such natural changes and movements, and (2) of the changing or moving objects themselves. It comprises, on the one hand, the study of things that are in eternal, unchanging movement—the heavenly bodies—and, on the other, the study of things that are subject to change and variation, both living creatures and inanimate objects, the elements and their compounds. The 'physicist' investigates, for example, the ultimate constituents of matter, the modes of combination of the elements, and their natural movements. Besides astronomy, φυσική, in Greek, includes not only the sciences we should call dynamics, physics and chemistry, but also all the various branches of biology.

The general principles underlying Aristotle's account of movement and change have already been outlined in ch. 3. Both the doctrine of the four causes, material, formal, efficient and final, and that of potentiality and actuality are introduced in the course of critical reviews of previous ideas on causation, and the latter doctrine, in particular, enables him to circumvent the problem that had perplexed Greek philosophers since Parmenides, of how anything can be said to change or come to be at all. But we must now discuss how Aristotle applies these principles in practice, first in his account of the heavenly bodies and then in that of the sublunary region.

The fifth element

First the distinction between a 'heavenly' and a 'sublunary' region needs to be explained. The latter is the region constituted by the four elements, earth, water, air and fire, which have, in Aristotle's view, natural movements either upwards—in the case of fire and air—or downwards—in the case of earth and water—in a straight line. But the region of the heavenly bodies, from the moon to the outermost circle of the fixed stars, is constituted not by any of these four elements singly or in combination, but by a fifth element, aither, which has the property of moving naturally in a circle. It is hard for us today, on coming across this theory for the first time, not to treat it as patently absurd. And Aristotle has often been blamed for introducing a distinction that was to lead astronomers down a blind alley for many centuries, until Newton at last reunited the two regions by showing that both celestial and terrestrial motions are subject to the same laws. But leaving aside the question of how far Aristotle can be held responsible for the mistakes of those who followed him uncritically, we should recognise that in postulating his fifth element he was swayed not merely by religious motives, but also by what must have seemed at the time strong evidence and arguments.

The problem, as he saw it, was to account for the eternal, unvarying, circular movement of the heavenly bodies. First in *Physics* VIII, chh. 7 and 8, he undertook a theoretical analysis of the different types of change to show that circular motion alone may be continuous. Briefly, all types of change, with one exception, take place 'from' one of a pair of contraries 'to' the other. When something is heated, for instance, there is a change from 'cold' to 'hot'. Or when water is boiled, which was, for Aristotle, a change from 'water' to 'air', this too was analysed in qualitative terms, water being considered cold and wet, and air hot and wet. The natural motion of the four terrestrial elements similarly takes place between the two contraries up and down. But none of these changes, he believed, can be continuous. He imagined motion in a straight line to be finite, for he held that the universe itself is finite, and he had argued elsewhere (*de Caelo* I, ch. 8) that infinite rectilinear motion is impossible on the grounds that an object accelerates as it approaches its 'natural place': if the motion continued to infinity, the speed, he believed, would be infinite, and this is impossible, because a body moving downwards with an infinite speed would have infinite weight. Rectilinear motion, then, may be continuous only in a shuttle-like way, motion from A to B being followed by motion from B back to A, and although this process can go on indefinitely, he denied that the movement can be called truly continuous, because at each extreme point (A and B) it is interrupted and the moving object is momentarily at rest. With locomotion in a circle, however, no such moment of rest is implied. This alone is not movement between contraries. He recognised, naturally, that clockwise and anti-clockwise motion are contraries, but neither of them individually is a motion between contrary extremes. And so he concluded that circular motion alone may be continuous.

But continuous circular motion was, for Aristotle, no mere hypothetical possibility, but a fact. 'There is something which is always in motion with a ceaseless, circular movement, and this is plain not only to reason, but also in fact' (*Metaph.* 1072 a 21 f.). He believed, indeed, that the unvarying nature of the movements of the heavenly bodies had been established by observations carried out over an extended period of time. 'Throughout the whole of past time,' he says at *Cael.* 270 b 13 ff., 'according to the records handed down from one generation to the next, no change whatsoever appears to have taken place either in the whole of the outermost heaven, or in any of its proper parts', and another text in the *de Caelo*, 292 a 7 ff., suggests that he was referring not merely to the observations carried out by Greeks, but to those of Egyptian and Babylonian astronomers as well.

How, then, could the supposed fact of the eternal, unvarying movements of the heavenly bodies be accounted for? He held that there are two basic kinds of motion, (1) natural and (2) enforced. Examples of natural motion are a stone falling, and flame rising, freely. A stone thrown upwards against the force of gravity illustrates enforced motion. But no enforced motion, he thought, could be eternal. He believed that whereas in natural movements the speed of the object increases as it approaches its 'natural place' (the acceleration due to gravity), the speed of an object propelled by force decreases the further it travels from the source that propelled it. Here he was, no doubt, influenced by observing two types of phenomena, especially, (1) the effects of gravitational forces retarding heavy objects thrown upwards, and (2) the effects of friction and of the resistance of the medium through which motion takes place, these being more obvious in cases of 'enforced', than in cases of 'natural', motion. But the circular motion of the heavenly bodies, being eternal, cannot be enforced. It must, then, be natural. Yet an object which moves naturally in a circle cannot, he argued, be one of the terrestrial elements or a compound of them. Their natural movements are upwards or downwards, from or to the centre of the earth. If they are moved in a circle, as when a stone is whirled round in a sling, this motion is in part, at least, enforced. And so there must be something, a fifth element, which moves naturally and continuously in a circle.

Believing that the movements of the heavenly bodies are continuous, natural and circular, and that the natural movements of the four terrestrial elements are rectilinear and discontinuous, Aristotle concluded that the heavenly bodies must be composed of a fifth element, aither. But while this is the main theoretical argument which led him to this conclusion, other empirical factors also influenced his doctrine. He was aware of the extreme distance of the heavenly bodies from the earth and of the vast expanse of the heavens compared with the volume of the earth and its surrounding atmosphere. One of the arguments which he uses to support his doctrine of the fifth element is that if either air or fire, for example, had been the constituent of the vast space between the earth and the outermost circle of the fixed stars, the earth itself would long ago have been destroyed (*Mete.* 340a 1 ff.). The four terrestrial elements are each either hot or cold and either dry or wet, and for these to continue to exist there must be an approximate balance between them. But the immense space of the heavenly region must, then, be filled by some other element which is not characterised by these opposite qualities, for otherwise the sublunary elements would be destroyed.

A combination of abstract arguments and empirical factors led Aristotle to suggest that there is a fifth element, aither, unlike the four terrestrial elements first in that it is not characterised by contrary qualities, and secondly in that its natural motion is circular and continuous, not rectilinear and discontinuous. But he was also influenced, on his own admission, by religious considerations. At *Cael.* 270b 5 ff., for example, he suggested that his doctrine of the immutable aither fits in with popular ideas concerning the divinity of the uppermost region, and at *Metaph.* 1074a 38 ff. he refers approvingly to traditional beliefs according to which the heavenly bodies are divine, even though he rejects the fantastic anthropomorphic and zoomorphic elements in those beliefs. For his own part he describes aither as a whole as 'more divine' and 'more precious' than the other four elements, and he considers the individual heavenly bodies to be alive and divine (*Cael.* I, ch. 2 and II, ch. 12).

The source of movement

Aristotle's doctrine of aither was, in part, a serious attempt to deal with what was undoubtedly a difficult problem, to account for the apparently unchanging movements of the heavenly bodies. But his theory of celestial motion is also closely linked with his account of the ultimate source or principle of movement. To deny the existence of motion, as the Eleatics had done, was, he believed, utterly mistaken. He considers and rebuts the arguments of Zeno at length in *Physics* VI, ch. 9 especially, and in any case he points out that to deny the existence of motion is not to speak as a physicist. 'To consider whether being is one and motionless', he says at *Ph.* 184b25ff., 'is not a part of physics.' And at *Ph.* 253a32ff. he puts it more strongly: 'to say that all things are at rest, and to seek arguments for this, disregarding the senses, is a sign of weak intelligence: to do so casts doubt on the whole inquiry, not just a part of it, and it attacks not only physics, but almost all the sciences and all ordinary opinions, since they all make use of motion.' He takes it as a datum of physics, then, that motion exists. Indeed it has always existed: he argues in *Physics* VIII, ch. 1, that motion or change itself cannot have had a beginning or have come to be, on the grounds that that coming-to-be itself would imply a previous process of change. More precisely, he holds that some things, the heavenly bodies, are in eternal motion, while others, the objects of the sublunary region, are sometimes in motion and sometimes at rest. Yet even if motion has no beginning in time, there must nevertheless be a source or principle of movement in the universe as a whole.

The unmoved mover

This is the starting-point from which Aristotle reasons to his famous doctrine of the unmoved mover. The problem is in origin partly a physical one, concerning movement and change, but the question of the source of movement leads to the ontological and theological questions of the nature of the primary substances and of god.

The conclusion of the argument in *Physics* VIII by which he establishes that there is an unmoved mover is clear enough: 'Since motion must always exist and must not cease, there must necessarily be something, either one thing or many, that first initiates motion, and this first mover must be unmoved' (*Ph.* 258 b 10 ff.). But how does Aristotle arrive at this conclusion? He assumes that in every instance of a thing moving or changing, there is a mover, something that initiates the movement or causes the change. Even with objects that move themselves, one may distinguish conceptually between that which is moved and that which initiates the movement. Whatever is moved, in fact, is moved by something. But is the primary cause of movement in the universe a mover that is itself in motion or unmoved? Two main considerations point to the conclusion that it must be unmoved. First if it is in motion, it too, according to the general principle already established, must have a mover that initiates its motion. Unless we assume that the prime mover is itself unmoved, we shall find ourselves in a vicious regress.

Aristotle's second main argument (*Ph.* 257b6ff. and *Metaph.* Λ, ch. 6) is that from the doctrine of potentiality and actuality. He constantly maintains that movement implies potentiality, and that that which brings about movement or change must in each case be something that is itself actual. (1) At *Ph.* 257b9f. he illustrates this second doctrine with an example of the operation of an efficient cause: it is that which is itself hot that heats something else. And it holds good as a general rule that the actualis-
.ing of a potentiality is brought about by something that is itself actual. Moreover (2) that which is the primary source of movement in the universe must be actual, not merely potential, since 'if there is something that is capable of causing movement or acting on things, but is not actually doing so, there will not [necessarily] be movement; for that which has a potentiality need not exercise it' (*Metaph.* 1071b12ff.). Both arguments indicate that the prime mover must be actual. But *qua* actual it is unmoved. Movement and change being the actualising of potentialities, an object changes or is moved in so far as it possesses potentiality, and if the prime mover were itself in movement, it would to that extent partake in potentiality. Again, then, from the doctrine of actuality and potentiality, we must assume that the prime mover is itself unmoved.

The prime mover is pure actuality. But two major questions which remain are: how does it cause movement? And what is its nature, that is, if it is actuality, what is its actuality?

The prime mover as final cause

The answer to the first question is given in *Metaph.* Λ, ch. 7. The unmoved mover causes movement not as an efficient, but as a final, cause, as the object of desire and love. Why, we might ask, did not Aristotle make his prime mover an efficient cause? This seems to be because the efficient cause generally acts, in his view, by coming into contact with that which comes to be. But wherever there is contact, there is, he believes, reaction. So if the prime mover had been an efficient cause similar to the efficient causes in sublunary change, it would itself have been in some measure affected or changed by the movement it brings about, and this Aristotle could not allow. There is, however, another possibility, that it causes movement as final cause. 'The object of desire and the object of thought', he says at *Metaph.* 1072a26ff., 'move in this way: they move without being moved... What appears to be good is the object of appetite, and what really is good is the primary object of wish.' The good moves us, in a sense, because we desire it or aspire to it, and it is this model, rather than the model of a craftsman or efficient cause, that Aristotle uses to describe the mode of operation of the unmoved mover. It is a final cause, but not in the sense of the object or being whose good is aimed at in a particular action, but in the sense of the good that is aimed at in the action: it is not a final cause in the way in which the owner of a house, the person for whose sake the house is built, is a final cause, but one in the way in which health is a final cause, when health is the object for which we take exercise and the good we aim at in our action. We are to imagine that the unmoved mover moves the heavenly bodies as the good moves us, as the object of their desire and love: κινεῖ δὴ ὡς ἐρώμενον (*Metaph.* 1072 b 3).

In summary, Aristotle's doctrine concerning the source of movement and change is as follows: the ultimate source of movement in the universe as a whole is a mover that is itself unmoved. This moves the heavenly bodies as final cause, as the object of their desire and love. But these in turn transmit movement as efficient causes. The heavenly bodies are 'moved movers', being moved by the prime mover, but themselves in turn moving other things, the lower heavenly bodies and eventually the sublunary sphere. The heavenly bodies move with an eternal and unchanging movement. Change exists only in the region below the moon. Both movement and change in the sublunary sphere are ultimately derived from the movements of the heavenly bodies. (1) Movement is transmitted to the sublunary region by its contact with the lowest of the heavenly spheres, that of the moon. (2) But change and variation also occur in the sublunary region as the product of the 'oblique course' of the sun, that is its movement in the ecliptic. This is the efficient cause of the seasons and of the continuous cycle of coming-to-be and passing-away in the sphere below the moon. And so it comes about that whereas each of the heavenly bodies moves with an eternal, circular motion, other types of locomotion also take place in the sublunary region and so too do generation and destruction, growth and decay, and qualitative changes of all kinds.

The prime mover as god

The unmoved mover causes movement as the object of love. But what is its nature? It is, of course, the highest being. In much of the discussion in *Metaphysics* Λ it is referred to in the neuter as τὸ ἀκίνητον κινοῦν. But then at 1072 b 24 ff. we find the masculine used. Aristotle slips from talking about the unmoved moving cause to talking about god: θεός. The highest being must, he believes, be alive. It is pure actuality, but it cannot be merely inert. This poses something of a problem, since any activity or life might be thought to imply a lack of fulfilment, a lack of actuality. We might suppose that in so far as any activity is ascribed to the highest being, this could only be done at the cost of diminishing its claim to the title of pure actuality. But this is not the case. There is one activity that is consistent with continuous actuality, namely intellectual activity or thought, νόησις. Thought involves neither movement nor change. Aristotle interprets it as the reception, by the mind, of the intelligible forms: this activity can be, and in the case of god is, continuous, and what is more it is supremely pleasant. This, then, is the actuality of the unmoved mover. At *Metaph.* 1072 b 13 ff., he says:

On such a principle, then, the heavens and nature depend. And its life is like the best which we have for a short time. For it is always in this state, whereas that is impossible for us...

And thinking in itself is concerned with that which is best in itself, and thinking in the highest sense with what is best in the highest sense...And contemplation is what is most pleasant and best. If, then, god is always in that good state in which we are sometimes, this is wonderful. And if he is in an even better state, it is even more wonderful. And he is indeed so. And life also belongs to him. For the actuality of reason is life, and he is that actuality, and his essential actuality is the best and eternal life. We hold, then, that god is a living being, eternal and most good, and so life and continuous and eternal duration belong to god. For this *is* god.

So far we have seen that the unmoved mover moves as a final cause, that he is pure actuality, and that his actuality is that of reason or thought. But then in ch. 9 of *Metaphysics* Λ Aristotle raises certain difficulties about the nature of the divine thought. It is important to recognise that this is an aporetic chapter, one in which he is more concerned with airing difficulties than with developing positive doctrines. And in some cases it is hard to say what his final and definitive answer to some of the problems he raises would have been. In ch. 7 he had already noted that thought and the object of thought are identical, and this is in line with the doctrine worked out in the *de Anima*, where he suggests that just as in sensation the sense-organ receives, and becomes identical with, the sensible forms, so too in thought, the reason—or rather that part of it which he calls the passive reason—receives and becomes identical with the intelligible forms. But then in *Metaph.* Λ, ch. 9 he says that god is a thinking about thought, νόησις νοήσεως. What does Aristotle mean by this admittedly sterile-seeming formula?

The chapter begins by raising the question of what the divine thought thinks: what is the object of its thought? If it thinks of nothing, it will be no better than a man asleep. But what then does it think? The object of its thought must be the best thing there is: but that is itself. 'And so it thinks itself, seeing that it is the best thing, and its thinking is a thinking of thinking' (*Metaph.* 1074 b 33 ff.). But as he goes on to point out, all cognition seems to be of something else, and only of itself by the way. The knowledge that a doctor, for example, has is knowledge about health: it is only secondarily knowledge that his knowledge is about health. He suggests, however, that this is not so in every case. Sometimes the knowledge itself is the object that is known. 'Where what is thought about is not material,' he says when touching on the same problem in the *de Anima* (430 a 3 ff.), 'that which thinks and that which is thought about are identical. Theoretical knowledge and what is theoretically known are one and the same.' An example might be knowing the law of contradiction or a geometrical theorem. Such knowledge may, it is true, be merely potential. But when it is actual, and we possess knowledge not only in the way that a sleeping man has sight, but in the way that a man who is actually seeing does, then the object known is indistinguishable from the knowing of it. Here, then, thinking is identical with its object, and this is also the case with god, the object of whose knowledge is himself.

How much does this chapter in the *Metaphysics* contribute to the doctrine of the unmoved mover? Certainly when Aristotle shows that the object of the divine thought can be nothing other than itself, this doctrine has one very important consequence. It becomes clear that god can have no knowledge whatsoever of the world of human experience. But the formula 'a thinking of thinking' seems less a positive contribution to our understanding of the nature of the unmoved mover, than a rather dramatic and paradoxical way of re-stating the same point, that as the object of the divine thought must be what is best, it must be itself. The upshot of his discussion of this topic seems to be to show that the problem of whether the divine thought is the activity or the content is an apparent, rather than a real, one. Where what is thought about is not material, the thinking and the object thought about are indistinguishable. We can see this in examples of actual theoretical knowledge. So too in the case of the divine thought, Aristotle seems to suggest, to ask whether it is the activity or the content is to pose a false dilemma, for the two are identical.

The number of unmoved movers

So far I have spoken of the unmoved mover as one. But in between ch. 7, which first defines the mode of operation of the unmoved mover, and ch. 9, which raises a number of difficult problems about the nature of the divine thought, there is a chapter which is largely devoted to the question of the number of unmoved movers. While the movement of the outermost sphere of the fixed stars is simple, the motions of the planets, sun and moon are complex. One unmoved mover, the first, brings about the movement of the outermost sphere as final cause, and this sphere moves the spheres below it in turn. But this will not account for the various independent movements of the planets, sun and moon, for which other unmoved movers are necessary, one for each of the simple movements that go to make up their complex apparent courses.

The problem of determining the number of these movements is, as he points out at *Metaph*. 1073 b 3 ff., a question of astronomy rather than of the science that deals with substance *qua* substance. But he goes into it in some detail, beginning with a summary of the theories of Eudoxus and Callippus.

In the history of early attempts to account for the complex motions of the planets, the work of Eudoxus is especially important.[1] Plato is reputed to have set to his pupils in the Academy the problem: what uniform and orderly movements have to be assumed in order to account for the apparent motions of the planets? Eudoxus' solution was highly ingenious. He assumed that the complex apparent paths of the sun, the moon and each of the planets were, in each case, the product of the simple circular movements of a certain number of concentric spheres. The earth is at rest at the common centre of all the spheres, but their axes are inclined to one another and the speeds with which they rotate differ. For each of the planets he postulated four such spheres. The planet itself is

[1] The classic work on the history of Greek astronomy is T. L. Heath's *Aristarchus of Samos*, Oxford, 1913, but an excellent brief summary and explanation of Eudoxus' system is available in Marshall Clagett's *Greek Science in Antiquity*, London, 1957.

imagined as lying on the equator of the lowest sphere, but its visible course is determined by the combined movements of all the spheres. This model enabled him to account for a remarkable number of the phenomena which are now, of course, explained quite differently. Briefly, the first or outermost sphere in each case accounted for the phenomena caused by the daily rotation of the earth about its axis. The second produced the apparent movement of the planet along the zodiacal band. The third and fourth spheres were intended to explain the main apparent irregularity in the motion of the planets, namely what are known as their stations and retrograda-tions, when their apparent easterly course through the constellations is interrupted and they travel westwards for a time. The figure produced by the combined move-ments of these two spheres was called the 'horse-fetter'—a sort of three-dimensional figure of eight—and indeed this can give a quite good approximation to the apparent paths of the planets through the constellations.

The details of Eudoxus' theory need not be entered into, but the total number of spheres he required was twenty-six, or twenty-seven if one is included for the outermost sphere of the fixed stars itself. He had four spheres for each of the five known planets and three each for the sun and moon. Callippus, however, evidently appreciated that Eudoxus' system was inadequate to explain certain of the phenomena. Two of the major difficulties were the inequality of the seasons, and the retrogradations of the lower planets, particularly Mars. And this led him to add two spheres each to the sun and the moon, and one each to the three lower planets, Mars, Venus and Mercury, bringing the total number of spheres in his version of the system to thirty-three.

Both these theories were purely mathematical constructions. Neither astronomer said anything about the mechanics of the heavenly movements, about the nature of the concentric spheres or about how their movements were transmitted from one to another. Aristotle's contribution was to turn what had been a mathematical theory into a fully mechanical model. As we have already seen, he *was* concerned to account for the transmission of movement from the outermost sphere to the sublunary region. But as soon as the spheres of Eudoxus are conceived as connected in a mechanical system, the movement of each of the heavenly bodies will be affected not only by its own spheres, but by all the spheres above it. So Aristotle was forced to introduce a number of 'reacting' spheres, the purpose of which was to cancel out the movements of certain of the primary spheres: this was achieved by assuming (1) that each reacting sphere has the same axis as the primary sphere it counteracts, and (2) that it rotates at the same speed in the opposite direction. He thought that in every case except the moon, which being the lowest heavenly body needs no spheres to counteract its movement, the reacting spheres will be one less in number than the primary spheres which he took over from Eudoxus and Callippus. The total number of spheres, primary and reacting, comes to fifty-five—or fifty-six including the sphere of the fixed stars itself—using the Callippan version of the system: or if no extra spheres are added for the sun and moon the total is rather less.[1]

At first sight the whole apparatus of concentric spheres seems extremely clumsy. But given the complexity of the phenomena to be accounted for, the system is remarkably economical in the number of *principles* it employs, even if the total number of *spheres* needed for all the heavenly bodies is high. However the credit for the mathematical ingenuity that the system shows belongs to Eudoxus, not to Aristotle.

As far as Aristotle's version of the theory is concerned, some of the details present difficulties. The number of spheres seems too high, since on analysis it turns out that the first primary sphere of each planet exactly reduplicates the movement of the last reacting sphere of the planet above: both move with the motion of the outermost circle of the fixed stars. Furthermore when we read at *Metaph.* 1074a12ff. that 'if the extra movements we referred to for the moon and the sun are not added, the

---

[1] The number of spheres required in the three astronomical systems of Eudoxus, Callippus and Aristotle may, for the sake of clarity, be set out in the form of a table:

	Eudoxus	Callippus	Aristotle	
			primary	reacting
Saturn	4	4	4 +	3
Jupiter	4	4	4 +	3
Mars	4	5	5 +	4
Venus	4	5	5 +	4
Mercury	4	5	5 +	4
Sun	3	5	5 +	4
Moon	3	5	5	
	26	33	33 +	22 = 55

total number of spheres is forty-seven', either the text is corrupt, and we should read ἐννέα, nine, instead of ἑπτά, seven, or else Aristotle seems to have slipped up. The extra spheres referred to are the two for the sun and two for the moon that Callippus had introduced, plus the corresponding reacting spheres: but it is here that the mistake may lie, for there will be not four of these, but two, since the moon has no reacting spheres. If we subtract the four primary and the two reacting spheres, the total number will be six, not eight, less than the original fifty-five.

It would, however, be a mistake to assume that Aristotle either claimed or believed that he had given an exact and definitive solution to the astronomical problem in *Metaphysics* Λ, ch. 8. The object of his discussion is to discover the number of unmoved movers required to account for the independent movements of the heavenly bodies, but the spirit in which he approached this problem can be judged from two passages. First when he begins his discussion (1073b10ff.) he says that he will give an account of what certain of the mathematicians—that is the astronomers—say about the movements of the heavenly bodies 'so that there may be a definite number for the mind to grasp. But for the rest we must investigate some things ourselves, and learn others from those who investigate them, and if those who study these things come to some conclusion which conflicts with our present statements, we must love both parties, but believe those who give the more exact account.' And then at 1074a14ff., after expounding his own version of the system, he concludes: 'let this, then, be the number of the spheres: so it would be reasonable to assume as many unmoved substances and principles. But we must leave to more powerful thinkers the demonstration of necessity'—that is the proof establishing both how many spheres there are, and why they must be just so many. Aristotle makes it plain that on astronomical matters he speaks more or less as a layman. Although his theory was often treated as an *ex cathedra* statement by later writers who were themselves dogmatic thinkers, he himself was evidently far from dogmatic about the details of his astronomy. Indeed he makes it clear that his account of the problem is to be treated as a provisional one.

Physics and theology

The interconnections between physics and theology are one of the striking features of Aristotle's cosmology. The theory of aither is both a religious doctrine and an attempt to account for certain phenomena. So too the prime mover is the ultimate source of movement in the universe and so the foundation of the physical system, but at the same time he is god, and the culmination of both the ontological and ethical systems. Wherever possible Aristotle incorporates traditional religious beliefs, purged of their fantastic mythical elements, into his own theory, or shows how his own doctrines fit in with popular ideas. At the same time the attention he pays, in his account of the heavenly regions, to the facts as he took them to be established by observation is evident. Thus his doctrine of the fifth element owes much to his belief that the records established that the movements of the heavenly bodies are unchanging and to his appreciation of the minute size of the earth in relation to the heavens as a whole. And when it came to determining the number of the unmoved movers he developed a system which would, he hoped, account for all the varied and complex phenomena of planetary motion. But if his discussion of the physics of the heavens has an undeniable empirical foundation, his main arguments about the source of motion are abstract ones. The most important argument by which he establishes that the prime mover is unmoved is one drawn from one of the fundamental principles of his physics, the doctrine of actuality and potentiality. His account of its mode of operation depends on the distinction between efficient and final causes, and his theory of its activity is based on his philosophical analysis of the nature of thought.

In the doctrine of the prime mover ideas from physics, from psychology and from theology are welded into a single complex whole. Yet many obscurities and difficulties, sometimes serious ones, remain. Although he airs a number of questions about the nature of the divine thought in *Metaphysics* Λ, ch. 9, the answers he gives are seldom satisfactory and this part of his doctrine remains highly obscure. Again we found that the astronomical theory of the fifty-five unmoved movers in ch. 8 can be criticised as uneconomical. A further major question that this theory poses is whether it can be reconciled with what Aristotle says about the unity of the prime mover. This too is a difficult and controversial topic, made more obscure by the ambiguity of the term πρῶτον in the key passages, where it may mean either 'first' in a series, or 'prime' in the sense of ultimate: the unity of the 'first' unmoved mover in the former sense does not, but in the latter does, preclude a plurality of other unmoved movers. But without entering into the technicalities of this issue, I may note that a text at *Ph.* 259a6ff. seems to show that Aristotle started out with a general preference for a single unmoved mover. There he says: 'since movement is eternal, the first mover, if it is one, will be eternal also, and if there are more than one, there will be more than one eternal mover. But we should suppose that it is one rather than many, and a finite rather than an infinite number.' Here too the term πρῶτον is unclear. But it remains difficult to conceive why Aristotle should have considered for a moment whether there was more than one mover of the outermost circle of the heavens, and we should probably conclude that this passage, at least, was composed before he had worked out the details of his final theory of fifty-five unmoved movers, at a stage when he envisaged the possibility of a plurality of such movers, but tended still to prefer to believe that there was only one.

But apart from the question of a possible development in his thinking on the number of unmoved movers, it is even more difficult to explain how a plurality of such beings is possible on his doctrine of matter and form. In the sublunary world the individual object, this table or that chair, is a complex of form and matter, but it is because their matter is different that two individuals of the same species are distinguishable, since their forms are the same. How, then, can there be several unmoved movers, when these possess no matter whatsoever? Some of the ancient commentators saw the difficulty and suggested that each of the fifty-five unmoved movers is an individual species, and while this suggests a possible, if rather desperate, way round the difficulty, it is a purely conjectural one. Aristotle nowhere discusses the problem, and we cannot know what his solution to it would have been.

But in spite of the difficulties and obscurities that remain —and after all no cosmological system is free from imperfections—Aristotle's doctrine is a remarkably complete and coherent whole. As a physical theory it is an attempt, and on the whole a successful one, to describe the ultimate source of motion in line with his general account of causation and change. And it includes an astronomical theory which is both more detailed than any pre-Eudoxan account, and also in one respect more ambitious than Eudoxus' own theory, in being an attempt to give a fully mechanical model for the movements of the heavenly bodies. While he believes the heavenly bodies to be alive and divine, he does not simply assume that the apparent irregularities in the movements of the planets were the result of their having independent wills, for he explains their movements on the same physical principles as apply to the rest of the heavenly bodies.

Finally as a theological doctrine its chief originality lies in its being so abstract. Aristotle was evidently less concerned to paint a morally uplifting picture of god, than to give an account of the ultimate cause on which the universe depends. His conception of god is certainly not an entirely impersonal one. He is alive, and his activity, contemplation, is described as supremely pleasant. While Aristotle proves at *Metaph.* 1073a5ff. that the primary substance has no magnitude, and so can hardly be located in space, he is not fully consistent on this point, and sometimes associated god, more conventionally, with the outermost sphere of heaven. But while in certain respects Aristotle was a conservative in theology, his original contribution was the conception of the unmoved mover acting as a final cause. This doctrine has often been criticised as cold and inhuman. Certainly Aristotle's god does not inspire, even though his activity, contemplation, is one that men should imitate if they are to lead the best and happiest life. The idea of a god remote from the world, in no sense its creator, and indeed knowing nothing about it, may well seem repugnant to those brought up with Christian beliefs about god. And yet Aristotle's doctrine is in the main the consequence of carrying the principle of god's perfection to its logical conclusion, and it has always proved difficult for other, less inhuman, theologies to explain the relation between a perfect god and an imperfect world. Moreover while Aristotle's god is not affected by the universe, as the final cause it is the principle on which the universe depends and to which it aspires. 'On such a principle', he said at *Metaph.* 1072b13f., 'the heavens and nature depend.' And at *Metaph.* 1075a11ff. he asks whether the good belongs to the universe as something separate from it—as we might say transcendently— or in the arrangement of the parts—as we might say immanently—and he answers that it does so in both ways, drawing a comparison with an army whose good lies partly in its arrangement and order, but also and more especially in the general on whom the order in the army depends. If his god is remote from the world, Aristotle believes nevertheless that the whole of nature seeks and desires the good: final causes are at work throughout nature, and god is the ultimate final cause.

CHAPTER 8

THE PHYSICS OF THE SUBLUNARY
REGION

The transmission of movement

The ultimate source of movement, in Aristotle's system,
is the unmoved mover who acts as a final cause, by being
loved. The 'moved movers'—the heavenly bodies or
more properly the spheres that carry them—transmit
movement in turn as efficient causes. But whereas throughout the heavenly region movement is eternal and unchanging, in the region below the moon there is both
movement and change. Change is brought about primarily because the course of the sun in the ecliptic is oblique
to the axis of the earth. This oblique course of the sun
causes the changes in the seasons, the ceaseless pendulum-
like movement between the two extremes of the heat and
dryness of summer and the cold and wet of winter,
changes which are, of course, a good deal more striking
in the Mediterranean than they are in our own more
temperate climate.

In making the sun the source of change in the sublunary
region Aristotle was no doubt chiefly influenced by the
manifest fact that the generation and decay of many living
things, especially plants, are closely linked with the
seasons. There are, however, several serious difficulties
both in his view of the relation between the heavenly and
the sublunary regions, and in his theory of the trans-

mission of movement from one to the other, and these must be considered before we discuss his account of the sublunary region as a whole. First he attempts no explanation of the *join* between the two regions. He assumes that the four sublunary elements naturally move either upwards or downwards, defining upwards as away from, and downwards as towards, the centre of the universe, and he maintains that there is a limit to both these movements, not only the movement to, but also that from, the centre. The region up to the moon is constituted by the four sublunary elements, and these four continually interact with one another since they possess contrary qualities, being either hot or cold, and either wet or dry. But at, or just below, the sphere of the moon, the sublunary elements give way to the fifth element, aither, and yet how this happens poses some unresolved problems for his theory. Aither moves naturally in a circle and is not qualified by the contraries hot/cold, wet/dry, and yet it must transmit movement to the sublunary elements and indeed do so without itself in any way being affected by them or reacting to them.

Then a second difficulty for Aristotle's theory is that it is not the lowest heavenly body, the moon, but the second lowest, the sun, that is responsible for change in the sublunary region. Yet how, we may ask, can the sun's movement in the ecliptic be transmitted to the sublunary region when the moon intervenes, and when he had deliberately introduced 'reacting' spheres to nullify the effect of each of the higher heavenly bodies on the movements of those below? Again he provides no satisfactory answer:

indeed he nowhere discusses the problem and we cannot say how he might have attempted to resolve the difficulty.

Thirdly, how can the heavenly bodies emit light and, in the case of the sun, heat, when if they consist of aither they cannot themselves be hot? This problem is discussed in the *de Caelo* (II, ch. 7) where he suggests that the heat and light they emit are produced by friction. He draws a comparison with flying missiles, and indeed it is true that at high speeds the friction encountered by objects moving through the air is accompanied by great heat, as is dramatically illustrated when a space rocket re-enters the earth's atmosphere. But he sees that the analogy of flying objects cannot be an exact one, since they themselves become hot, and he denies that this can happen to the heavenly bodies. He suggests, however, that the air and fire in the region immediately below the aither are somehow affected by the movements of the heavenly bodies.

We can point to a number of serious problems which Aristotle's theory of the relationship between the heavenly bodies and the sublunary region leaves unresolved. But although he was aware of some at least of these difficulties, they did not lead him to modify any of the essential features of his theory. The sun obviously is responsible for seasonal changes on earth, and the heavenly bodies as a whole evidently do emit light. Even though they consist of aither, then, the higher heavenly bodies do, somehow or other, affect the sublunary region: but the doctrine of aither itself could not be abandoned without leaving a far greater difficulty unresolved, namely how to account for their continuous circular movement.

The earth

In the sublunary region the main masses of the four simple bodies are arranged in the descending order, fire, air, water, earth. Each of these elements has a natural tendency to move upwards or downwards to its 'natural place', but the variations caused by the sun in the sublunary region, notably variations in temperature, ensure that the elements do not become completely separate. The main mass of the earth in Aristotle's system, as in all earlier systems except the Pythagorean or Philolaic, is imagined as at the centre of the universe. In this Aristotle was largely influenced by the observed fact that heavy objects fall downwards in straight lines, and he argued that earth, and things made of earth, must behave always and everywhere in the same fashion: where nothing prevents them, they must move downwards towards their 'natural place'. This led him to conclude that the earth is at rest in the centre of the universe. But Aristotle was no flat-earther. On the contrary, he provides us with the first reasoned exposition of the doctrine that the earth is spherical. He based this doctrine on various considerations. First he drew attention to the fact that eclipses of the moon, which he knew to be caused by the interposition of the earth between the sun and the moon, show a curved outline (*Cael.* 297b24ff.). Secondly, he noted that quite small changes in the position of the observer lead to perceptible differences in the stars that are visible above the horizon, from which it may be inferred (1) that the earth's surface is convex, and (2) that the earth is minute in comparison with the sphere of the fixed stars (*Cael.* 297b30ff.). Here, then, were two telling pieces of evidence that pointed to the conclusion that the earth is spherical. Yet his main argument, or at least the one which he spent most time elaborating (*Cael.* 297a8ff.), is a theoretical one. The path of a falling body is a straight line directed at the centre of the universe. So two bodies dropped side by side do not fall in parallel lines, but in lines at a small angle to one another which when produced would converge at the centre of the universe. He imagines how earth would behave if distributed throughout the universe, and he suggests that the result of this imaginary test would be the formation of a roughly spherical body at the centre of the universe. If there were a greater mass in one part than in another, the greater would push the smaller until equilibrium about the centre was produced. So however the total amount of earth was originally distributed, the mass of the body resulting from the earth collecting to-gether must be similar on all sides. The body must, in fact, be a sphere.

The earth is a spherical mass of no great size at rest in the centre of the universe. It follows from the doctrine of the natural tendency of earth to move towards the centre of the universe that the earth is unique, and indeed this doctrine provides the basis of one of the arguments by which Aristotle establishes the uniqueness of the universe as a whole (*Cael.* I, ch. 8). As regards the size of the earth, this is described as 'not large in comparison with the other stars' (*Cael.* 298a19f.), and he records an estimate of its circumference, telling us that the mathematicians had calculated this at 400,000 stades. Although he does not tell us the method by which this figure was arrived at, we may presume that it was, like later estimates, based on a measurement of the difference in elevation of the same stars observed from different points on the same meridian. The actual result obtained is, hardly surprisingly, wide of the mark. On the most likely interpretation of the value of the 'stade' in question, the circumference was made out to be nearly twice its actual length, about 46,000 English miles, as compared with the real figure for the equatorial circumference of about 24,902 English miles. Later Greek astronomers were to make much closer approximations to the true figure, but bearing in mind that this is the first recorded estimate of the circumference of the earth, we may consider it a creditable achievement. As an interesting addendum to this, Ross and others have noted that the chapter in the *de Caelo* in which he discusses the size of the earth provided a stimulus to the voyage of Columbus. Although Aristotle's own estimate of the circumference of the earth was far too large, he reported that there were some who believed 'that the region around the Pillars of Heracles joins on to that round India, and so the ocean is one', and he expressed the cautious opinion that this view 'is not entirely incredible' (*Cael.* 298a9ff.).

The elements

It is now time to turn to the physics and chemistry of the sublunary region, and first to Aristotle's theory of the elements. How did he arrive at the doctrine of the four 'simple bodies', earth, water, air and fire? As early as

Empedocles it had been suggested that these four substances are the 'roots' of all things, and Plato too had assumed that other substances were compounds of these four, although he believed that they themselves were not elemental, but were composed of different combinations of the primary triangles. Other physicists, however, had ignored Empedocles' theory. The atomists, in particular, had suggested that all the apparent differences between physical objects derive ultimately from differences in the shapes, positions and arrangements of solid, unalterable, homogeneous particles, the atoms. Moreover while Plato's account of compounds was indebted to Empedocles, his doctrine of the ultimate constituents of material objects owed far more to the theory of the atomists and shared with it a mathematical basis. For Plato other kinds of differences were ultimately derived from differences in the geometrical shapes of the primary triangles and of the solids composed of them.

Aristotle's return to a qualitative theory of matter, after the quantitative, mathematical accounts of the atomists and of Plato, has often been represented as retrograde. But this is not entirely just. The atomic theories of Democritus and Plato were undoubtedly most ingenious, but they too were, of course, pure speculations, incapable of being brought to any experimental test. Granted that atomism was, in the long run, to prove far more fruitful than any qualitative theory of matter, in the short term the doctrine that Aristotle proposed must have seemed in some respects more promising. Certainly his accounts of the ultimate constituents of matter and of the changes affecting the elements must have seemed to stay closer to what could actually be observed. It is obviously true that any physical object may be said to be either hot or cold, and either wet or dry, while to associate the physical properties of substances with geometrical shapes must always have appeared rather arbitrary. Equally the qualitative accounts which he gave of such observed changes as the evaporation of water and its condensation again as rain must have seemed more plausible than any mathematical interpretation of those changes. If we bear in mind that we are not dealing with pure chemical elements, it is not too misleading or inaccurate to associate three of the four simple bodies with the three primary states of matter, 'earth' with the solid, 'water' with the liquid, and 'air' with the gaseous, state: and fire, considered as a substance rather than as a process, was, naturally enough, treated as a fourth simple body on a par with the other three. Finally Aristotle's doctrine provided the basis for some fairly detailed and extensive physical investigations, not only his own, but also those of other theorists who took over his doctrine. Whereas the atomic theory of Democritus was of little use so far as practical research into the constitution of natural substances was concerned, Aristotle's qualitative theory served as a working hypothesis, even if only a very vague and general one, in several such inquiries, beginning with those whose results are recorded in the fourth book of the *Meteorologica* and in Theophrastus' *On Stones*.

Aristotle's account of the constituents of material objects was less ambitious and less speculative than the main rival theories in one respect, at least, that it stayed closer to what could be directly observed, the perceptible qualities of things. And yet the argument by which he establishes his doctrine of the four simple bodies in the *de Generatione et Corruptione* is a highly abstract one. Perhaps the most important feature of that argument is the way in which the problem was formulated. 'We are seeking', he says, 'the principles of perceptible body, that is of tangible body' (*GC* 329b7f.). The problem is to find the principles of perceptible bodies, and the discussion remains throughout a discussion of the *sensible* qualities of physical objects.

He analyses tangible qualities, like all other qualities, in terms of pairs of contraries, namely the two opposite ends of the scale. He claims therefore that the principles of perceptible body will be certain tangible contrarieties, but of these there are a great many, for example hard and soft, rough and smooth, heavy and light, viscous (or sticky, γλίσχρον) and brittle (κραῦρον) (*GC* 329b18 ff.). He then engages in an ingenious analysis in which he reduces the other types of tangible contraries to two pairs, hot and cold, and dry and wet. Thus the brittle, he suggests, is derived from, and can be reduced to, the dry, and the viscous derives from the wet. Again the soft is reduced to the wet and the hard to the dry. He concludes his discussion at *GC* 330a 24 ff. by saying: 'it is evident that all the other differences are reduced to the first four [hot and cold, dry and wet]: and these cannot be reduced to any lesser number.' He goes on to consider the possible combinations of his two primary opposites. Logically these are six in number, but two combinations, hot and cold, and dry and wet, are impossible as contraries cannot be coupled, and this leaves four possible combinations, (1) hot and dry, (2) hot and wet, (3) cold and wet and (4) cold and dry, which he then identifies with the four simple bodies, fire, air, water and earth respectively.

However much Aristotle owed to earlier doctrines based on fire, air, water and earth, the way in which he constructed and attempted to justify his theory is original. Physical bodies are analysed in terms of tangible contrarieties and the reason why there are *four* simple bodies is that it is impossible to derive all the tangible contraries from less than two primary pairs, hot and cold, and dry and wet. While fire, air, water and earth are the simplest natural substances, each of these is conceived as possessing, and consisting of, a pair of qualities. Quality-less matter, as I have remarked before, is an abstraction: although logically matter can be imagined without qualities of any sort, in fact it never exists in such a form. The building-blocks from which other material objects are constructed are the four simple bodies.

The main outlines of his theory of the ultimate constituents of matter are clear enough, but we must now consider how his ideas are applied in practice in his account of the changes and combinations that the simple bodies undergo. First he held that changes may and do take place between the simple bodies themselves; water may become air, for instance, or air water. In this his theory differs from that of Empedocles, but resembles Plato's which allowed changes to take place between three of the four simple bodies, the exception being earth. Indeed Aristotle's theory of the primary qualities was partly designed, one might suggest, to enable him to give an account of such changes. Take the change that he would have described as water becoming air, when water is evaporated by the sun, for example, or when a kettle boils. This is interpreted as a change from the cold and the wet to the hot and the wet, that is a substitution of hot for cold. And this change may take place in the reverse direction, when cold is substituted for hot, as, for example, when water-vapour, as we should say, condenses to form rain, or when the steam from a kettle condenses on encountering a cold surface. Likewise air becomes fire, according to Aristotle, by a substitution of dry for wet, and water comes from earth by a substitution of wet for dry.

Some of the changes that Aristotle mentions obviously relate to, and are attempts to interpret, common phenomena. But other transformations which he says occur strike us as fantastic, as for instance the suggestion that water comes from earth or earth from water. How far does the theory tally with experience? First it must be repeated that Aristotle's simple bodies are not pure chemical substances. Water is defined merely as a cold and wet fluid, and most metals are said to be composed predominantly of water, no doubt because they are fusible. Earth in turn covers a wide range of cold and dry solids. When Aristotle spoke of water becoming earth, and he was far from being the only Greek physicist to do so, he might have counted as an example the formation of residues of salt from the evaporation of sea-water, or even the silting up of rivers. It is a feature of his theory that some changes between the simple bodies are easier or more direct than others. Thus the change from air to water or *vice versa* involves the substitution of a single quality. On the other hand, a change from water to fire, or *vice versa*, or from air to earth, or *vice versa*, involves the substitution of both qualities in each case, and this can only take place, in Aristotle's view, in two stages, for example by water changing first to air and then to fire. By good fortune the transformations that the theory precludes from taking place directly, water ↔ fire and air ↔ earth, are far removed from ordinary experience. Yet we may be sure that once Aristotle had worked out the basic doctrine that each of the simple bodies consists of two primary qualities, he arrived at the details by a process of deduction, and while there are certain lucky correspondences between what the theory admits and what superficial observation might suggest, many anomalies remain. Thus it is difficult to say how we should interpret the production of fire from earth which is mentioned at *GC* 331a33 ff., unless perhaps he was thinking of the way in which certain hard stones give off sparks when struck. Finally the theory is silent on what seems to us an all-important point, namely what happens when one quality is substituted for another, and the cold and the wet, for example, becomes the hot and the wet. Aristotle does not explain the nature of this transformation, nor does he give any clear account of the nature of the distinction between air, which is hot and wet, and hot water, or again of the distinction between cold air and water.

Compounds

Compounds are formed from the simple bodies by combination. There are, Aristotle suggests, two types of composite substances, which he calls τὰ ὁμοιομερῆ and τὰ ἀνομοιομερῆ, literally 'substances with similar parts' and 'substances with dissimilar parts'. This distinction seems more obscure than it really is. These two terms enable him to draw attention to the difference between a uniform natural substance, such as hair or bone, on the one hand, and a composite object, such as a face or a hand, on the other. Hair is homogeneous: if you cut it into parts, the parts will all be alike, and like the whole. But a face consists of unlike parts, eyes, nose, mouth, hair and so on. Under the uniform substances are included the vast majority of natural substances, both organic and inorganic kinds, as for example flesh, blood, semen, skin, milk, nail, horn, bark, the metals, the various kinds of stones, salt, soda and pitch.

These compound substances are composed of different combinations of all the simple bodies, as Aristotle says at GC 335 a 8 f. But how, writing many centuries before the discovery of the science of chemistry, does he conceive the combination and separation of the simple bodies? He draws useful and important distinctions between various modes of mixture. First there is simple agglomeration, for which his term is σύνθεσις. One of the illustrations he gives is that of a pile of seeds of different sorts, such as barley and wheat. The resultant mixture is not homogeneous, and indeed in this case it is easy enough to separate the component substances again by mechanical means, by sieving them. Secondly, there is μῖξις or combination, the combination of liquids being termed κρᾶσις. Under this head Aristotle includes a number of instances of what we should call chemical combinations, as for example the formation of the alloy bronze from tin and copper. But some of his examples are of mixtures, such as that of wine and water, where no chemical reaction takes place. μῖξις is, however, clearly distinguished from σύνθεσις by several criteria, the chief of which is that in μῖξις a change of quality, ἀλλοίωσις, takes place. The constituent substances interact with one another to produce a substance with properties that may be quite different from those of the constituents taken individually. And this resultant compound, unlike the end-product of 'agglomeration', is homogeneous throughout.

Aristotle may be credited with having drawn clearer distinctions between the different modes of mixture than any earlier writer, even though, as is hardly surprising, his distinctions do not correspond exactly to those we draw between mechanical mixture and chemical combination. But there is a second point in which his theory of compounds marks a new advance, and that is that he goes much further than any of his predecessors in attempting to determine the actual composition of specific natural substances. The de Generatione et Corruptione (I, chh. 6–10) contains his theoretical discussion of the modes of mixture. But the fourth book of the Meteorologica examines the question of the constitution of natural substances, and sets out a good deal of information concerning their physical properties. He considers, for example, which substances are combustible, which incombustible, which can be melted, which solidified, which are soluble in water or in other liquids, and so on. And he attempts to classify natural substances according to which of the simple bodies predominates in them. Thus he suggests that those substances that solidify in cold, but are dissoluble by fire, consist predominantly of water, while those that are solidified by fire have a greater proportion of earth. The actual conclusions that he advances are, as these examples show, unsophisticated, and he attempts no precise estimate of the proportions of the simple bodies in the various compounds he considers. But even so the fourth book of the *Meteorologica* may be considered the first important attempt, in antiquity, to begin the incredibly complex task of collecting and collating information about the physical properties of natural substances and their reactions to various simple tests.

The fourth book of the *Meteorologica* sets out Aristotle's view on the material constituents of a variety of natural substances, and, as in other fields of inquiry, the researches that he had begun were carried on and developed by his successors in the Lyceum, notably in this case by Theophrastus, whose short treatise *On Stones* contains a detailed account of the properties of various stones and earths. But in Aristotle's view the physicist or student of nature must be concerned not merely with the material cause of natural substances, but also and more especially with their formal, final and efficient causes. As he points out in the introductory methodological chapters in the biological treatise *de Partibus Animalium*, the biologist must study the parts of the body from both points of view, and especially from the latter. If we were describing a bed, he says at *PA* 640b22ff., we should try to describe its form and what makes it a bed, rather than the matter, the bronze or wood. If we describe the matter at all, we do so as belonging to the concrete whole. Similarly the biologist must investigate the formal cause of the parts of the body. Again when at *PA* 645a30ff. he justifies the study of the internal parts of the living body, blood, flesh, bones, blood-vessels and the like, he says that we should not suppose that 'what we are talking about—and the object for which our inquiry is undertaken—is their material, but rather the whole form, just as in discussing a house, it is the whole form, not the bricks and mortar and timber in themselves, that is our concern'.

For Aristotle, the investigation of the material constitution of natural substances is preliminary and subordinate to the study of their formal and final causes. The *de Generatione et Corruptione*, which sets out his doctrine of the simple bodies and of the various modes of mixture, and the fourth book of the *Meteorologica*, in which he attempts a rough classification of compound natural substances, lead on naturally to the psychological and biological treatises, where he considers the vital functions of living creatures and their parts. The study of the 'chemical' composition of blood, that is of its material elements, is subordinate to the study of its function in the living body, the role it plays in growth and nutrition, and it is in accordance with Aristotle's expressed preference for the examination of formal and final causes that his biological treatises are a good deal more important and more extensive than his work devoted to a discussion of the material constitution of natural substances.

Dynamics

The next main topic to be studied is, then, Aristotle's theory of the vital functions of living beings, his doctrine of soul. But before doing so it is worth adding some brief notes on a rather neglected and often misunderstood part of his account of change in the sublunary region, namely his contributions to the science we should call dynamics. His work in this field has tended to be ignored, partly, perhaps, because there is no single book or set of books in which he presents his views on natural and enforced movement in a systematic and comprehensive fashion, as the *de Generatione et Corruptione*, for instance, sets out his doctrine of the simple bodies together with the arguments by which he hoped to establish it. And such dynamical theories as he is generally known to have held have often been dismissed as aberrations unworthy of so great a thinker. It is certainly true that those theories are often mistaken, yet his work in this field was far from valueless.

The general distinction between natural and enforced motion has been mentioned before. Aristotle considers that, as a general rule, fire and air move upwards, water and earth downwards, when nothing prevents this. But objects may also be moved in a direction contrary to, or different from, their natural tendency by force. Thus a stone may be hurled upwards into the air, or a ship floating on the water may be moved horizontally through it. But he not only draws this general distinction between two types of locomotion, but also proposes certain general rules concerning the factors governing the speed of the moving object in either type of case. He recognised that the speed of an object may be influenced by its shape, for example, but he believed that the two main factors that determine an object's speed are (1) its weight, and (2) the density of the medium through which it travels. His general rules may be expressed as follows: (1) in natural motion—that is in the case of freely falling or freely rising bodies—the speed is directly proportional to the weight of the body and inversely proportional to the density of the medium. And (2) in forced motion, the speed is directly proportional to the force applied and inversely proportional to the mass of the body moved: however he appreciated that if a force A moves an object B a distance C in a time D, it does not necessarily follow that half the force $A/2$ would move the same object B half the distance $C/2$ in the same time D, since it may be the case that half the force is insufficient to move the object at all. And as I have noted earlier, he suggested that whereas in natural motion the speed of the object increases the nearer it comes to its 'natural place' (the acceleration due to gravity), in forced motion the speed decreases as the object progresses further away from the propelling agent.

Before Aristotle the nearest that natural philosophers had come to developing dynamical theories was in such vague generalisations as the doctrine of 'like-to-like'. But this doctrine embraced a wide range of phenomena, for it might include not only the action of gravitational forces, when heavy objects such as stones 'seek their like' in falling downwards, but also the behaviour of gregarious animals: this example was one actually used by the Atomists to illustrate how like is drawn to and known by like. Again Plato's doctrine of 'circular thrust' was used not merely to account for the movement of projectiles, but also to explain certain phenomena connected with partial vacua, as well as such vital processes as respiration. Although Aristotle's propositions seem crude, they represent, in fact, the first extant attempt to establish the relation between the various factors governing the speed of moving objects.

The gulf between Aristotelian and modern, post-Newtonian, dynamics is, however, immense. And yet Aristotle's propositions are less at variance with observed phenomena than might at first be supposed. He has often been condemned for assuming that the speed of a freely falling body varies directly with its weight, but it is as well to be clear where his mistake lies. The fact is that in *air* heavier bodies do fall more rapidly than lighter ones of the same shape and size, although this is not true, of course, in a vacuum. He was correct in assuming that there is *some* relationship between weight and speed in motion that takes place in a medium, although the relationship is not a simple one of direct proportion. Then too it is an obvious fact of experience that motion through a dense medium is slower than through a rare one, but again Aristotle may be said to have oversimplified the relationship between the density of the medium and velocity.

He certainly realised that in arriving at general propositions concerning the speed of moving objects a number of factors may, indeed must, be discounted. He takes it for granted, for example, that the medium through which movement takes place is completely homogeneous, although this is never the case in fact. And while he notes that the speed of an object is influenced by its shape, he leaves this too out of account when proposing his general doctrines of natural and forced motion. And yet the main difference between Aristotelian and Newtonian dynamics is that in the latter the process of abstraction is carried much further. Newtonian dynamics relates to the ideal case of frictionless movement through a void. But the propositions of Aristotelian dynamics refer to movement taking place through a medium. Indeed because he assumed that speed is inversely proportional to the density of the medium, he explicitly denied that motion through a void is possible, for the speed would be infinitely great. While we should say that the effects of the resistance of the medium should be discounted in considering the relation between force, mass and velocity, Aristotle assumes throughout his discussion that motion must take place through a medium. But the problem he thereby set himself, and took to be the central problem in dynamics, is one that we now know to be of extraordinary complexity. To determine the precise effect that the resistance of the medium has on the velocity of a moving body, we have to take into account not only the density of the medium, but also the velocity, mass and shape of the body in question.

The main shortcoming of Aristotle's dynamics is not so much a failure to pay attention to the data of experience, as a failure to carry abstraction far enough. In assuming that motion necessarily takes place through a medium, he may be said to have stayed too close, rather than not close enough, to the data of experience. The paradigms of motion in his dynamics are such cases as a ship being hauled through the water, or a leaf falling from a tree, or a ball being thrown up into the air and falling again. The ship can be hauled more easily when unladen; it moves more rapidly when the force applied to it is increased; the leaf shows the influences of shape and weight on speed, and so on. But the paradigm of motion in Newtonian dynamics is one that we never observe except under artificial conditions, namely frictionless movement through a void. Nevertheless it is true both that Aristotle failed to carry out certain simple tests that would have indicated the inaccuracy of some of his generalisations, and that there are certain logical inconsistencies between his propositions that might have suggested to him that he had oversimplified certain problems. To some extent better experimentalists and better mathematicians were to remedy these shortcomings in later antiquity, as when Philoponus, anticipating Galileo by some thousand years, provided experimental evidence to refute the doctrine that the speed of a falling body is directly proportional to its weight: he observed that when two objects of different weights are dropped from the same height the ratio of the times required for the motion is not equal to the ratio of the weights. But if there are undoubtedly grave inadequacies in Aristotle's dynamics, his achievement in this field, in being the first to advance general propositions concerning the factors governing the speed of moving objects, is still remarkable enough. And if there is a lesson to be learned from his work in dynamics for his method and approach to scientific problems as a whole, it is not, as has sometimes been maintained, that he blandly ignored the observed facts in constructing his theories on *a priori* principles, but rather that his theories are hasty generalisations based on admittedly rather superficial observations.

CHAPTER 9

PSYCHOLOGY

In many ways Aristotle's doctrine of the ψυχή is the linch-pin of his whole philosophy: certainly it is the key to his philosophy of nature and it provides an important link between his physics, his ethics and his theology. Of all natural objects, it is those that are alive that provide the clearest and most dramatic illustrations of the role of the final cause—the young animal and the seed of the plant growing into mature specimens. The doctrine that different living creatures possess different vital functions plays, as we shall see, an important part in his conception of happiness: happiness and the good for man are defined in terms of the activity of the ψυχή, but particularly in terms of that faculty which man alone among the animals possesses, namely reason. So the highest activity for man is the activity of reason, contemplation. Living creatures are arranged in a hierarchy according to the faculties of the ψυχή they possess, and this scale extends upwards to include the gods. While men have reason along with other, lower faculties of the ψυχή, the gods possess reason alone, and the activity of the unmoved mover is, as we have seen, described as continuous untrammelled contemplation.

Conventionally translated 'soul', the term ψυχή has a range far wider than either 'soul' or 'mind' in English, for it covers every vital function from reproduction, through sensation and locomotion, to reason. The three books of the *de Anima* and the minor treatises grouped under the title *Parva Naturalia* contain much more than what we should describe as 'psychology'. They deal with the cognitive faculties, sensation and reason, but much space is devoted, particularly in the *Parva Naturalia*, to what we should consider physiological questions, as for example sleep and waking, and even respiration. These treatises lead on naturally to the biology proper: as the 'psychology' of the *de Anima* and the *Parva Naturalia* includes much 'physiology', so conversely living creatures are studied in the biological treatises partly, indeed in places principally, from the point of view of the ψυχή. In the *de Partibus Animalium* (641 a 21 f.) Aristotle says that 'it is the business of the natural philosopher to speak and know about the ψυχή', and in the *de Anima* (402 a 4 ff.) he says that 'knowledge of it [the ψυχή] evidently contributes a great deal towards the truth as a whole, and particularly to our understanding of nature'.

Earlier views

As is his custom, Aristotle begins his discussion of the soul in the first book of the *de Anima* by examining earlier views, and this examination serves not merely as a historical survey of earlier doctrines, but also to identify the main problems that he intends to deal with. His discussion ranges over the whole field of Presocratic and fourth-century speculation on the topic, and he offers some interesting interpretations and criticisms of his predecessors' views. He suggests, for example, that the two main characteristic marks of soul, for earlier writers, had been movement and cognition, and he has some telling criticisms to make of those who had failed to distinguish clearly enough between inanimate substances and animate ones. He asks pertinently why, if soul is identified with water or fire, for example, in the way that some of the Presocratics had tended to suggest, these elements do not form living creatures wherever they exist. To identify soul as fire is to provide an answer to the question what it is made of, but it does not contribute to our understanding of the distinction between what is, and what is not, alive.

But two of the controversies of the time are particularly important for the interpretation of Aristotle's own doctrine of soul. The first is the question of whether or in what sense the soul has parts, and the second the problem of the relationship between the soul and the body and in particular the question of whether the soul is capable of separate existence. Both these topics were much debated in the fourth century, and both were raised and discussed by Plato. Having enunciated the famous doctrine of the tripartite soul in the fourth book of the *Republic*, Socrates remarks, at the end of that dialogue (611 b), that 'it is not easy for a thing to be immortal that is composed of many parts and not put together in the best way', and he goes on to suggest that his previous account of the soul refers merely to its present appearance and to what happens to it in its human existence, and that its true nature is very different from this. The question of whether the soul is manifold or simple is not expressly answered in later dialogues, although so far as the human soul is concerned the *Timaeus* (69c ff.) suggests that the three parts of the soul are located in different areas of the body and that only the reasoning part is immortal.

The second, more fundamental, problem bequeathed by Plato was the question of the relation between the soul and the body as a whole. Here Plato's doctrine is clear-cut and definite. The soul is different in kind from the body. The soul is invisible and immaterial, while the body, of course, is both visible and material. Moreover, the soul is separable from the body and immortal. This was Plato's firm conviction, whatever his opinion may have been about whether this thesis could be demonstrated to the satisfaction of a sceptic. But while Plato affirmed the soul's immortality and its separability from the body, this posed two difficult problems. First if the soul is immaterial, how does it move the body? This is a question that is raised in connection with the soul and the body of the sun in *Laws* x, 898 d ff., although neither there nor anywhere else does Plato resolve the difficulty satisfactorily. And secondly there is the even more obscure question of how or why the soul becomes incarnate in the body, and here Plato's doctrine has to be gleaned from hints in the eschatological myths of the *Phaedo*, the *Republic* and especially the *Phaedrus*, since this is evidently not a problem that can be tackled in any other than mythical terms.

General definition of soul

These were the main issues that form the background against which Aristotle's own doctrine of the soul should be judged. When at the beginning of *de Anima* II he sets

out to give his own positive views about the soul, he defines it in the unpromising and obscure-seeming formula:
'the first actuality of a natural body that potentially has
life' (412a27f.). What does this mean? The doctrine of
soul as an actuality—ἐντελέχεια—is introduced after he
has applied the more familiar distinction between form
and matter to living creatures. A living being is a composite whole, possessing both matter and form, body being
the matter and soul supplying the form. But, he goes on,
matter is potentiality and form actuality, and one can
speak of actuality in two ways which he illustrates by
drawing a distinction between (1) possessing a piece of
knowledge—as it might be of Pythagoras' theorem—and
(2) actually using that knowledge—as it might be in a
piece of reasoning in geometry. Soul is actuality, Aristotle
suggests, in the former sense, the 'first' actuality: 'for
both sleeping and waking involve the presence of soul,
and of these waking corresponds to actual knowing, sleeping to knowledge possessed but not being used' (de An.
412a23ff.).

Two illustrations help to make his view of the relationship between body/matter and soul/form clearer. The
first is that of the axe (412b11ff.). If a tool such as an axe
were a living creature, then what makes it an axe—the
capacity to hew, cleave and chop, one might say—would
be its soul: whereas the matter from which the axe is made,
the metal, would be the body. He then gives a rather better
illustration, that of the eye (412b18ff.): 'Suppose the eye
were a living creature: sight would have been its soul, for
sight is the substance of the eye that corresponds to the

definition [i.e. of what it is to be an eye]...And once sight is removed, the eye is no longer an eye except in name: it is no more a real eye than a stone eye or an eye in a drawing', just as a dead animal, as he says elsewhere, is an animal in name alone. Unlike Plato, who had spoken of soul and body as separable entities, Aristotle insists that the soul is the form of a composite whole whose matter is the body. It is just as impossible, then, to separate soul from body, as it would be to separate the sharpness of the axe from the metal it is made of, or the sight of the eye from the physical organ. 'Therefore there is no need', he says at 412b6f., 'to inquire whether the soul and the body are one, any more than one would do so in the case of the wax and the shape given to it [by the signet ring].'

The originality and importance of this theory lie in the conception of the living creature as a single complex whole. Soul is not a separate entity that merely inhabits the body during the lifetime of the animal. It is the actuality of the body—that which makes the living creature a living creature. While Plato stands as the first major exponent of the dualist view on what has come to be called the mind-body problem, Aristotle may legitimately be considered the first major exponent of the opposite, monistic view, according to which mind and body are considered not as different substances, but rather as different aspects of a single complex entity.

So far as the general definition of soul is concerned, Aristotle's position both on the relation between soul and body, and on the question of immortality, is perfectly clear. His general theory excludes the possibility of the soul as a whole being separable and immortal, for if it is the actuality of the body, it clearly cannot exist except in conjunction with the body of which it is the actuality. Yet as we shall see Aristotle qualifies this theory in one very important respect: he makes an exception to his general rule that the soul cannot have separate existence in the case of one of its faculties, namely reason. Already in *de An.* II, ch. 2, 413 b 24 ff., he says:

Concerning reason and the faculty of contemplation nothing is clear as yet. But it seems that this is another kind of soul, and that this alone may be separable, as that which is eternal from that which is perishable. But as far as the other parts of the soul are concerned, it is evident from what we have said that they are not, as some hold, separable, although it is clear that they are distinguishable in definition.

How far Aristotle is able to justify his doctrine that reason is immortal is a question we shall be considering shortly.

The faculties of soul

After giving what he calls an outline account of the soul in the opening chapter of *de Anima* II, Aristotle goes on to identify its various faculties. These are clearly not parts in the sense of separate entities. True, he sometimes uses the term μόρια, parts, of them, but the stricter term to describe what they are is δυνάμεις, faculties. There is no single authoritative passage that sets out a definitive list of the faculties he recognises, but ignoring the minor variations that exist between his different accounts we may say that the six main faculties he distinguishes are as follows:

nutrition and reproduction (θρεπτικόν)
sensation (αἰσθητικόν)
desire (ὀρεκτικόν)
locomotion (κινητικὸν κατὰ τόπον)
imagination (φαντασία)
reason (νοῦς or τὸ διανοητικόν).

This general classification of vital faculties enables broad distinctions to be drawn between living creatures of different sorts. The higher up the scale of (terrestrial) creatures one goes the greater the number of faculties of soul the creature possesses. This becomes clear when we consider each faculty in turn. All living things have the ability to nourish themselves and to grow, and all natural species, excluding certain abnormal or hybrid specimens, are able to reproduce themselves. The 'nutritive' faculty is, accordingly, the most widespread of all the faculties of soul, being found in all animals and plants. But that is the only faculty of soul that plants possess, according to Aristotle. Animals have at least one other faculty in addition to θρεπτικόν, namely sensation. But not all animals possess all of the five senses, touch, taste, hearing, smell and sight. They all have touch, for this sense is indispensable to them in their search for and recognition of food. But as regards the other senses, Aristotle discusses at some length in the psychological and biological treatises such detailed questions as whether the bee can smell, the mole see and fish hear.

Desire

The next three faculties, desire, locomotion and imagination, are closely interrelated. First the faculty of desire accompanies sensation, that is to say whatever has sensation also has desire. This is explained at *de An.* 414 b 4 ff., where Aristotle says that whatever has sensation experiences pleasure and pain, and whatever experiences pleasure and pain, also experiences appetite, appetite being simply desire for what is pleasant. Moreover, as we have just seen, all animals have the sense of touch and can perceive their food and drink: and hunger and thirst are the names given to the specific desires for food and drink. Naturally Aristotle recognises other desires besides these, and it is particularly striking that he should insist that the faculty of ὄρεξις cuts across the Platonic division of the soul into three parts. As he says at *de An.* 432 b 3 ff.: 'desire would seem to be different both in definition and in capacity from all [the other parts of the soul]. And it is absurd to break this faculty up: for wish is in the rational part, and appetite, ἐπιθυμία, and spirit, θυμός, in the irrational. And if the soul is tripartite, there will be desire in each part.'

Locomotion

Next there is locomotion, the power of originating movement in place. As with the sense of sight, for instance, some but not all animals possess this faculty. Aristotle believes that certain marine animals, particularly among the shellfish, do not have the power of moving themselves. Just as he is prepared to go into the question of which animals have which senses in some detail, he devotes two studies to the problem of the ways in which animals move, the two short treatises the *de Motu Animalium* and the *de Incessu Animalium*. So far as the *de Anima* is concerned, having identified locomotion as one of the faculties of the soul in book II, he discusses it in general terms in a subtle, but abstruse, analysis in book III (chh. 9–11). He insists that it is a separate faculty, distinct from the others he recognises, but he points out its close connection both with desire on the one hand, and with reason and φαντασία, 'imagination', on the other. At 433 a 9 f. he considers what initiates movement in animals, and suggests that this is 'either desire or reason, if imagination can be considered a sort of reasoning'. The point here is that while he does not allow animals to have reason in the strict sense, they may, and many of them do, possess φαντασία, the ability to form mental images. Both imagination and reason itself— in this case the 'practical', not the 'theoretical' reason— may be the stimulus to movement, but he goes on to point out that when imagination initiates movement, it does not do so without desire being present also, and the same is true of the practical reason too: 'for wish is [a form of] desire, and when movement is produced according to a calculation, it is also according to a wish' (433 a 23 ff.). So in a sense the source of movement is one thing, namely desire, and he concludes (b 27 ff.): 'an animal is capable of moving itself in so far as it has the faculty of desire; but desire presupposes imagination, and imagination may be rational or it may belong to sensation, and of the latter kind the other animals too [besides man] have a share.'

Imagination

This takes us to φαντασία, conventionally translated 'imagination', although our term has creative associations which are absent from Aristotle's use of φαντασία. This too, like locomotion and all the senses except touch, belongs to some but not all animals. He denies that ants, bees and larvae, for instance, have the ability to form mental images or presentations. Imagination presupposes sensation, but it is different from sensation, as can be seen from two facts, especially: first we can imagine something without perceiving anything, for example when we have our eyes shut, or when we dream. And secondly imagination is fallible, while sensation itself is not: Aristotle holds that the sensation of this white colour, or of that shrill sound, is infallible, and that error arises mainly in the judgements we make concerning what we perceive, as for example when we associate a particular sensation with a particular external object. He says that imagination is a movement produced by sensation, similar to the sensation itself: 'it is a movement imparted by the sense when the sense is in a state of actuality. And since sight is the principal sense, φαντασία gets its name from light, φάος, since it is impossible to see without light. Because imaginings persist and resemble sensations, living creatures do many things under their stimulus, in some cases (the animals) because they do not have reason, in others (man) because their reason is sometimes clouded by some affection or disease or sleep' (de An. 429 a 1 ff.). In summary, imagination derives from sensation, but unlike sensation itself, it is true or false. And it has two important roles to play: first it is the basis of memory, for memory does not take place without mental images; and secondly it acts as a stimulus to action and movement, for as we have seen desire presupposes imagination.

Sensation

The two cognitive faculties of the soul are sensation and reason, and Aristotle's accounts of these two contain some of his most ingenious, as well as some of his most obscure, ideas. We may begin with sensation. Here he appeals once again to the distinction between form and matter, which had already played an important part in his general definition of soul. When sensation occurs, the sense-organ or αἰσθητήριον receives what Aristotle calls the 'perceptible form', without the matter, of the object perceived. He illustrates this by referring to a piece of wax which receives the imprint of a signet ring, but not the actual iron or gold of which the ring is made. So, when we see something, the eye receives the perceptible form of the object, but not its matter. But what does he mean by 'perceptible form'? The primary objects of sensation, according to Aristotle, are colours, sounds, smells and so on. Each sense has its own corresponding primary sense-objects. When we see something white, the eye, which is potentially able to receive the perceptible form 'this white colour', does so, and indeed the perceptible form and the recipient organ coalesce and become one during the act of perception. The sense-organ is described as an intermediate, which can be acted on by a range of sense-data, as for example, in the case of sight, the range from white to black. And Aristotle recognises that if the sense-object exceeds the range that the organ can perceive, the organ itself suffers damage, being dulled or even destroyed, as is shown by such examples as the eye being temporarily blinded by bright light or the sense of touch being destroyed by something extremely hot. Here then there is an obvious analogy between his account of sensation as a mean between opposite extremes and his ethical doctrine of moral virtue as a mean between two vices.

In general, sensation is explained as the activation of the sense-organ by 'perceptible form', but one of the valuable parts of his analysis is the distinction he draws between different types of sense-objects and the account which this leads him to give of what it is to make a mistake about what we perceive. At *de An.* 418a7ff. and elsewhere he distinguishes between three types of sensible objects. (1) Primarily what we perceive is this or that colour, this or that sound, and the sensation of these 'special' objects of sense is infallible, or as he puts it rather more guardedly in one passage (428b19) 'subject to the minimum of error'. 'Thus sight is of colour, hearing of sound and taste of flavour...But each sense judges of its own objects and is not deceived as to the fact that there is a colour or that there is a sound, although it may be deceived about what or where the coloured object is or what or where the object is which produced the sound' (418a12ff.). Whereas we cannot be mistaken in registering the impression of a colour or a sound, we can and do make mistakes in our interpretations of our sensations, in identifying, for example, this white colour as a dove, or in judging that that shrill sound comes from a trumpet. (2) Secondly there are what he calls the 'common sensibles' (κοινὰ αἰσθητά). There are certain things we perceive, such as movement, rest, number, figure and size, which are not the special objects of any one sense, but common to all. Whereas a white colour belongs to sight and cannot be touched or smelt, movement, for instance, may be perceived both by sight and by touch. (3) The third type of sensible object is what is perceptible 'accidentally'. The example given at *de An.* 418a20f. is the son of Diares. What we see is, strictly speaking, a colour, or rather perhaps a collection of colours, but what we see also happens to be a particular person, namely Diares' son. Individuals, such as Diares' son, the Parthenon, this table and so on, are, then, objects of sense 'accidentally'.

In both (2) and (3) error is possible. There is, however, a difference between these two cases. The common sensibles are not perceived merely 'accidentally', like Diares' son. On the contrary they are clearly stated to be perceived by the senses directly, καθ' αὑτά. There is no *special* sense that perceives movement, figure and so on: at *de An.* 425a13 ff. Aristotle explicitly denies that there is a *sixth* sense to perceive the common sensibles. But even though they do not belong to any particular sense, they are directly perceived by the senses acting in common, that is by the faculty of sense as a whole. There is, however, as he notes but does not fully explain at *de An.* 428b 23 ff., a much greater chance of error in perceiving the common sensibles than there is in seeing a colour or perceiving any of the other special objects of sense.

Reason

This analysis of sensation is relevant to the next and final topic, the most difficult and hotly debated part of Aristotle's theory of soul, his account of reason. His discussion of the other faculties of soul leaves no room for doubt on one point: they cannot exist in separation from the body. But he makes an exception of reason. At *de An.* 413 b 24 f. he had remarked that concerning reason 'nothing is as yet clear'. Unfortunately the two main chapters he devotes to the subject, book III, chh. 4 and 5, cannot be said to resolve all the difficulties.

He begins in book III, ch. 4, with the analogy between reason and sensation. Sensation involves the receiving of the perceptible form without the matter of the object perceived. Reasoning similarly involves the receiving of what he calls the 'intelligible form', without, of course, any matter. But then Aristotle qualifies this analogy by pointing out that whereas too great a stimulus from the object of sense dulls or destroys the organ, the equivalent does not happen with reasoning. When the mind comes into contact with what is especially 'knowable' or 'knowable' in the fullest sense, this does not destroy it or make it less able to apprehend lesser subjects: on the contrary it apprehends them better. Here then is one indication of the separability of reason and its objects. But he still has not made clear what 'intelligible form' is. 'Perceptible forms' turned out to be primarily the special objects of sense, colours, sounds and so on. The 'intelligible form' is the essence of a thing, the 'what it is to be that thing', or its definition. Aristotle's example is that of flesh. Sensation discriminates hot and cold and the other perceptible qualities of flesh, but we judge what it is to be flesh itself by a different faculty, by reason. If colours, sounds and so on are perceptible forms, the definition of flesh as matter of a certain sort with a certain form, the definition of man as a rational animal, the definition of a circle as a plane figure bounded by a curved line everywhere equidistant from a point, are examples of the objects of reason, the intelligible forms. Like the sense-organ, reason is potentially capable of receiving its objects, and actually becomes one with its objects in the act of reasoning, just as the sense-organ becomes one with the perceptible form in the act of perception. But the important difference between the two cognitive faculties lies in this: sensation depends on a part of the body, the sense-organ, the eye in the case of sight, for example, and in the case of touch the flesh as a whole. But reasoning, in Aristotle's view, does not (*de An.* 429a24f., b4f., 430a7f.). νοῦς is not, in fact, an organ of the body. Aristotle has no equivalent to our notion of the brain as the seat of mental activity, even though he considers the heart to be the common sensorium, or seat of the faculty of sense. Accordingly the activity of νοῦς, reasoning, is carried on independently of the body. And it is primarily because he believes that the body is in no way involved in reasoning that he speaks of reason as being a different kind of soul and as being separable from the body. Reasoning alone is not an actuality of a *part* of the body.

The doctrine of ch. 4 is clear in the main. The chapter ends with Aristotle noting some difficulties, such as how mind can know itself (it must be an intelligible object itself), and what is a much more difficult question and one that he never satisfactorily answers, why mind does not think continually. But we understand reasoning to be at once similar to and different from sensation: similar in that it is thought of as the reception of form without matter—in this case the 'intelligible forms' such as 'what it is to be a man'—but different in that while sensation depends on a part of the body, reasoning does not. But Aristotle then turns to consider at greater length the question of what acts, and what is acted upon, in reasoning, introducing in ch. 5 the complex and obscure theory which has come to be known as the doctrine of the active and the passive reason.

Here he begins with the familiar distinction between matter and moving cause. As these distinctions exist in everything natural, so too, he suggests, 'these differences must necessarily exist also in the soul': the ambiguous phrase καὶ ἐν τῇ ψυχῇ at 430a13 is best translated for the moment by an equally ambiguous English one. 'So then there must be one sort of reason that is such as we have described by virtue of becoming everything, and there is another sort of reason that is such by virtue of making everything.' He calls the former παθητικὸς νοῦς or passive reason: the latter, the reason that is such 'by virtue of making everything', is conventionally termed the 'active' reason, although Aristotle never uses the term ποιητικός to describe it, and the associations of the English word 'active' are potentially rather misleading. He then continues (430a15ff.): 'It [that is the 'active' reason] is a sort of condition, ἕξις, like light: for in a way light too makes what are potentially colours actual colours. And this reason is separable and impassive and unmixed, and its being is actuality...And when it is separated it appears just as it is, and this alone is immortal and eternal. But we do not remember, because although this is impassive, the passive reason on the other hand is perishable.'

How much can be gleaned from this, possibly the most disputed chapter in the whole Aristotelian Corpus? First it is clear that whereas he had elsewhere treated reason as a single entity both throughout the *de Anima* and in his other treatises, he here draws a general distinction between two sorts of reason. It is again largely with the help of the analogy with sensation that we are, it seems, to understand the distinction. In sight, the objects are the visible forms, and the percipient is the sense-organ, the eye, but sight cannot take place without a third thing, light: light is the necessary precondition without which the visible forms cannot be perceived. So in reasoning, the objects are the intelligible forms, and what apprehends them is the passive reason, but a third thing is again necessary, according to Aristotle, namely the 'active' reason, without which the intelligible forms cannot be known. For the sake of clarity the analogy may be set out in the form of a table:

Mode of cognition	Sight	Reasoning
Object	Visible forms	Intelligible forms
Recipient	Eye	Passive reason
Necessary precondition	Light	'Active' reason

The role of the passive reason is for the most part clear.

Its function is to receive the intelligible forms; in that sense it 'becomes' everything. It evidently belongs to the individual person, as the sense-organs do, and it is explicitly said to be perishable. The passive reason, in fact, is brought into line with Aristotle's doctrine concerning the other faculties of soul which also cease to function on the death of the individual.

But the role of the 'active' reason is much more difficult to grasp. It is imagined, apparently, as activating the intelligible forms. It makes what is potentially intelligible actually intelligible: this is presumably what he means when he says that it 'makes' all things. But we might ask what exactly its relation is to the individual soul. In particular, is it always external to the individual? Or does it exist in the individual at any rate during his life? Here the ambiguity which I drew attention to in the phrase καὶ ἐν τῇ ψυχῇ at 430a13 proves an embarrassment. The dispute could be definitely settled if this phrase bore the sense 'within the soul', for then Aristotle could be said to have stated quite explicitly that both passive and 'active' reason are within the individual. Unfortunately, however, the phrase might simply mean 'in the case of soul', and as he has just used the expression ἐν ἁπάσῃ τῇ φύσει at 430a10 in an equivalent sense, 'in the case of every natural object', it seems possible or even probable that this is what Aristotle did mean. The argument cannot be determined by an appeal to the phrase καὶ ἐν τῇ ψυχῇ, and indeed it is doubtful whether we can settle the matter definitively one way or the other. On the one hand the analogy of light might, if pressed, suggest that the 'active' reason is something external to the individual. And when we reflect that the activity of god and the unmoved mover is described in *Metaphysics* Λ as reason, and he is pure actuality (*Metaph.* 1072 b 22 ff. and 26 ff.) and eternal and impassive, it might be argued that the 'active' reason is not human at all, but divine. On the other hand, there are indications that point in the opposite direction, to the conclusion that the 'active reason' is thought to exist within each individual person. Thus it might be thought that when at *de An.* 430 a 22 he refers to the 'active' reason as not merely separable, χωριστός, but separated, χωρισθείς—that is, presumably, from the individual—this implies that it can also exist *in* the individual. And when having noted that it is eternal Aristotle goes on to say (430 a 23 f.) that *we* do not remember, since the 'active' reason is impassive, and the passive reason perishable, this too seems to indicate that we as individuals each have a share in the 'active' reason.

Aristotle's texts hardly allow a firm answer to be given to our question, but in the final analysis it may be that the divergence between the two views is not very great. Whether the 'active' reason is thought of as entirely divine, or merely as the divine part in us, in either case as that which makes the intelligible forms actually intelligible it is certainly impersonal in the sense that it does not depend on the individual person. Furthermore when we consider that the 'active' reason is neither material nor, presumably, extended, the question of *where* it is to be located, in us or outside us, may in any case be thought a paradoxical one. Finally on the question of immortality, it is clear first that the 'active' reason is the *only* part that is immortal, and secondly that the sort of immortality accorded to it is in no way a personal or individual one.

What may be said about the doctrine of the soul in the *de Anima* as a whole? As regards the lower faculties Aristotle introduces a new and important conception of soul as the first actuality of the natural body that potentially has life. Here he puts forward an original interpretation of the relationship between soul and body which is in marked contrast to the dualist view of Plato. Moreover it is a striking feature of Aristotle's treatment of the soul in the *de Anima*, again in marked contrast to Plato, that he discusses it neither from a religious nor from an ethical point of view, but very much from the point of view of the naturalist. Thus he does not attempt to lay down dogmatic general rules about sensation in animals: he recognises that different animals possess different faculties of sense and is prepared to go in detail into this question. But as regards the highest faculty of soul, we see that Aristotle nevertheless believes in immortality of a sort. Reason is made an exception to the general rule that the faculties of soul are inseparable from the body, because reason, he holds, is not dependent on the body and is not an actuality of a part of the body. Even so the passive reason is said to be perishable, and it is only the impersonal 'active' reason that is described as immortal and eternal. However much of the Platonic doctrine of soul Aristotle rejected, he shared with Plato and with other earlier Greek writers the belief that part of the soul is immortal, and more particularly the belief in the divinity of reason, which was thought of both as the seat of intelligence in us and the source of intelligibility in the world as a whole.

CHAPTER 10

ETHICS

Three separate ethical treatises are included in the Aristotelian Corpus, the *Magna Moralia*, the *Eudemian Ethics* and the *Nicomachean Ethics*. Of these the *Magna Moralia* is far from certainly authentic. Some scholars consider it an early work, composed while Aristotle was still much influenced by Plato, but it is more usually thought to have been written by one of Aristotle's pupils. Of the two other ethical treatises the *Eudemian Ethics* is generally held to be the earlier and it is useful both for the additional evidence it provides concerning some of Aristotle's ethical theories and more especially for the light it throws on their development. Our main source for his mature moral philosophy is, however, the *Nicomachean Ethics*, and it is with this that I shall be chiefly concerned in this chapter.

The plan of the 'Nicomachean Ethics'

This is one of the most coherent and systematic of Aristotle's treatises and it is probably the easiest and most rewarding of all the major works for the student to tackle first. Unlike the *Physics* and the *Metaphysics*, which are collections of books that are often quite loosely connected to one another, the *Nicomachean Ethics* forms a coherent whole. Aristotle defines the subject and states the problem in book I. Books II to V deal with moral virtue, first in general, then, after a discussion of choice and responsibility, in detail. Book VI deals with intellectual virtue, VII with moral weakness. Books VIII and IX form a digression from the main subject and contain a detailed examination of friendship. In X he picks up the discussion of pleasure which he had begun in VII and then returns, finally, to the topic of happiness, the central subject of ethics, which he had considered in outline in book I. We find, too, that he develops and modifies points as he goes along. For example, the general account of moral virtue in book II must be understood in the light of his later discussion of the intellectual virtues, particularly of φρόνησις or practical intelligence, and the second account of pleasure, in book X, modifies the earlier, in VII, as well as supplementing it.

Stylistically the *Nicomachean Ethics* has more of the quality of a Platonic dialogue than any other of Aristotle's extant works. Yet his views on the nature and aim of ethics and on the method to be used in discussing moral questions are, in certain respects, fundamentally different from Plato's, and these differences must be borne in mind if we are to avoid seriously misconstruing either philosopher's contribution.[1] Three major points should be brought out here before we turn to Aristotle's ethical theories themselves.

[1] Among those who have commented on the differences between Plato's and Aristotle's ethics Renford Bambrough has contributed several particularly important and helpful discussions, the most accessible of which is the introduction to the section on ethics in the Mentor selection of texts in translation, *The Philosophy of Aristotle*.

Plato and Aristotle as moralists

(1) The first is that Aristotle insists that ethics is not an exact science. At *EN* 1094b 11 ff., for instance, he says:

Our discussion will be adequate, if we make it as clear as the subject-matter permits. The same degree of precision should not be demanded in all inquiries...Fine and just actions, which are the subject-matter of politics, admit of plenty of differences and variations, so that the view has arisen that they are matters of convention, and not of nature...We must be content, then, in dealing with this subject, to indicate the truth in broad outline, and when speaking about things which are true only for the most part, and using premisses which are of the same kind, to reach conclusions which are also of the same sort...It is the mark of an educated man to seek precision in each kind of inquiry just so far as the nature of the subject permits. It is as inappropriate to demand demonstration in ethics as it is to allow a mathematician to use merely probable arguments.

The contrast with Plato could hardly be more pointed. Where Plato had used mathematics as the paradigm for knowledge, and mathematical certainty as the standard which the statesman should try to attain in ethical and political matters, Aristotle mentions the example of mathematics only to draw a fundamental distinction between the two types of inquiry. Rigorous proofs and certainty are appropriate in mathematics, but quite out of place in ethics and politics, where we should attain simply as much precision as the subject-matter allows. To bring out this point Aristotle refers to the view that morality is conventional, as this highlights the extent of possible disagreement in ethics. He does not, however, subscribe to this view himself. His own position here is a subtle one, since he denies both that right and wrong are matters of convention, and that they can be made the subject of absolute rules and rigorous proofs. The distinction between right and wrong is, he believes, a natural one: but ethics, like medicine, deals with individual cases, and while generalisations are possible on moral questions, just as they are on the subject of diseases, they are true only for the most part, not without exception.

(2) The first point to be made about Aristotle's conception of ethical inquiry is that in ethics we should aim merely at the degree of precision that the subject permits. But he also differs from Plato in his view of the method to be used in this inquiry. Plato insisted that only the philosopher is truly happy, and that very few people will attain to this state at the end of a long and arduous training in which they learn to turn away from the confusing world of ordinary experience to contemplate the Forms. Aristotle's view is more mundane. First he does not set moral virtue so far out of the reach of ordinary men. Secondly, in examining moral questions as a whole he is prepared to consider, indeed he thinks it essential to consider, the views of ordinary men. 'Perhaps there is little point in reviewing all the opinions that have been held,' he says at *EN* 1095 a 28 ff., 'and it is enough if we take the most common and those that seem reasonable.' The starting-point, for Aristotle, is an examination of current views about what happiness or virtue consists in.

Again the contrast with Plato is marked, for Plato, like

Socrates, evidently had a profound distrust of popular notions on such subjects as virtue and generally considered them quite incoherent and worthless. Aristotle, for his part, does not underestimate the inconsistencies of popular morality, but he clearly believes that in attempting to discover the truth it is important to examine what he calls τὰ φαινόμενα, a phrase which in the context of ethics is usually equivalent to 'what is generally thought to be the case'. Moreover he sees his task as being to stay as close as possible to the generally accepted opinions, and to take over as much as possible from popular morality. He describes his method at *EN* 1145b2ff., for instance, as follows: 'as in all other cases, we must posit τὰ φαινόμενα and after first discussing the difficulties go on to prove, if possible, all the common views, ἔνδοξα, about these affections, or, failing that, most of them and the most authoritative ones. For if we resolve the difficulties and leave the common views unshaken, we shall have proved the case sufficiently.'

Aristotle pays far more attention and respect than Plato had done to the common opinions or what was generally thought reasonable on questions of morality. But we can distinguish their methods in another respect as well. At *EN* 1095a30ff. he says that Plato was right to raise the question of whether any particular inquiry was 'from' or 'to' first principles, and although he does not suggest which approach he thinks Plato himself preferred, he does have more to say about his own method. 'We must begin from what is known: but this has two senses, first what is known to us, and secondly what is known absolutely', and he points out that they must evidently begin with the former. But, as he explains elsewhere, what is better known 'to us' is what is closer to sensation, or the particulars, while it is the universal or what is prior in definition that is better known 'absolutely'. Although no single term, whether 'deductive' or 'counter-inductive', adequately describes the complexities of Plato's procedure, it is clear that Aristotle considered the correct method in ethics, as in other inquiries, to be, broadly speaking, an 'inductive' one, one that proceeds from what is confusedly given in experience to the reasoned universal judgement.

(3) This difference in method corresponds to a further difference in the aims of the two philosophers in their discussions of ethical questions. This lies in the different proportions of description and prescription, or of analysis and recommendation, in their work. There is certainly an important element of search and inquiry in the discussion of moral issues in Plato's dialogues: yet his underlying intention is to recommend and to persuade. Without writing sermons, he moralises through the mouth-piece of Socrates, and the need for men to change is a powerful theme in his writings. With Aristotle the mixture contains the same two ingredients of description and prescription, but in very different proportions. He will reject what the common-sense view suggests only if he has to, and much of the *Nicomachean Ethics* is devoted to analyses of particular examples that throw light on the nature of such things as choice, responsibility, friendship and pleasure. Far more than Plato, Aristotle takes human nature as he finds it and speaks of how men do behave as much as, or

even more than, how men ought to behave. Yet he too has his persuasive and prescriptive role. He too, like Plato, often forcefully advocates his own point of view, and this is especially true in the last book of the *Nicomachean Ethics* where he sets out his own ideal of the supremely happy life.

Criticism of Plato's Form of the Good

We have seen that Aristotle contrasts ethics and the exact sciences, while Plato wishes to equate the two: and speaking in very general terms, we may say that Aristotle's ethics are both more purely inductive and more descriptive than Plato's. That Aristotle himself was well aware of certain fundamental differences between his own conception of ethical inquiry and Plato's is clear from the fact that he devotes a whole chapter (ch. 6) in the first book of the *Nicomachean Ethics* to a criticism of the key Platonic doctrine of the Form of the Good. He attacks the theory of Forms on various counts in this chapter, but two of his objections are particularly important for our understanding of the differences between the ethics of the two philosophers and indeed between their general philosophical stand-points.

First at *EN* 1096a19ff. he argues that 'good' is not a univocal term, that is that there is no single definition of 'good' that applies to it in every context in which it is correctly used. It has different senses in different categories. Thus in the category of substance he says that it is predicated of god or reason, in the category of quality, of the virtues, in the category of quantity, of the right measure and so on. 'Good' has, he suggests, as many senses as 'is'. There cannot be a single Form common to all 'goods', for if there had been, the term could not have been predicated in all the categories, but only in one.

Then at *EN* 1096 b 31 ff. he maintains that even if there were such a thing as the Form of the Good, knowledge of it would be useless. First the Form itself, separate and independent, would be unattainable, whereas their inquiry is directed towards discovering something that is attainable. Secondly, he considers the argument that by knowing what is good in the absolute sense we shall have greater knowledge of those things that are good relative to us, and if we know them, obtain them. But on this he comments:

The argument has a certain plausibility, but it seems to conflict with what happens in the case of the sciences. For in all of them men aim at some good and try to find out where they fall short of it, and yet they disregard getting to know the Good. Yet if it were so useful, it is hardly likely that all the craftsmen would be unaware of it and not even try to find it. And it is hard too to see how a weaver or a carpenter will benefit in his art by knowing the Good itself, or how a man who has seen the Form itself will be a better doctor or general. Doctors do not seem to study even health in this way: they study the health of man, or rather the health of this individual, for it is individuals that they cure (*EN* 1097 a 3 ff.).

These criticisms provide good illustrations of the differences between the two philosophers in their approach to ethics. Plato had insisted that 'good' has a single definition. Thus when Meno suggested, in the dialogue named after him, that the virtue or excellence of a man is

different from that of a woman, and these in turn differ
from those of a child or a slave, Socrates complained that
he did not want to be given a swarm of virtues: he wanted
to know what makes them all virtues (*Meno* 71e ff.).
Aristotle takes, in effect, Meno's side in this argument. He
insists that 'good' has different senses in different
categories. Yet he does not conclude that 'good' is
merely ambiguous—that the term is an equivocal one like
the word 'box' in English. Once again, as in the dispute
between nature and convention, Aristotle takes up a position intermediate between two opposed extremes. Like
'is', 'good' is neither univocal, nor equivocal. The point
is a subtle one, and Aristotle himself considers it too technical to go into in any detail in the context of a discussion
of ethics, merely mentioning that 'goods' may be one by
being derived from, or contributing to, a single thing, or
they may be one 'by analogy' (*EN* 1096 b 27 f.): but he had
explained elsewhere how a term may be neither univocal
nor equivocal in his analysis of the use of 'being' and
'healthy' in the *Metaphysics* (Γ ch. 2, see above, pp. 127–8).

At *EN* 1096a 19 ff. the argument brought against the
Form of the Good is a logical one, based on the distinction
between the different ways in which the term may be used
as a predicate. But at *EN* 1096b31 ff. the objection is
based on practical, empirical considerations. Aristotle
refers to the evidence provided by the arts and the crafts,
and notes first that craftsmen do not in fact attempt to
investigate the Form of the Good, and secondly that even
if they apprehended it, it would be doubtful whether they
would benefit from this at all in practice. Here, as often

elsewhere in the *Ethics*, he refers to the example of medicine. Both ethics and medicine are, in his view, practical, not theoretical, disciplines, whose aim is not merely understanding, but action. Just as the doctor has an individual patient to cure, so the politician or statesman is concerned with particular, practical decisions, and Aristotle suggests that in neither case will knowledge of the Platonic Form of the Good serve any useful purpose.

The comparison between Plato and Aristotle reveals how their conceptions of the nature and aims of ethical inquiry differ. But it is now time to turn to Aristotle's particular moral doctrines themselves. We may begin with his statement of the problem in book I, leading up to the definition of moral virtue. His account is so clear that I shall follow his order of exposition closely.

The problem: happiness

The subject of their inquiry, Aristotle says, is the good for man, specifically the chief or highest good. But on the *name* of the good, almost everyone is in agreement (*EN* 1095 a 17 f.). Both the general run of men and persons of culture call it happiness, εὐδαιμονία. But the trouble is that there is so much disagreement about what happiness is. The man in the street considers it to be something simple and obvious, like pleasure or wealth or honour. And often the same man gives different answers at different times, saying when he is ill that happiness is good health, and when he is poor that it is wealth and so on. Aristotle summarises current views on the best life by reducing them to the three ideals of pleasure, honour and contemplation.

The nature of the 'good' is disputed. It appears to be something different in each activity, one thing in medicine, but another in generalship. How, then, are these difficulties to be resolved? In each activity, he suggests, the good lies in the end, or what the activity aims at. In medicine, for example, this will be health. Furthermore we can distinguish between (1) ends that are pursued for the sake of something else, that is ends that are themselves means to some higher end, and (2) ends in themselves. Honour, pleasure and virtue all fall in the former category, while happiness falls in the latter, for while we pursue honour, pleasure and virtue for the sake of happiness, happiness alone is an end in itself, a self-sufficient good.

To grasp some idea of happiness, Aristotle continues (*EN* 1097 b 22 ff.), we must consider the function of man, his ἔργον. If we consider any craftsman, say a sculptor, the 'good' will be found in his function or activity, that is sculpting, and not merely in sculpting, but in sculpting well. The same will apply, Aristotle suggests, to man as a whole. But what is the function of man as such? Man clearly possesses several vital functions, or functions of the 'soul' in Aristotle's terminology, but some of these he shares with other living beings; nutrition and growth, for example, are common to all living beings, and he shares sensation with the animals. It is not these we should consider, then, so much as man's specific function. What marks man out from all the other animals is that he alone is rational. The characteristic function of man is described at *EN* 1098 a 7 f. as 'activity of soul according to reason, or not without reason'. But we must add that the activity must be in accordance with virtue or excellence, for man's happiness will not consist in activity as such, but in activities performed well, just as the excellence of a flute-player consists not merely in playing the flute, but in playing it well. This leads to the preliminary definition of the good for man, at *EN* 1098a16ff., as 'activity of soul according to virtue, and if there are several virtues, according to the best and most complete. And in a complete life. For one swallow does not make a summer, nor does one day. And so too one day, or a short period, does not make a man blessed and happy.'

Aristotle turns aside to consider whether his own view tallies with what others had held on the subject of happiness, and he claims that his own doctrine incorporates other opinions, such as that happiness resides in virtue or wisdom or pleasure. He notes indeed that views that have been held by many people from ancient times or by individuals of high repute are unlikely to be completely mistaken: rather 'they probably hit the mark in one respect or several' (*EN* 1098b27ff.). He recognises, too, that for complete happiness not only the goods of the soul are necessary, but also those of the body, such as beauty and health, and external goods, such as wealth, at least in moderation. A person cannot be completely happy if ugly, or poor: to which one may remark that had Aristotle known Socrates he might not have expressed this conventional view so confidently.[1] Friends, good birth and fine children are also mentioned among other external goods the lack of which will take the lustre from happi-

---

[1] I owe this observation to Mr J. E. Raven.

ness. But while certain external goods are the preconditions of happiness and these depend to some extent on chance, happiness itself is defined as an activity of soul and as such is not a matter of chance but something that arises from human effort. It follows that neither children nor animals can be said to be happy, since they are not capable of such 'activity of soul according to virtue'. We need, Aristotle says at *EN* 1100a4f., complete virtue and a complete life. But he firmly rejects the common, if paradoxical, Greek idea that a man can only be said to be happy when dead. Happiness, he insists throughout, is an activity, not a mere disposition nor a state of mind. Moreover the happy life in itself is pleasant. Happiness, as he says at *EN* 1099a24ff., is 'the best and noblest and most pleasant thing': the happy life is self-sufficient and it comprehends virtue and pleasure, with which other people had identified happiness.

Moral virtue

Defining the good for man Aristotle said that it is activity of soul according to virtue. But this means that virtue or excellence itself, ἀρετή, has to be investigated. Leaving aside the lower functions of the soul, such as nutrition, he distinguishes two main types of virtue, the intellectual virtues, such as wisdom and practical intelligence, and the moral ones, such as liberality and temperance, and after some preliminary remarks about the distinction between these two types he turns to consider moral virtue first in general and then in detail.

His discussion begins with the important general point that while the intellectual virtues are generally acquired by teaching, the moral virtues come from habituation (*EN* 1103 a 14 ff.). No virtue is innate in the sense that the faculty of sight is innate. But if the moral virtues are not innate, they are not contrary to nature either. They arise in us, as he puts it at *EN* 1103 a 24 ff., because we are fitted by nature to receive them, but they are perfected by training and habit. We acquire virtue by practising virtuous acts. We become brave, for example, by doing brave deeds.

Aristotle's thesis is not as circular as it might appear. His main point is that it is impossible to acquire a virtuous disposition otherwise than by practising virtuous acts. But the obvious problem is how can we do brave deeds without being brave already? There are two parts to Aristotle's reply. First the immediate answer to the question of how the moral virtues arise in us is that they are the result of training and habituation. Correct upbringing makes all the difference. A man becomes brave because he is trained as a child to act bravely. Secondly we should note that the word 'brave' has two uses, one in respect of the person who does certain acts, and the other in respect of the acts themselves. 'Brave' applied to a person, the primary use, refers to a settled character-trait. But 'brave' can also be used of those acts that conduce to the formation or confirmation of the disposition in the persons that perform them. In Aristotle's view the person who does the acts may or may not have the firm disposition. His standard of moral virtue is, we may observe, a high one. To do a couple of 'brave' deeds is not enough. First of all the agent must know the quality of his acts: otherwise animals would be called brave, and this Aristotle was not prepared to allow. Secondly the action must be the result of choice. And thirdly it must be an action that reflects a firm and settled disposition (EN 1105 a 31 ff.).

These remarks about 'choice' and 'disposition' lead naturally to the next topic, the definition of moral virtue itself. This must be one of three things that take place in the soul, an affection, πάθος, a faculty, δύναμις, or a habit or disposition, ἕξις. Under affections are included such emotions as anger, fear and joy. Under the faculties he includes, for example, the capacity to feel pleasure and pain. And by dispositions he refers to the way we are disposed in relation to the affections: we may, for instance, feel anger weakly or violently. But moral virtue cannot be either an affection or a faculty, since neither of these involves choice or carries any praise or blame, while both of these are true of virtues and vices. Moral virtue must, then, be a disposition. Specifically it is a disposition involving choice, προαιρετική, in the matter of pleasures and pains: it is concerned with pleasures and pains since it is on account of pleasure that we do bad things and on account of pain that we refrain from fine actions (EN 1104 b 8 ff.). But so far this has simply identified the genus of moral virtue without establishing its differentia or saying how it may be distinguished from vice—for vice too is a 'disposition involving choice in respect of pleasures and pains'. The differentia of moral virtue is provided by the famous doctrine of the mean, together with the notion of practical intelligence, φρόνησις, and the definition Aristotle offers runs: 'virtue is a disposition involving choice and lying in the mean relative to us as defined by reason and as the man with practical intelligence would define it' (*EN* 1106b36ff.).

The doctrine of the mean

How does he arrive at this doctrine, and what is the intention behind it? The antecedents of the doctrine of the mean may be traced, in Greek popular morality, in such sayings as the Delphic 'nothing too much', and it also owes a good deal to the common medical and physiological doctrine that health lies in a mean state between opposite extremes, such as, for example, 'the hot' and 'the cold'. In introducing his doctrine Aristotle uses two analogies, one referring to the arts and crafts in general and the other to medicine, but both rather far-fetched. Good craftsmen aim at the mean in the sense that they try to avoid what is disproportionate: we say of fine works of art that it is impossible to add anything or take anything away, and this implies, he believes, that excess and defect destroy the beauty of the work, while the mean preserves it (*EN* 1106b9ff.). The second analogy is slightly more plausible. The health and strength of the body are impaired by either too much or too little food, and again by either too much or too little exercise, while the right amounts of food and exercise create and preserve health and strength (*EN* 1104a11ff. and cf. 1106a 36ff.). Similarly, virtues and vices relate, he suggests, to affections and actions in which there is an excess, an intermediate and a defect. Thus we may feel fear, anger, pity and so on, and pleasures and pains in general, in different degrees, but both to feel them too much and to feel them too little are bad. 'To feel them at the right time, about the right things, in relation to the right people, with the right motives, and in the right way, is what is intermediate and best, and this is what virtue consists in' (*EN* 1106b16–23).

The general rule that virtues and vices relate to affections and actions in which there is a scale of excess, intermediate and defect, virtue lying in the intermediate between the two extremes, is stated in *EN* II, ch. 6. But Aristotle introduces important qualifications and modifications into his doctrine which we have to consider carefully if we are to understand how he means us to apply the general rule. First of all he acknowledges that there are some vices which have no corresponding virtue. Among the affections, spitefulness, shamelessness and envy, and among actions, adultery, theft and murder are not excesses or defects. 'In such matters,' as he puts it, 'there is no good or bad in the sense of committing adultery with the right woman, at the right time and in the right way. Quite simply doing any of these things is wrong' (*EN* 1107a15ff.). There are, then, certain exceptions to the rule that virtues and vices stand on a scale of excess, intermediate and defect.

Secondly, the mean that we are to aim at is not an arithmetical one, but, as he says, the mean 'relative to us'. One cannot determine where virtue lies by doing a sum, adding together two figures each representing a value for one of the extremes, and then dividing the total by two. In the analogy Aristotle uses (*EN* 1106a36ff.), if ten 'minae' of food—we might say 10,000 calories—is too much for a man to eat, and two 'minae' too little, it does not follow that six 'minae' will be the correct quantity. For this may be too little for a professional athlete, and too much for someone who is just beginning to train. We must, in fact, take the individual into account. But here too we must be careful not to jump to the conclusion that Aristotle went to the opposite extreme and held that moral virtue is merely subjective. The right amount of food will be different for the trained athlete and for the beginner. But there is a *right* amount of food in each case. Similarly when determining where the mean lies, we must take into consideration the particular disposition of each individual: but while Aristotle recognises that moral virtue will not consist in having the same feeling or doing the same action in every case for all people, he certainly believes that it will consist in having a particular feeling or doing a particular action in each individual case.[1]

The mean is 'relative to us', but also 'as defined by reason and as the man with practical intelligence would define it'. The mean and what is good is not merely a matter of having certain feelings and doing certain actions, but having them and doing them at the right time, in relation to the right people, with the right motives and in the right way (*EN* 1106b21ff.). As he observes at one point (*EN* 1109a26ff.), 'anybody can get angry, or give money away, or spend it—that is easy: but to do this to the right person, to the right extent, at the right time,

---

[1] Here again this important point has been emphatically brought out by Renford Bambrough, see above p. 203 note.

with the right motives and in the right way, is not something that just anyone can succeed in, nor is it easy.' Throughout his discussion of moral virtue he repeatedly stresses that we must take all the individual circumstances of each case into account. It follows that to find the mean is an intricate and difficult task, and this too is something to which Aristotle explicitly draws attention on several occasions. At *EN* 1137a4ff., for instance, there is an eloquent passage in which he points out how difficult it is to know where justice lies, how this involves more than merely understanding the law, and how as in medicine, and even more than in medicine, knowing what contributes to justice is not merely a question of knowing certain general rules, but of understanding what will bring about the desired result in the particular circumstances of each case.

Men think that to know what is just and what is unjust requires no great wisdom, because it is not difficult to understand the matters dealt with by the laws. But the actions prescribed by law are only accidentally just actions. But to know how actions should be performed, and how distributions should be made, in order to be just, is harder than to know what is good for health. And even there, while it is easy to know what honey, wine, hellebore, cautery and surgery are, to know how and to whom and when they should be applied in order to produce health is no less a task than that of being a physician...But to be a physician and to effect cures is not a matter of using or not using surgery or medicines, but of doing so in a certain way.

The doctrine of the mean has been extensively criticised, but many of the objections that have been made arise from what seems a mistaken view of the aims of the doctrine. It is often criticised as if it were intended as an absolute rule, as if Aristotle having once noticed a scale of excess, intermediate and defect in certain virtues and vices, generalised his observation and then set out to apply the rule dogmatically to every case. This is certainly a much exaggerated view, if indeed there is any truth in it at all. The fact that Aristotle makes exceptions of such vices as adultery and murder should put us on our guard. He is evidently not proposing a rule that applies to every case without exception. Moreover we have seen that while he suggests that virtue lies in a position intermediate between two extremes, he allows that this position will vary from individual to individual. We should, he believes, become aware of our own personal propensities and compensate for them: if we tend to be cowardly, we should aim more towards the opposite extreme of rashness, and so on. He nowhere suggests that the doctrine of the mean provided, of itself, the solution to the problem of determining where virtue lies. All that the general doctrine can do is to indicate, as it were, where we should begin to look in the search for virtue, to suggest that it will be found within a certain range or within certain limits. But as for each individual decision, and it is of the nature of ethics that it deals with *individual* situations, we must take note of all the particular circumstances of the case. As Aristotle repeatedly, and rightly, stresses, finding the correct solution is no easy matter.

But then a second type of criticism is made of the doctrine, that it applies a quantitative scale to what are essentially qualitative differences, and that to do so is inappropriate and artificial. This criticism clearly has some force. Generosity and miserliness, which may involve a quantitative factor such as an actual amount of money, lend themselves more readily than do other virtues and vices to Aristotle's schematic analysis in terms of an excess, an intermediate and a defect. But whether it is misleading to apply such an analysis to virtue as a whole is a moot point. Our own vocabulary for passing moral judgements incorporates many terms whose primary connotations are quantitative ones. We apply the terms 'too much' and 'too little' to an extensive range of feelings, activities and dispositions, as for example to love, pride and ambition: we may say of someone that he suffers from too much ambition, for instance. And indeed we use the simple adverb 'too' even more generally to qualify adjectives referring to vices and virtues, such as vain, self-indulgent, irascible, humble, modest, magnanimous. Aristotle's scheme of virtues and vices is certainly an elaborate one, and sometimes when he finds it necessary to coin a new term to refer to an excess or a defect in order to complete his schema he cannot be said to supplement any real deficiency in the Greek language. Yet the doctrine is neither intended nor used as a dogmatic rule from which the nature of any particular virtue may be derived by a process of deduction. It is a descriptive generalisation, an attempt to produce a general formula to express what is common to a number of virtues, and while some of Aristotle's examples are questionable, it must be granted that his theory has some application to a wide range of cases.

The doctrine of the mean supplies the general framework for Aristotle's discussion of the individual virtues and vices. That discussion itself is undogmatic, subtle and penetrating. Among its chief merits are the readiness with which he recognises the complexities of the subject-matter he is dealing with, and the skill with which he reveals both the distinctions, and the connections, between the different uses of many terms that refer to moral virtues. Courage, for instance, is defined as a mean with respect to certain things that inspire either confidence or fear, and in particular with respect to death. But that is only one aspect of his treatment in book III, chh. 6–9, which includes, for example, an interesting analysis of the various evils that may be the objects of fear: not to be afraid of poverty or disease does not, in Aristotle's view, entitle one to be called brave. Moreover he draws distinctions between courage in the strict sense and no less than five other kinds, among which are the seeming courage that merely reflects experience, the passion that is also shown by some wild animals, and the confidence exhibited by those of a sanguine disposition or, temporarily, by those who are drunk. Similarly in his long account of justice, to which the whole of book V is devoted, he draws important distinctions between the general and the particular senses of the term. In one sense justice[1] is equivalent to the whole of moral virtue, but more particularly it is used

[1] In his contribution to *New Essays on Plato and Aristotle*, London, 1965, pp. 159 ff., Renford Bambrough both elucidates Aristotle's conception of justice and argues that his treatment of the subject in *Nicomachean Ethics*, book V, may be considered a paradigm case of a philosophical discussion.

of distributive and rectificatory justice, and he also discusses, for example, political justice and the difference between natural and merely conventional justice.

Intellectual virtue

The detailed examination of moral virtues and vices in books III–V contains much else that is of interest but beyond the scope of this discussion. After it, Aristotle returns to consider the second type of virtue or excellence that he had identified at the end of book I, namely intellectual virtue. At *EN* 1139b16ff. he defines five kinds of intellectual virtues, τέχνη, ἐπιστήμη, νοῦς, φρόνησις and σοφία. These cut across our own categories, but they may be conventionally translated 'art', 'scientific knowledge', 'rational intuition', 'practical intelligence' and 'wisdom'. Very briefly 'art' alone is related to a capacity for making rather than one for acting or doing, but it is an 'intellectual virtue' nevertheless since it involves a true process of reasoning. 'Scientific knowledge' concerns what is unchanging and cannot be otherwise: it is a state of capacity to demonstrate the connections between things in that sphere. νοῦς is here used of the faculty whereby we get knowledge of the first principles or starting-points from which such demonstrations begin, and the fuller accounts that are given of both 'scientific knowledge' and of νοῦς in the *Posterior Analytics* have already been discussed in ch. 6. 'Practical intelligence', unlike 'scientific knowledge', concerns things that can be otherwise, that is the contingent: it is by 'practical intelligence' that we reason out the right means to secure the ends we aim at. And 'wisdom' Aristotle considers to be a combination of νοῦς and 'scientific knowledge' related to the highest and most valuable objects.

These definitions provide a very rough guide to the five intellectual virtues, but only two of the five, namely practical intelligence and wisdom, play an important part in his ethics. The topic of wisdom will be covered when we consider the description of the highest form of life, the life of contemplation, in book x. But our immediate concern is with the doctrine of practical intelligence and the relation between this and moral virtue.

Practical intelligence

The definition of moral virtue ran: 'virtue is a disposition involving choice and lying in the mean relative to us as defined by reason and as the man with practical intelligence would define it.' Courage, for example, consists not merely in having the right feelings of confidence, but in having them in relation to the right objects, from the right motives, in the right way and at the right time. But deliberation about all these factors, the circumstances of the individual action, falls within the province of practical intelligence.

Moral virtue, as Aristotle says at *EN* 1144a7ff., is what makes us aim at the right mark, practical intelligence is what makes us take the right steps to achieve the right end. The relationship between the two excellences is a close one: indeed he suggests that the two are inseparable. One may distinguish logically between the two elements, (1) deliberation about means, and (2) desire for ends, but Aristotle believes that in practice it is impossible to have the one excellence without the other. Practical intelligence without moral virtue to supply the right end would be mere astuteness or cunning, δεινότης. Practical intelligence itself, the 'eye of the soul' as he calls it at *EN* 1144a29f., is much more than this, and one cannot have it without also having moral virtue, for the reasoning that practical intelligence undertakes starts from the ends that are determined by moral virtue. Conversely moral virtue without practical intelligence is at best what he calls 'natural virtue', a natural disposition which even children and animals may share, but which needs training and reason to develop into virtue.

The sort of reasoning that practical intelligence undertakes is made clear as he proceeds. The right end, he assumes, is supplied by moral virtue, which is itself the result of training and habituation. But to see how to achieve the right end involves a process of deliberation, βούλευσις, in which we work out the steps that will lead, directly or eventually, to what we want. Aristotle imagines that this may be a quite complex process. Practical intelligence is a matter of recognising that Y leads to the end desired Z, that X leads to Y, that W leads to X and so on, until we arrive in our reasoning at something that is actually in our power. There deliberation stops, and we act. He illustrates this process with a concrete example. Health is an end which we naturally desire. But to know that health is good does not help to determine what we should do to acquire or preserve it. In Aristotle's example we need to know, for instance, that light meats are easily digestible and contribute to health. But this knowledge, knowledge of the universal, still does not provide us with an answer to the question of what we should actually do, for we may or may not know what types of meat are 'light'. We have, then, to take our reasoning back to the particular. Health is good; light meats are wholesome and contribute to health; chicken is a light meat; this is chicken. Then when we have arrived at something we can do—eat this chicken—we act. Admittedly this example of a process of deliberation seems far-fetched. But it enables Aristotle to bring out the common-sense point that, for practical purposes, experience may count for more than theoretical knowledge (*EN* 1141b16ff.). A man who knows that light meats are wholesome but does not know which meats are light is less able to produce the desired results than a man who knows that chicken is wholesome but cannot give the theoretical explanation of this. In Aristotle's view, however, both types of knowledge together constitute, and are necessary for, practical intelligence.

Choice and responsibility

The interrelated conceptions of moral virtue and practical intelligence are linked, in turn, to Aristotle's views on choice and responsibility. Here too, as with the doctrine of the mean, his theory has been severely criticised, in particular for its apparent failure to recognise what we refer to as the will. This is a complex subject, but if we are not to misconstrue Aristotle's doctrine of choice, we must first consider this alleged shortcoming or omission, asking, to begin with, what role the notion of will plays in those thinkers who employ it. However much the debate between free will and determinism may be an issue in theology, it seems safe to say that it is of little practical relevance to questions of behaviour. At least it is usually the case that both the proponents of free will and the proponents of determinism agree that we have the illusion of being free agents in the sense that we believe that we can choose between one course of action and another, although they go on to differ about whether this is a mere illusion or not. Indeed in terms of practical ethics society as a whole assumes that everyone is responsible for their behaviour except the very young, the deranged and those suffering from such a disease as epilepsy. The normal non-epileptic adult citizen is put into jail for wrong-doing in a way that would be patently absurd if he had no control whatsoever over his actions or responsibility for them. The theological problem, then, is not one with which Aristotle need be concerned, at least so long as his discussion remains at the level of the actual factors which influence or appear to influence behaviour. But what does concern anyone who deals with ethical questions at any level is the question of moral responsibility. It is here that Aristotle's doctrine of choice, προαίρεσις, comes in. The notion of will is an opaque one. Certain contexts in which it is used would seem to be strictly irrelevant to the type of discussion Aristotle aims to give. But where will is relevant to questions of behaviour, we find that Aristotle has a fairly complex and subtle theory covering not only the subject of choice, but also such related topics as self-control, self-indulgence and the distinctions between voluntary and non-voluntary action.

Aristotle's first discussion of these topics comes in book III, ch. 1, 1109 b 30 ff., where he distinguishes between four classes of action, (1) τὸ ἑκούσιον, voluntary or willing actions, (2) τὸ οὐχ ἑκούσιον, non-voluntary or not-willing actions, (3) τὸ ἀκούσιον, unwilling actions—the translation 'involuntary' is inappropriate, since in English this term is usually contrasted with 'intentional' rather than with 'voluntary'; and finally (4) τὸ βίαιον, compulsory actions. Voluntary actions, first, are those in which the motive comes from the agent himself and he knows precisely what it is he is doing. Non-voluntary actions are those in which the agent supplies the motive, but is ignorant of some of the circumstances of what he does, and unwilling actions Aristotle identifies as that class of non-voluntary or not-willing actions where the agent afterwards feels distress and repentance at what he has done. One of his examples is that of a man who strikes another with a spear in the belief that the spear has a button on it: another is that of a man who gives a patient a drink not knowing what the effect of this will be, and the patient dies as a result. In neither case is the action voluntary or willing in the full sense, for the agent was not aware of all the circumstances of what he was doing: these are, rather, unwilling actions, at least when the agent repents what he has done. Lastly there are compulsory actions, where the motive is not supplied by the person who does the action, but by someone else, as it might be by the tyrant who forces a man to do something evil against his will.

These distinctions are on the whole well drawn. To differentiate between unwilling and not-willing actions on the basis of the emotions that the agent feels after the action may strike us as a little artificial. But it is obvious that Aristotle establishes clear and useful general distinctions between voluntary, non-voluntary and compulsory actions, and he provides an acute analysis of certain complex cases, such as that of the man who throws cargo overboard to lighten a ship in a storm, where the action is voluntary in one sense, but not voluntary in another: no one throws cargo overboard voluntarily, but in particular circumstances one may choose to do so, for example to save the ship. He recognises, too, that there comes a point where we should resist doing certain deeds at all costs, however much we may be threatened with force (*EN* 1110a26ff.). He suggests that rather than perform such an act as matricide, even under compulsion, we should face torture and death.

Then he draws further distinctions within the class of voluntary actions. Here again the conventional translation of the Greek terms may be rather misleading. ἑκούσιον, 'voluntary', is, for Aristotle, a generic term applicable to actions done by any living creature, but he restricts προαίρεσις, conventionally translated 'choice' or 'purpose', to certain acts within the sphere of human behaviour. Children and animals can perform voluntary acts, and acts done on the spur of the moment may also be described as voluntary. But not all voluntary acts are 'chosen', for 'choice', in his view, involves deliberation: furthermore, according to the doctrine later developed in book VI, ch. 2, 'choice' also implies moral character. Here we come to what is perhaps the key to Aristotle's conception of moral responsibility. He maintains that we are responsible not only for our individual acts, but also for our moral character or disposition, which determines the ends we wish for or desire. He considers various cases where a plea might be offered that the agent cannot be held responsible for his acts. He discusses the case of an offence committed in ignorance because the agent was drunk. But, he argues, the man was responsible for his action, nevertheless, since it was in his power not to get drunk. And in general he points out that we are held responsible for being ignorant of anything in the law that the law requires us to know (EN 1113 b 30 ff., 33 ff.). But then he also considers the more difficult and interesting case of a person who is the sort of man who does not bother to know the law, and here he replies that we are each responsible for the sort of person we are. The self-indulgent man may be held responsible for becoming self-indulgent, for his character is the result of repeated voluntary acts of self-indulgence, and so too the man who is unjust is responsible for having become so. 'For it is the activities concerned with particular objects that create the corresponding character' (EN 1114 a 7).

This doctrine helps Aristotle to counter the sophistic dilemma of the 'apparent good'. Some people had argued that each person only aims at what appears to him to be good, not at the good in an absolute sense. But Aristotle rebuts this by saying that we are responsible for what appears to us to be good (EN 1114 b 1 ff.). He strongly resists the conventionalist view that good and evil are subjective terms. As he sees it, we are primarily and directly responsible for our individual actions, and it is through our actions that we are responsible also for our moral character as a whole. He recognises that the process by which we develop a settled disposition is a gradual and imperceptible one. Moreover he observes that while we can modify our particular actions with little difficulty, it is much harder to alter our engrained habits. Men may be said to become unjust or self-indulgent voluntarily in that they voluntarily perform certain acts that they know to be unjust or self-indulgent. But it does not follow that they can automatically become just again merely by wishing this. 'To begin with,' as Aristotle says (*EN* 1114a 19ff.), 'it was possible for them not to become men of this sort..., but once they have become so, it is not possible for them not to be so.'

Aristotle asserts emphatically that both virtue and vice are within our power. Against the Socratic view that no one does wrong voluntarily he uses two cogent arguments. He points out, first, that as a matter of fact the law punishes those who do wrong, unless they acted under compulsion or in a state of ignorance for which they were not themselves responsible. And in addition to this pragmatic, common-sense argument, he adduces a logical one, pointing out that if no one can be said to be acting voluntarily when doing wrong, it follows that no one can be praised for acting virtuously either. If virtue is voluntary, so too is vice. If we can be praised for the one, we can be blamed for the other (*EN* 1113 b 6ff.).

Interestingly enough, however, he concedes that Socrates was in a sense right. This is the conclusion he reaches when he discusses the problem of ἀκρασία—the lack of self-control. How is it that men sometimes act against their better judgement? In what sense can they be said to know that what they do is wrong? Here he begins by distinguishing between actual and merely potential knowledge (*EN* 1146b31 ff.). We may know something, but the knowledge may be only latent, not consciously present in our minds. For example, we may know (1) a general rule such as that 'dry food is good for men', and also know both (2) that 'I am a man' and (3) that 'food of such and such a sort is dry', but yet not know, or not consciously realise at this particular moment, (4) that the particular food in front of us is food of the sort in question. His other main example exhibits more clearly the role of desire. He takes a case where we know a general rule 'no sweet food ought to be tasted': the illustration is again banal but it serves to bring out his point well enough. But we also know, say, that 'sweet food is pleasant' and faced with some particular food, this piece of cake, we desire it as something pleasant, and do not realise, or ignore, that it comes under the general rule 'no sweet food ought to be tasted'. When we are 'overcome' by desire, it is the judgement that the particular comes under the general rule that we lack. And so Socrates was right in a sense when he argued that if a man has knowledge this cannot be overcome by passion, for in a failure of self-control what is mastered by the desire is not knowledge in the true sense, but a judgement about a particular.

Naturally his account of responsibility has its limitations, and difficulties remain. In his account of ἀκρασία he appears to place more emphasis than we might on the lack of certain knowledge, as if the agent would have behaved differently if he had been more fully aware of certain facts of the case. Yet at the same time he recognises that in general men act against their better judgement when overcome by desire, and he draws a useful distinction between the man who lacks self-control, the ἀκρατής, and the positive voluptuary, the ἀκόλαστος: both give way to their desires, but the former does so against his better judgement, the latter of set purpose. There is a problem, too, for Aristotle's theory, in the transition from childhood irresponsibility to adult responsibility. How, we may ask, if childhood training counts for so much in developing moral virtue or vice, and we ourselves are not responsible for the training we receive, can we be held to be fully responsible for the sort of people we become? Yet at least we should generally agree that such a transition from irresponsibility to responsibility does take place, even if the boundary between the two cannot be defined precisely. On the whole, however, Aristotle's treatment of the problem of choice and moral responsibility is both lucid and helpful, and like so much of his ethics it is punctuated with perceptive observations concerning imaginary examples, such as the cases that were mentioned of the man who throws cargo overboard in a storm, and of the man who strikes someone with a spear in the belief that the spear has a button on it.

Pleasure

Moral virtue and vice are, as we saw, concerned with pleasures and pains. It is on account of pleasure or pain that we sometimes act against our better judgement, and good education consists in being trained to enjoy what we ought to enjoy and to dislike what we ought to dislike. Pleasure occupies, then, a very important role in Aristotle's ethics. He discusses it at some length on two occasions, in book VII, chh. 11–14 and in book X, chh. 1–5. The treatment in book VII takes the form of a preliminary survey of some current views concerning pleasure, particularly of certain arguments against pleasure, and the tone of much of the discussion is rhetorical. He considers three views about pleasure, (1) that no pleasure is good, (2) that some pleasures are good but most are bad, and (3) that, even if some pleasures are good, pleasure is not the chief good, the summum bonum. The whole discussion is related to and reflects contemporary debates in the Academy, where Speusippus, for instance, had adopted the position that no pleasure is good, and Eudoxus the view that pleasure is the supreme good. We should not assume that in refuting a particular thesis Aristotle himself wishes to endorse its contrary. Most of the time he is primarily concerned with showing where the arguments that had been advanced for one thesis or another are invalid. We should not be misled, either, when at one point (*EN* 1153 b 25 ff.) he says that 'the fact that all men and animals pursue pleasure is some indication that it is in some way the chief good'. Here too the tentative views of book VII are both clarified and modified by the later discussion in book X.

There Aristotle makes his own views about pleasure explicit. First it becomes evident that he did not in fact endorse the Eudoxan view that pleasure is the chief good. Yet unlike Plato, who despised and rejected those pleasures that are common to men and animals, Aristotle maintains that the fact that all animals pursue pleasure suggests that it is at least *a* good. 'Those who object', he says, 'that what all things desire is not good are very likely talking nonsense' (*EN* 1172b35f.). His own conception of pleasure is that it 'perfects' or 'completes' natural activity. He points out that the natural functioning of a sense-organ, for example, is accompanied with pleasure, at least when the sense-organ is in good condition; and 'the pleasure is most perfect when the organ is in the best condition and active in respect to the best of its objects'. Pleasure accompanies any conscious natural activity, not only sensation, but also and more especially thought. But when he says that pleasure 'completes' the activity, it is not that the activity itself is incomplete: rather the pleasure supervenes on it, as he puts it in a rare poetic phrase, 'like the bloom of youth on those in the flower of life' (οἷον τοῖς ἀκμαίοις ἡ ὥρα, *EN* 1174b33). So long as both the objects perceived or thought about and the percipient or thinking subject are as they should be, the activity will be accompanied with pleasure. But the pleasure ceases when the activity ceases. It follows that human beings, who are incapable of continuous activity, are incapable of continuous pleasure. But no such restriction applies to the gods.

The doctrine that pleasure completes natural activity has some important consequences. Activities differ, of course, in their moral quality, being good, bad, or morally neutral. So too, Aristotle suggests, the moral quality of pleasures varies, being dependent on that of the activities which they accompany. The interest and importance of this view become apparent when we compare the general tendency shown by most earlier writers—and by a good many later moralists too—to tackle the question of the moral quality of pleasure by considering whether pleasure *as a whole* is good, bad or indifferent. Such an approach no doubt underlies Speusippus' doctrine that no pleasure is good, for example, and Plato, who distinguishes clearly enough between different types of pleasures, pure, impure and mixed, frequently portrays the speakers in his dialogues generalising about the moral quality of pleasures taken as a whole, as indeed often happens in ordinary conversation. In contrast to any attempt to find a simple answer to the global question of whether pleasure is good or not, Aristotle insists that the moral quality of pleasures varies with that of the activities of which they are the pleasures (*EN* 1175a21ff.).

At the same time, however, he develops the view that it is the good man (ὁ σπουδαῖος) who is the judge of what is truly pleasant, as indeed he is of what is truly good. As a sick man may have a mistaken opinion about what is sweet, bitter, hot, cold and so on, and the judge of these things is the man in health, so, Aristotle suggests, the morally sound man provides the criterion of what is or is not truly pleasant (*EN* 1176a12ff.). Other pleasures, he argues, are only apparently pleasant, and this leads him to draw the paradoxical conclusion that certain admittedly disgraceful pleasures are not real pleasures at all, but pleasant only to those who are corrupt or depraved (*EN* 1176a19ff.). Pleasures then, are good, bad or indifferent according to the quality of the activities they complete. But in judging both the activities and the pleasures, we should refer to the good man as the standard and measure of what is truly good and truly pleasant.

The highest life

Aristotle set out the central problem of ethics, the nature of happiness, in book I. Happiness, he there pointed out, depends on man's function, and this is activity of the soul according to virtue, and this led him into a detailed discussion first of the moral, and then of the intellectual, virtues. But then in the closing chapters of book x (chh. 6–8) he takes up once again the subject of happiness and the highest life. If happiness is activity according to virtue, he says, it is reasonable that it should be according to the highest virtue (*EN* 1177a12f.). But the highest virtue will be that of the highest part of the soul, that is reason, νοῦς, the activity of which is here called 'contemplation', θεωρητική. The highest life and the true end for man is, then, the contemplative life or the life of the philosopher. Indeed this is not only the highest life, but also the most pleasant and the most self-sufficient. Like everyone else, the philosopher must be provided with the necessities of life, at least in moderation. But whereas to be just, for example, one needs people to whom to be just, the philosopher can carry on his activity by himself—although it may be better, Aristotle adds, if he has fellow-workers. Practical activity, he believes, is undertaken for the sake of leisure, while philosophical activity is an end in itself. As he puts it at *EN* 1177b30ff.:

> if reason is divine in comparison with man, then life according to reason is divine in comparison with human life. But we must not follow those who tell us as we are men to have human aspirations, as we are mortal to have mortal aspirations, but we must, so far as we are able, make ourselves immortal, and do everything we can to live in accordance with the best thing in us.

This famous passage shows that for all Aristotle's frequent references to, and obvious respect for, the common-sense point of view, when it comes to expressing his ideas concerning happiness, he is capable of highly idealistic sentiments. He writes on the life according to reason in a manner which immediately puts one in mind of Plato. Yet the conception of happiness he puts forward differs in certain respects from Plato's, and it is not only consistent with, but follows naturally from, his own views on the nature of the soul.

To take this second point first, Aristotle's conception of the highest life for man reflects his idea of man's place in the scale of living creatures. Plants, animals, man and even gods are, as we have seen, arranged in a single continuous scale according to the faculties of soul they possess, plants possessing simply the nutritive and reproductive faculty, animals sensation, and in most cases locomotion, desire and 'imagination', in addition.

Man in turn has not only the lower faculties, but also reason, which he shares with the gods. The best life depends in some measure on the proper functioning of the lower faculties of the soul: thus at *EN* 1178 b 34 f. Aristotle observes that our bodies must be healthy if we are to pursue the life of contemplation. Yet when he seeks to define the highest form of life, he naturally refers to the faculty which marks man out from the other animals.

The exercise of reason is the highest form of activity, but reason, Aristotle said, is 'divine in comparison with man', and it is not in so far as one is a man that one will live the life according to reason, but 'in so far as there is something divine in us' (*EN* 1177 b 26 ff.). As a man, the philosopher will also exhibit the social and political virtues, doing just and brave acts, performing his duties with regard to contracts and so on, these activities and their corresponding virtues being, in Aristotle's eyes, typically *human*. For Aristotle, as for Plato, man is a composite being, part animal part divine. But there is this difference between the two philosophers' views of his nature, that while Plato writes in the *Republic* 519 c ff., for example, as if it were something of a degradation for the philosopher to descend into the political arena after the vision of the Good, for Aristotle practical activity in the social and political sphere is typically human. Both philosophers agree in holding the contemplative life to be superior to the life of action, but Aristotle takes the virtues associated with the latter to be characteristic of human beings as human beings, while he considers the life according to reason to be something super-human.

Aristotle's eulogy of the life of contemplation accords with his conception of the soul, and it is a point where ethics, psychology and theology overlap. At *EN* 1178 b 8 ff. he considers the life of the gods. What sort of actions can be ascribed to them? Hardly acts of justice, for it is absurd to think of the gods making contracts, returning deposits and so on. Equally they cannot perform acts of bravery, for it is absurd to imagine them confronting dangers and running risks. Nevertheless they are alive and active, not asleep like Endymion. But if they cannot be engaged in practical activity, still less in production, it is clear that their activity is contemplation. They enjoy continuously what men can achieve only from time to time, namely the pure happiness that accompanies contemplation. In the *Ethics*, as in the *Metaphysics*, Aristotle concludes that the activity of the gods is contemplation, but he arrives at this conclusion by a slightly different route, not by considering the conditions of change and the necessity for a first mover that is unmoved and pure actuality, but by taking as an assumption that the gods are alive and active, and then considering and rejecting all other possible activities, except for contemplation, as unworthy of the divine.

The value of argument in ethics

After the eulogy of the life of contemplation in book x, chh. 6–8, in which the life of the philosopher is compared with the activity of god, Aristotle turns in the very last chapter of the *Nicomachean Ethics* to give a highly realistic assessment of the value of argument in ethics.

If [he asks] we have dealt adequately in outline with these matters and with the virtues..., should we consider our purpose to have been fulfilled? Or rather, as we say, in the practical sphere the end is not to contemplate the various things and to know them, but rather to do them. As regards virtue, it is not enough to have knowledge of it, but we must try to possess and use it, or try any other way to become good.

Once again, then, Aristotle stresses the practical objectives of his discussion. But he goes on:

now if arguments were enough to make men good, then, as Theognis said, they would justly have won many and great rewards...But as things are, while they seem to have power to encourage and spur on liberal-minded young men..., they are powerless to encourage the mass to noble behaviour. For they [the many] do not naturally obey the sense of shame, but only fear, and they refrain from evil deeds, not because the deeds are shameful, but because of the penalties involved. They live by emotion and pursue their own pleasures and the means to them and avoid the opposite pains, but they have no inkling of what is fine and truly pleasant, since they have never tasted it. But what argument would reform such people? It is difficult, if not impossible, to remove by argument traits that have long been established in the character: and we must probably be content if, when all the factors by which men are supposed to become good are present, we obtain some share of virtue (*EN* 1179a33–b20).

Aristotle is under no illusions about the practical results that can be hoped for from his own, or any other, work in ethics. Nature, habituation and argument each contribute something towards making us good. But nature is beyond our control. And argument or teaching influences only a small number of persons, those whose characters are naturally disposed towards virtue and have been further developed by good habits. As regards the mass of people, Aristotle does not suppose that they have listened, or ever will listen, to argument. They are not amenable to reason, only to force. And the force that will compel them to be good, or at least dissuade them from wrong-doing, is represented by the law, which stimulates those of a good disposition to virtue, prevents those inclined to disobey by punishments, and banishes those who are beyond correction. The study of ethics, then, leads towards and is continuous with the study of politics, that is the study of human society as a whole, its laws and customs and its social and political institutions. It is through good legislation, and through good legislation alone, that a society can ensure the good conduct of its citizens. But what the study of ethics and human nature can achieve is to determine 'the good for man' and the ends we should set before ourselves, so that like archers, as Aristotle had put it at the very outset of his treatise, we may have a mark to aim at in our lives.

Aristotle's moral philosophy is characterised by four themes especially. The first is that virtue and vice, justice and injustice and so on, are neither matters of convention, nor subject to universally valid rules. Good and bad are not arbitrary terms, but nor are they terms that can be defined with the precision appropriate to mathematics. Aristotle's view is that while the 'right amount' in which moral virtue consists will vary within a certain range from one individual case to another, there will nevertheless be a *right* amount in each case. This important feature of his ethics has been called its objectivity.

Secondly goodness and happiness itself lie not in states of mind or dispositions, but in activities, not merely in having a capacity to act, but in exercising that capacity to the full. Here, and in the related idea that pleasure accompanies natural activity, there is what may be called a vitalist tendency in Aristotle's ethics. In sharp contrast to those other-worldly philosophies or religions that have bewailed the human condition and preached the vanity of human wishes and desires, Aristotle believes that the full realisation of man's faculties is both a worthy and a satisfying end to set before ourselves.

Thirdly there is the close interrelation between the intellect and the moral character. While we may distinguish logically between the moral disposition and the deliberative faculty, the good man must have both the character to desire the right things and the practical intelligence to work out the right means to those ends, and the two excellences are in fact inseparable. Here Aristotle's ethics takes neither an exclusively emotionalist nor an exclusively intellectualist view of morality, but strikes a balance between the two.

Fourthly and finally there is the idea that man has affinities both with the animals and with the gods. The exercise of reason is the highest activity, and it is in contemplation that man finds the purest happiness. But as a man the philosopher will carry on practical activities and exhibit the practical virtues in the social and political sphere. And as an animal he has a body with a variety of functions and with needs that must be satisfied. Aristotle emphasises that man alone of the animals is rational, but he does not forget that man is still an animal. Here then he advances what may be described as a philosophy of the whole man.

The particular **moral** doctrines that pervade Aristotle's ethics are of considerable and lasting interest. But in the long run his conception of the nature of ethical inquiry is even more important than the particular views that he advocated on various topics. The moral philosopher studies human nature as it is. His first duty is not to preach, but to analyse, and his method begins with a careful examination of what men generally believe on matters of right and wrong. The *Nicomachean Ethics* is obviously less impressive as literature than the great ethical dialogues of Plato. But Aristotle's treatise is designed for a quite different purpose. Its aim is not primarily to convert, but to investigate the whole subject of human behaviour, to discuss the difficulties that are encountered in dealing with moral questions and to arrive at the most adequate solution to the problems: and if the conclusions reached have not the certainty of mathematical demonstrations, this is because in the nature of the case such certainty is not to be expected in ethical inquiry. The achievement of his discussion is not to engage the emotions, which it rarely does, but to shed light. And if we may read Plato with greater enjoyment, we should go away from Aristotle with a clearer and more sober understanding of the issues.

CHAPTER 11

POLITICS

Programme and methods

The last chapter of the *Nicomachean Ethics* points out that it is only by good legislation that society can ensure the good conduct of its citizens. The study of the behaviour of the individual is continuous with the study of society as a whole, and Aristotle mentions some of the main questions that need to be investigated under the second head. He complains that his predecessors had left the topic of legislation unexamined and he sketches out how he will deal with the subject. First he will review earlier ideas where they seem to have something to contribute to the subject. Then he will investigate, 'in the light of the constitutions that have been collected', what factors preserve or destroy constitutions and the reasons that some states are well, others badly, governed. Finally he will consider what constitution is best and what laws and customs the best state should have (*EN* 1181 b 12–23).

From the programme outlined here one might suppose that Aristotle undertook the detailed histories of individual constitutions, such as the *Constitution of Athens*, before writing the *Politics*, in which he deals with the causes of the changes in constitutions, the best possible form of state and so on. It might even appear that he followed, or claimed to be following, an idealistic work-plan, first completing the descriptive studies, and then and only then proceeding to the theoretical treatise. But even if such a plan were feasible, how far would it represent Aristotle's actual method? The precise relation between the descriptive and the theoretical works on politics cannot be settled since neither the main books of the *Politics* nor the *Constitutions* can be dated exactly. But some points are reasonably certain. First the collection of 158 constitutions was a joint effort on the part of members of the Lyceum. Not all, and perhaps not even very many, of these studies were actually composed by Aristotle. He was responsible for initiating the programme of research, but no doubt he delegated much of the work to pupils, and the programme almost certainly continued after his death. Secondly—an obvious point—while the passage in the *Nicomachean Ethics* suggests that some constitutional histories had been completed, it does not specify how many. Even if the passage is genuine—and some scholars have suspected that it may be a later editorial addition—it does not imply that the entire collection of 158 constitutions had been completed before the *Politics* was begun. And thirdly, even though Aristotle complains about his predecessors' neglect of the topic of legislation, in politics, as in so many other fields, many of the problems he discusses are a legacy from Plato. Such are, for example, the nature of the ideal state and the causes of changes in constitutions. Aristotle must have been interested in many of the issues he deals with in the *Politics* from the moment he entered the Academy and heard such works as the *Republic* read.

When we consider the *Politics* itself, the extent to which the various books appeal to particular historical examples varies a great deal, and how much the evidence cited presupposes, or derives from, the constitutional studies is problematical. But the method he adopts is broadly similar to that of the ethical treatises, in that throughout the work general issues are discussed in connection with, and with frequent references to, particular instances. The possibility of making a systematic collection of political case-histories has no exact equivalent in the field of ethics proper; the nearest parallel in Aristotle is the collections of data concerning natural species in the biological works. But since the idea of a systematic collection of the relevant material is a natural extension of Aristotle's normal practice of referring to the particular case or the concrete example whenever the occasion offers, the question of how many constitutions had been completed before, how many after, any particular book of the *Politics* becomes a rather academic one. Recent research has tended to endorse what common-sense by itself would suggest, that neither the theoretical nor the descriptive works on politics wholly preceded the other: here as elsewhere throughout Aristotle's work there is a constant interaction between his theoretical assumptions and the empirical data at his command.

Scope of the 'Politics'

The discussion in the *Politics* ranges over the whole field of what today we should call sociology. Aristotle deals with the πόλις and the life of its inhabitants in all its aspects, and as is well known the Greek term refers not merely to a city, but to what we should call a sovereign state. He begins with the question of what a state is. How should it be defined, and how is it to be distinguished from other types of community? He considers what other writers, Plato, Phaleas and Hippodamus, had had to say on the ideal state, and he describes the three existing states that were reputed to enjoy the best constitutions, Sparta, Crete and Carthage. He then turns to the citizen and considers how he should be defined. What are the rights and obligations of citizenship, and who should enjoy it? How many types of constitution are there? What are the main causes that bring about the constitutional changes that affect states? In particular, why do revolutions occur? Finally he turns to give his own views on the best state, discussing among other things the proper education of its citizens.

These are the main topics dealt with in the separate books of the *Politics*, but there is much else besides. We find Aristotle giving us his views on the institution of slavery, on the degree of separation of political functions that is desirable, on the problem of whether the rule of law or the rule of the individual is better, and so on. For our purposes the most notable features of his political thought may be discussed under three main heads, the concept of the state, the classification of constitutions and the theory of the best possible state.

The state

Aristotle describes the state as the highest form of community: more precisely it is a self-sufficient community that exists not merely to supply the bare necessities of life, but for the sake of the good life. It differs from an alliance because it has a moral aim, to ensure the good of the community as a whole, whereas an alliance exists merely for mutual protection. It differs again from a nation, ἔθνος, for a nation is a group of indefinite size linked by race, whereas a πόλις forms a unified entity of limited size: indeed the optimum size of the state, in his view, is, as we shall see, very small. A state is more than a mere aggregate of individuals: it is a community under a single constitution and law. The unity of the state consists neither in the location—for the citizen-body may move and still form a state—nor in the population—for the citizens are never the same individuals, since the generations are always succeeding one another: it lies rather in the constitution. When and only when this is modified, the state itself is affected.

He believes that the state is a natural institution. He bases this idea on a largely conventional view of how civilisation developed (*Pol.* I, ch. 2). The first and simplest association to be formed is the household. When several households come together for the sake of something more than their daily needs, the village is formed. Finally when several villages unite and form a complete and self-sufficient community, this constitutes a state. Each of these associations is natural, the product of man's natural instinct to form societies, referred to in the often quoted dictum ὁ ἄνθρωπος φύσει πολιτικὸν ζῷον (for example, *Pol.* 1253 a 2 f.). Other species of animals are naturally gregarious, but man, who alone is endowed by nature with the gift of speech, is the only animal with a sense of right and wrong, and he alone forms societies. The state is, then, a natural development, yet it is a development none the less, and Aristotle hails the unknown law-giver who founded the first state as one of man's greatest benefactors (*Pol.* 1253a 29ff.).

The rulers and the ruled: slavery

But Aristotle maintains not merely that man by nature possesses a social instinct, but also that the distinction between ruler and ruled is a natural one. In book VII he adduces historical examples to show that the organisation of the state into ruling and subject classes is widespread and ancient (1329a40ff.). But in book I he argues that just as there is a natural distinction between male and female, and again one between father and child, so too there is a natural distinction between master and slave. He maintains, indeed, that the distinction between ruler and subject is everywhere to be seen in nature, and it exists even within the individual person, where the soul by nature rules and the body is ruled.

This has often been cited as a particularly striking and sad example of a great philosopher being misled into taking a temporary, man-made institution for something natural and permanent. And so indeed it is. But this is not a momentary lapse on Aristotle's part nor a doctrine that he adopts without reflection. On the contrary he recognises and discusses the opposite point of view, namely that the distinction between master and slave is purely conventional and arbitrary. Indeed he agrees with this view up to a point. He acknowledged that many people became slaves by accident, as for example prisoners of war, and he says that no one who did not deserve to be a slave should be thought of as one. There is, then, 'conventional' as well as 'natural' slavery, but, he continues (*Pol.* 1255a 31 f.), 'it must be admitted that some are slaves everywhere, others [he is thinking particularly of the Greeks themselves] nowhere'.

Moreover while he suggests that nature would like to distinguish between the bodies of slaves and those of freemen, adapting the former to servile labour and the latter to the life of the citizen, he recognises that the opposite often comes about, and that those who have the body of a freeman do not necessarily have a freeman's 'soul' (*Pol.* 1254b27ff.). Yet this admission is not so damaging, at least in Aristotle's own eyes, as it might seem to us. While nature aims for the most part at what is best, he often remarks that it does not always achieve this. The idea of a scale of perfection is, as we have seen, an integral part of his conception of the animal and vegetable kingdoms, and the less perfect the species the further it falls short of the ideal standard set by man. Thus it is better for the male and female sexes to be separate, but in many animals there is no sex differentiation. Again he notes elsewhere in the *Politics* (1259b1ff.) that males are not always more powerful than females, and yet he continues to maintain that the male sex is the 'natural' ruler. He concludes, then, that despite the frequent failure of nature to mark the distinction between slaves and masters in men's bodies, this is nevertheless a natural distinction, one that corresponds to the distinction in function between ruling and obeying.

It is natural, right and expedient for the slave to practise obedience, and for the master to exercise authority, but the abuse of this authority is bad for both parties. There is a community of interest between them just as there is between the body and the soul of an individual person (*Pol.* 1255 b9 ff.). And so Aristotle contrasts the role of the slave favourably with that of the lowest type of manual worker or artisan. The slave's life is naturally linked with that of the master, while the artisan, in Aristotle's view, has no such natural role to perform.

Unity of the state

The state is a unity, but one composed· of dissimilars. Aristotle argues against an excessive unification of the state (*Pol.* II, ch. 2). The citizens that compose it will naturally differ in birth, wealth and moral virtue, and he considers it mistaken either to ignore these differences or to attempt to bring about complete equality by legislative measures. What ensures the good government of people of unequal merit and capacity is the law. Whereas individuals are always liable to be swayed by their emotions, the law is the embodiment of reason (*Pol.* 1287 a 32). The laws provide, however, no more than general rules, and matters of detail—the application of the rules to particular instances—must be left in the hands of the magistrates. Pursuing a topic much discussed by Plato he considers whether the rule of the best law or that of the best individual is to be preferred. He allows that very occasionally there may be a quite exceptional citizen who should have supreme power, although normally the rule of more than one man is better. But in general he maintains that good laws and good magistrates each have a different contribution to make to good government. He recognises that the laws vary a great deal from one constitution to another, and that it is far from being the case that they are all good. And the main criterion he uses to distinguish between good and bad laws is whether they ensure the good of the whole state or merely that of the ruling class.

The varieties of constitution

The distinction between constitutions that do, and those that do not, aim at the good of the state as a whole plays an important part in one of the attempts Aristotle makes to classify the different types of constitutions. At *Pol.* 1279 a 22ff. he suggests a six-fold classification, embracing three good constitutions and three 'deformed' or 'perverted' types, which he calls παρεκβάσεις. The three good ones are (1) the rule of a single man, or monarchy, (2) that of a few, or aristocracy, and (3) that of the many, which he calls constitutional government, using the same term, πολιτεία, that he uses generically for 'constitution'. The three deformed types are (4) tyranny, which aims at the good of the tyrant alone, (5) oligarchy, which aims at the good of the few, specifically of the wealthy minority, and (6) democracy, which aims at the good of the many, specifically of the poor majority. But this is not the only way in which constitutions are classified in the *Politics*. At 1290a 13 ff. in particular, he refers to the popular way of dividing constitutions into two main types, oligarchy and democracy, and while he criticises this idea, he grants that it has some validity and he observes that constitutional government may be described as a mixture of these two (*Pol.* 1293 b 33 f.).

There are, then, slight shifts in Aristotle's position on this problem, and this has been taken to suggest that his views on the correct way of classifying constitutions underwent a development. However that may be, this subject provides a good illustration of two important, but sometimes opposing, tendencies in Aristotle's thought, the tendency to schematise, and the amassing of empirical data. As an example of the first tendency one may note that he introduces into his political theory a counterpart to his ethical doctrine of the mean: he suggests at *Pol.* 1295 b 1 ff. that the best constitution is a mean between two extremes in that in it the power is in the hands of the 'middle class'—that is the citizens who avoid the extremes of wealth and poverty. More surprisingly he writes at one point (*Pol.* 1290 b 23 ff.) as if he thought it possible to deduce the various kinds of constitutions by first analysing all the different elements in the state and then considering all the combinations of these that are theoretically possible. Moreover in this passage he explicitly compares the problem of classifying constitutions with that of classifying animals: and the fact that he thinks such a deductive method applicable in that field shows that at the time of writing he still had some highly impracticable ideas on the problems of zoological taxonomy.

At the same time Aristotle at many points demonstrates his awareness of the complexities of political forms. He recognises, for example, that there are several distinct types of democracy and oligarchy (*Pol.* IV, chh. 4–6). The common people include many different groups, farmers, artisans, traders, sailors and so on, and different forms of democracy may be distinguished according to who has a share in political power, and according to whether the people or the constitution is supreme. Similarly he identifies four different types of oligarchy according to the composition of the ruling minority and the power it exercises, and he also notes that the way in which the constitution is administered may differ markedly from its outward form, a democratic constitution being administered oligarchically or *vice versa* (*Pol.* 1292 b 11 ff.).

His analysis of these and other types of constitutions in book IV is interspersed with references to existing states, to Athens and Aegina, for instance, as examples where the sailors form a considerable class, to Sparta to illustrate a mixed constitution and so on. His references to concrete examples are especially frequent when he discusses in book V the changes that occur to constitutions. In ch. 5, for instance, he considers what brings about revolutions in democracies. Having suggested that one of the main causes may be the excesses of demagogues when these provoke a reaction on the part of the wealthy class, he cites the cases of Cos, Rhodes, Heraclea, Megara and Cyme in turn to prove his point. Again his discussion of the rise and fall of tyrannies in chh. 10–12 is full of information about particular cases, and while some of his generalisations in this passage are strongly reminiscent of Plato's vivid but unsystematic treatment of this theme in the *Republic*, these are now supported by extensive documentary evidence. When he comes to discuss the ways in which different constitutions are preserved, he again illustrates with case-histories the main economic, social and personal factors which may contribute to the maintenance of the *status quo*. Thus he suggests that tyrannies may be kept in being (1) by the tyrant engaging in external wars, or (2) by his increasing the level of taxation—as Dionysius of Syracuse had done—or again (3) by his engaging in massive expenditure in order both to impoverish the people and to keep them occupied: here he cites the construction of the pyramids by way of illustration along with several Greek examples. Whether or not Aristotle had composed many of the constitutional histories of individual city-states, his whole discussion of the factors that preserve or undermine different types of constitutions is a fine example of his use of detailed case-histories to support his theories and explanations.

The best possible state

Having criticised and rejected the ideas of Plato and other writers on the ideal state in book II, Aristotle returns to this topic to give his own views in books VII and VIII. There he begins by repeating that the object of the state is to secure the good of the community as a whole. The best constitution is that in which every man, whoever he is, can act best and live happily (*Pol.* 1324a23 ff.). But happiness, he insists, depends on virtuous activity, and so the extent to which a man is capable of happiness will depend on the extent to which he is able to practise virtue: the citizen alone is in a position to practise both the virtues of the statesman and those of the philosopher, and so he alone is capable of happiness in the fullest sense. But the object of the state as a whole may be said to be to enable its members to fulfil their various capacities for virtue.

He then describes not the best imaginable state, so much as the best that is consistent with what is practicable. He deals in turn with the number of the citizens, the size and nature of the country, the external relations of the state, even the town-plan of the city, as well as more fundamental questions such as who should enjoy citizenship, on what principles the relations between the classes in the state should be regulated, and how the citizens should be educated.

He begins with the important problem of the size of the state, that is the number of its full members, the citizens, and here he argues that there is a natural limit to the size of the state just as there is to the size of a living creature, whether animal or plant, or to the size of a tool (*Pol.* 1326a35ff.). A state must have enough citizens to ensure that it is self-sufficing, but not so many that the working of the constitution becomes impracticable. This limit will, he believes, be exceeded if the citizens are too many to be addressed at a single assembly: 'for who can be the general of such an excessive multitude, or who the herald, unless he has the voice of a Stentor?' (*Pol.* 1326b5ff.). And Aristotle also observes that in an over-populous state foreigners and μέτοικοι, resident aliens, will easily acquire the rights of citizenship and will be difficult to detect when they do so. He assumes that the number of citizens should be stable, but he recognises that to achieve this is much more of a problem than most writers had allowed. He criticises Plato on this score in book II, but this is hardly fair since the question is discussed in the *Laws* (740 b ff.). But he notes that the failure of Greek states to deal with the problem of controlling the size of their citizen-body was a general one which had grave consequences: over-population led to poverty which in turn led to revolution and crime (*Pol.* 1265 b 10 ff.). Like Plato, he believes that the laws should lay down general limits concerning the age at which citizens should marry and have children. Then to deal with the problem of excessive children he advocates first that no deformed child should be allowed to live, and secondly that abortion should be procured where necessary, this being preferable to the children being born and then exposed (*Pol.* 1335 b 19 ff.).

Self-sufficiency is also the key-note in his discussion of the size and nature of the territory required by the best state, and when he demands that this should be able to produce all that the city needs, we should remember that the needs in question were quite modest. Apart from agricultural produce, including both food and the raw materials for clothing, there was little that the Greek city-state used or required except for timber, stone and metal. But if the state should be self-supporting, he allows nevertheless that it will import certain products and export others: it will engage in foreign trade, without, however, turning itself into a market-centre for the sake of the revenue to be gained from doing so. On balance he believes there is an advantage in the city having access to the sea, but in general he imagines few contacts being made with other states.

He stresses the importance of a healthy climate, and notes the need for a good supply of pure water. On these topics, and on the question of the aspect of the city, which he says should face east, there is a close correspondence between his ideas and those of such medical writers as the author of the Hippocratic treatise *On Airs Waters Places*, although he does not mention this specific work by name. Concerning the city itself, he remarks that the modern fashion of laying-out cities on a regular plan, which was introduced by Hippodamus, is both convenient and beautiful, but that the older method of irregular construction has the advantage of greater security in war (*Pol.* 1330b 21 ff.). Both security and beauty will be achieved if the city is constructed with quarters of each of these two types. Against Plato, he argues that it is foolish to suggest that the city need not be fortified, and he notes that the walls must be strong enough to withstand the perfected siege engines of his day.

'*Proportional equality*'

So much for the material requirements of the best state, but Aristotle also deals with its social and political structure. The general principle which should regulate the relationships between the various classes in the state had been laid down in his earlier discussions of justice in books III, V and VI. This is the principle of 'proportional equality'. He criticises both the democratic and the oligarchic notions of justice on different but related grounds. The democrats considered all citizens to be equal because they are equal in one respect, free birth. The oligarchs, on the other hand, thought men unequal because they are unequal in another respect, namely wealth. But both views are wrong since both depend on too narrow a conception of equality and inequality. It is neither wealth alone, nor free birth alone, that should determine whether two men should be considered equal, for we must take into account all their qualities, not only wealth and birth, but also and more especially their moral and intellectual virtue (*Pol.* 1280a22ff., 1301a25ff. and b29ff.). Similarly between classes as a whole we should, he says, consider not only the number of people for or against any particular measure, but also the qualifications of those on either side, although he admits that it is difficult to work out an equation of this nature (*Pol.* vi, ch. 3).

Justice consists in every man getting what he deserves, but what he deserves will not be the same in every case. Equal men should have equal shares, but those who are superior in virtue should not be treated on a par with their inferiors. What ensures stable government is the principle of 'proportional equality' (*Pol.* 1307a26f.). Furthermore he considers the different classes that are necessary for the state and the different rights that each should enjoy. He nowhere gives a complete classification, but if we combine what he says in different passages and allow for certain minor discrepancies, he identifies the following essential functions in the state.

First, since there must be food, there must be farmers to produce it. Secondly, the state needs manufactured goods, and so artisans and craftsmen to produce them. Thirdly, trade is essential, and so there must be traders to look after the commercial life of the state. Fourthly, the state needs soldiers, for while peace is better than war and the object for which wars are waged, the state must be secure from attack both from outside and from within. Fifthly, he speaks of the need for a certain amount of property and wealth in the state, and so of a certain number of well-to-do citizens. Sixthly, there must be priests to attend to the religious services. Seventhly, and most necessary of all, there must be men to exercise deliberative and judicial responsibilities, in short to rule. And in addition to all these there must, he believes, be serfs, τὸ θητικόν (*Pol.* IV, ch. 4 and VII, ch. 8).

Having identified the various essential services to be performed in the state Aristotle asks in *Pol.* VII, ch. 9 how these should be divided up. Should one man have one or several occupations? Here he draws a general distinction between those occupations that are, and those that are not, compatible with the life of a citizen. In the best state the citizens will not be either farmers, or artisans, or traders, for none of these occupations is compatible with the best life which depends on the leisure necessary for the development and practice of moral and intellectual virtue. As far as the soldiers, the rulers and the priests are concerned, he suggests that these three functions will be performed by the same people, but not, however, at the same time. The state needs men in their physical prime as soldiers. But to rule the chief quality needed is wisdom, and this is not acquired until after the physical prime is past. Aristotle supposes, then, that the citizens, who alone will be the owners of property in the state, will be in turn first soldiers, then rulers, and finally, in their old age, priests.

There is a major division in the best form of state between citizens and non-citizens, between the rulers and the ruled. The latter included the farmers, the artisans and the traders, not to mention the serfs, all of whom are necessary for the state to exist, but who take no part in its government and so cannot be said to form part of the state in the full sense. In support of this policy he appeals to a series of concrete examples to show that the distinction between a ruling and a subject class is very common and of great antiquity; to illustrate the latter point he refers to the caste-system in Egypt, among other examples, at *Pol.* 1329 b 23 ff. But he also makes it clear that his doctrine is in line with his general physical principles. It is evident, he says in a later context (*Pol.* 1333 a 21 ff.), that both in nature and in art the inferior exists for the sake of the superior, and the superior is that which possesses a rational principle. The same is true of the individual man, in whom the soul is divided into a rational and an irrational part, and whose body exists for the sake of the soul as a whole. And the same is true again, clearly, of the state, for here too we may distinguish between the necessary conditions, and the true parts, of the state, and here too the principle holds true that what is necessary exists for the sake of what is good, the 'good' in this case being the life of moral and intellectual virtue that the citizens will lead.

Within the ruling class itself, the citizens take their turn in governing and being governed. He recognises as a matter of fact that those who carry arms can determine the fate of any constitution (*Pol.* 1329a11 ff.), but in the best state the soldiers are the younger men, and he argues that the young do not take offence at being ruled, especially if they know that they will enjoy this privilege themselves when they have reached the appropriate age (*Pol.* 1332b38 ff.). When he turns to consider, finally, how the ruling class should be educated, one of the main objects of the system he prescribes is to instil the spirit of obedience in the young, on the principle that he who is to learn to command must first learn to obey, although naturally enough their education includes much else besides: like a true Greek, Aristotle discusses how the body, too, should be trained, and the part that music should play in education.

Aristotle's political thought constantly reflects the circumstances and beliefs of the Greek city-state of the fourth century B.C. We have seen that he takes slavery to be a natural institution, a view typical of the vast majority of educated Greeks of his day, although Aristotle himself makes it clear that the idea that slavery is purely conventional had been put forward, and to give him his due, he agrees that there is something to be said for this point of view since many men became slaves unjustly or by accident. Again he assumes that the life of a farmer or a craftsman or a trader is incompatible with the life of a citizen, and here too he may well represent the majority view among Greek political theorists. And thirdly he manifests, at many points, an anti-barbarian bias, expressing his contempt for barbarian customs and asserting that the bar-

barians are naturally more servile in character than the Greeks (*Pol.* 1285a19f.), even though he allows exceptions to this rule and shows considerable respect for the political institutions of the Carthaginians in particular.

In none of these three cases could one claim that Aristotle was much, if at all, in advance of contemporary opinion. It is truer to say that the effect of his work was to provide some sort of rational justification for some deep-seated Greek prejudices. He believes the distinction between ruler and ruled, and between superior and inferior, to be part of the natural order of things. He arranges the species of living beings in a hierarchical structure according to the faculties of soul they possess, and he expresses the view that plants exist for the sake of animals, and animals in turn for the sake of man (*Pol.* 1256b15ff.). And he considers it valid to draw similar distinctions between ruler and ruled within the human species itself, first between male and female, secondly between the mature man and the child, and thirdly between the freeman and the slave. He compares the slave first with a tool, saying that he is as it were a living instrument (*Pol.* 1253b 27ff.), and then with a tame animal: for both slaves and domestic animals minister to the needs of life with their bodies (*Pol.* 1254b25ff.). Aristotle is egalitarian only to the extent that he advocates that everyone of equal merit should be treated equally, but this is at best a severely restricted egalitarianism, since it is qualified by his conviction that there are extensive differences in merit between different human beings.

Throughout his political work the city-state of the

fifth or fourth century provides his model and his ideal. This is obvious when, for instance, he sets such a low limit to the size of the citizen-body and suggests that when the citizens cannot all be addressed at a single assembly constitutional government becomes impracticable. His comments on the city of Babylon are also instructive, for he implies that so large a city should be considered a nation rather than a πόλις (*Pol.* 1276a27ff.). Although his knowledge of non-Greek states is not inconsiderable, his view-point remained that of a citizen of a Greek city-state. Yet we—with the advantage of hind-sight, of course—might well consider that the city-state was already past its heyday by the time Aristotle wrote; and its decline was undoubtedly accelerated by the major upheaval in the civilised world caused by the conquests of Alexander. Aristotle nowhere mentions Alexander in the *Politics*. There are, it is true, several references to the possibility of there being a man so far superior to his fellow-citizens in virtue that he is like a god among men (for example *Pol.* 1284a3ff., 1288a15ff.), and these have sometimes been taken to refer to Alexander. Yet depending on their date they might more naturally be taken to refer to Philip than to Alexander, and in any case it is far from certain that Aristotle had any specific historical personage in mind. But clearly at the time of writing the *Politics* Aristotle did not appreciate the significance of Alexander's conquests, which took place, after all, only in the last dozen years of Aristotle's life. Moreover had he appreciated their significance, he would certainly have regretted and opposed this or any

other political development that threatened the independence of the city-state. To judge from one passage (*Pol.*
1327b31ff.) where he speaks of the possibility of the
Greeks ruling the world if they were united politically
and 'had a single constitution', he may well have found
the idea of a Greek world-hegemony attractive, but not,
we may be sure, if that hegemony had to be bought at
the price of the destruction of the institutions of the
Greek city-state. The city-state provided the setting for
the individual to practise moral and political virtue, and
Aristotle's whole conception of the good life is indissolubly
linked with this supposition.

Aristotle shows a certain sense of the development of
history at several points in the *Politics*. His picture of the
growth of the state from the village in book 1, ch. 2 is
rather naive. But elsewhere he makes some perceptive
historical observations, as for example when he sketches
the evolution of Greek city-states from monarchical to
more democratic constitutions and comments on the part
played in this development by the rise of the hoplite class
and by the increase in the numbers of the 'middle' class
(*Pol.* 1297b16ff.). In book 1, ch. 9 he offers an interesting
account of certain economic developments that had taken
place in the past, particularly the change from primitive
barter to more complex forms of exchange, and in
several places he speaks of the benefits derived from man's
discovery and development of the arts and crafts in
general. Yet he does not extrapolate this development
with regard to the future, or imagine that much further
progress would or could be made. At *Pol.* 1264a3ff., for

example, he expresses the to us truly astonishing view that almost everything had already been discovered, and while he is thinking particularly of political institutions at that point, it is clear from *Pol.* 1329 b 25 ff. that he believed that every art had been invented and forgotten many times over in the course of human history (cf. *Metaph.* 1074 b 10 ff.). He does not imagine that political institutions will evolve beyond those of the city-state, certainly not in the direction of any improvement upon them. His ideal is a static one, a city-state with a permanent constitution and a stable population.

Aristotle shares some typical Greek prejudices of his time and he lacks the notion of progress as we understand it today. This is not surprising, but it limits the value of his political thought for the modern reader. Again we should say that he appeals too often to psychological and moral factors to explain political changes. He believes that the stability of states depends much more on the character of the citizens than on constitutional or economic factors. At *Pol.* 1263 b 15–27, for example, he criticises those who saw in the possession of private property the roots of evils whose real cause, he suggests, lies in human wickedness. Yet he does not entirely neglect the part played by non-personal factors such as economic, constitutional or even geographical considerations. He refers to these in his account of the causes of revolutions, especially, observing at *Pol.* 1308 a 35 ff., for instance, that property qualifications may be affected simply by the increase in the amount of money in circulation in the state, even though their nominal value remains unchanged.

But our gravest doubts concerning the viability of Aristotle's political theory relate to his reliance on the virtue of the citizens of the best state as the safeguard of its constitution. He certainly recognises that in the average state each class acts in its own self-interest. In book IV, ch. II, for example, he speaks of the struggles between opposing factions which were such a feature of Greek history, and he suggests that it was because of these factions that a moderate form of government, intermediate between democracy and oligarchy, had existed so rarely in Greece. Again when he notes how difficult it is to determine in theory what is just and equitable for those of unequal merit according to the principle of 'proportional equality', he goes on to remark that the practical difficulties in persuading those who were in a position to demand more than their fair share to desist from doing so are far greater (*Pol.* 1318 b 1 ff.). He observes, too, that those who hold office in the state should be capable, virtuous and loyal to the constitution, and that such a combination of qualities is hard to come by (*Pol.* 1309 a 33 ff.), and we saw that he was well aware that the fate of any constitution is in the hands of those who have the military power (*Pol.* 1329 a 11 ff.). Yet his solution to these difficulties, so far as the best state is concerned, lies in the virtue of its citizens. The young men who form the warrior class will be educated in obedience and so will not want to seize power unconstitutionally before the time appointed for them. Like many other attempts to picture the best form of state, Aristotle's is open to the criticism that the working of the constitution depends, at certain key points, on the goodness and self-restraint of the citizens, and indeed not merely on the moral virtue of the citizens, but also on the willingness of the non-citizen classes to accept the roles ascribed to them.

Many of Aristotle's political theories strike us as over-idealistic. Yet the positive aspects of his political thought should not be overlooked. First his conception of the state contains much that is valuable. He gives a forceful exposition of the theory that the state exists in the common interest, that is for the good of the whole, not that of a particular part, even though he holds that different people participate in the state to different degrees. And we may agree with him, too, when he treats political associations as the means to an end, rather than ends in themselves, the end being the happiness of individuals. But it is Aristotle's chief merit to have shown how political science may be investigated as an empirical study. He applies to his work in politics the principle he uses elsewhere throughout his ethics, that the starting-point of the study is what is better known to us and the particular instances. The business of the political theorist embraces both analysis and recommendation. His theory of the best state takes up two books of the *Politics*, and elsewhere his discussion is much influenced by his views about the role the state should perform. But in classifying the varieties of con-stitutions, for example, and in considering the factors that contribute to stability or instability in each of them, he refers repeatedly to particular concrete examples. Much of the *Politics* is devoted to analysing how existing states functioned. And the programme of histories of individual constitutions proves that far more than any earlier writer he appreciated the value of systematic studies of case-histories in this field. Here too we may observe, as we have done so often in reviewing other aspects of his work, that whatever criticisms may be made of the particular ideas he put forward, he made a fundamental and lasting contribution to the subject in his method of approach to the problems.

CHAPTER 12

LITERARY CRITICISM

Aristotle nowhere puts forward a developed aesthetic, nor even a complete theory of literary criticism. Yet despite the gaps and limitations of his discussion and the extreme obscurity of some of his ideas, he went further in his analysis of the aims and nature of poetry than any earlier writer. His defence of the usefulness of poetry provided an important antidote to Plato's criticisms and rejection of it, and his work in this field was to prove enormously influential.

The 'Rhetoric'

He discusses literary style in two treatises, the *Poetics* and the less well known *Rhetoric*. To deal briefly with the *Rhetoric* first, that work, as its name suggests, is an analysis of the art of public speaking. The scope of rhetoric and its relation to philosophy had been topics of some dispute which Plato had discussed at length in the *Gorgias* and the *Phaedrus*. Aristotle defines it as the faculty of discovering the possible means of persuasion with regard to any subject (*Rh.* 1355b26f.). It is a counterpart to or offshoot of dialectic, which he had discussed in the *Topics*. Both deal with probabilities, and as such they are both contrasted with the study of strict demonstration or scientific proof, the subject-matter of the *Analytics*. But while dialectic proceeds by question and answer, the orator uses continuous speech, exercising his skill in three main fields: (1) political, (2) legal, and (3) ceremonial, oratory.

The *Rhetoric* is concerned with methods of persuasion. Just as in the *Sophistici Elenchi*, for example, he considers how to deceive your opponent in argument and how to counter his attempts to do the same to you, so too in the *Rhetoric* he discusses the tricks of the trade, the various devices the public speaker may use to win his case. These include persuasive, but not strictly valid, arguments, and appeals to the emotions of his audience. A large part of the third book of the treatise is devoted to the question of style, for this too is relevant to public speaking. Aristotle suggests that the orator's style should be clear, vivid and appropriate both to the subject-matter and to the audience addressed; it should be neither too high-flown and ornate, nor too common and colloquial, and he discusses how these various aims are to be achieved, dealing in some detail with such matters as the right use of simile and metaphor, the avoidance of incorrect language, prose rhythm, the construction of periods and so on.

The 'Poetics'

The third book of the *Rhetoric* lays down some sensible rules concerning prose style from the point of view of effective public speaking. It is, however, the *Poetics* that represents Aristotle's main contribution to literary criticism. Even so, after the first five introductory chapters, the *Poetics* deals in detail with only one of the four main genres of poetry, namely tragedy. His remarks on epic are quite brief, he has even less to say on lyric poetry, and his promised discussion of comedy has not survived.

The style of his discussion of tragedy has much in

common with the method we have seen him adopt elsewhere. Just as in the biological, physical, ethical and political treatises his discussion of the problems is punctuated with frequent references to concrete examples, so too the *Poetics* is full of quotations from and references to actual Greek tragedies. At the same time his analysis of tragedy is highly abstract and technical. His aim is evidently not merely to describe the genre as practised in his day, but also and more particularly to put forward his own ideas about what makes a good tragedy and why. He is aware of what other writers had had to say on the subject and several of his principal theses appear to owe more to his theoretical disagreements with Plato than to his own direct observation and experience of Greek tragedy. Furthermore his own theory of poetry is closely linked with other parts of his philosophy, particularly with his ethics, and several of the terms he uses are obscure or liable to be misunderstood unless we take into account doctrines that are expressed more fully in other treatises.

The general term that Aristotle uses to describe not only all the various poetic genres, but also the fine arts, together with music and dancing, is μίμησις. By this he means a creative activity, not merely the mechanical copying of an original to produce as faithful a likeness as possible, and so 'representation' is often a closer English equivalent than 'imitation'. 'Representation', he believes, is a natural instinct in man from childhood (*Po.* 1448 b 5 ff.); he possesses this instinct to a greater degree than any other animal, and it is by imitating things that he learns, at least at first. Moreover it is an important part of Aristotle's doctrine that the poet and the artist represent things not merely as they are, but as they might be and as they should be. He traces the origin of poetry to two main sources, the natural instinct to imitate and represent things, and the delight we take in the product of such representations. The various genres of poetry evolved historically, he suggests, from crude improvisations, and he sketches the main stages in the development of tragedy, the increase in the number of actors from one to three, the decline in the role of the chorus, the introduction of effects such as scene-painting and so on (ch. 4).

The objects that poetry represents are defined quite narrowly as the actions of human beings, particularly actions as revealing moral character, the agents being not morally indifferent persons, but men who are good or bad. This provides Aristotle with the basis of his distinction between tragedy and comedy, for tragedy, he says, represents people who are better than the average, while comedy represents those who are worse than the average, but worse not in the sense that they are evil, but in that they are laughable and ridiculous.

Tragedy

When he turns in ch. 6 to deal with tragedy particularly in greater detail, he begins with a highly compressed general definition (*Po.* 1449 b 24 ff.): tragedy is a representation of an action that is serious and that has a certain magnitude and is complete in itself; in language that is embellished with ornament; in a dramatic, not a narrative, form; and it is a representation that through pity and fear effects a purging of these and similar emotions. Some but not all of the component parts of this obscure statement are elucidated in the discussion that follows. First he explains what sort of representation tragedy is. The tragedian's job is to relate not what actually happened, but what might happen, not in the sense of what might conceivably happen, but what might be expected to happen. The tragedian, one may say, represents neither actual past events, nor on the other hand random fantasies of his own devising, but ideal sequences of events, events as they would be likely to occur. This leads Aristotle to draw an interesting contrast between poetry and history in a digression in ch. 9. The difference between the two is not merely that the one is in verse and the other in prose. Even if Herodotus were put into verse, it would still be history. The real difference, Aristotle says, is that history deals with what has actually happened, poetry with what might happen. History deals with particular facts, poetry with the universal, and so poetry is more philosophical and serious than history (*Po.* 1451 b 5 ff.). To us this seems a very strange conclusion, but it is entirely consistent with Aristotle's view-point. In real life any chain of events is influenced by chance and accident. But the poet can and should represent an ideal sequence of events, the events as they would occur according to the general rules governing human behaviour. The contrast between Aristotle's view and the low opinion of poetry expressed by Plato is clear. Where Plato had condemned poetry as third in the order of reality, an imitation of particulars which themselves imitate the Forms, Aristotle brings to bear Plato's own favourite distinction between particular and universal to suggest, on the contrary, that what the poet represents is not the mere particular, but the universal. He uses particular events as the means to represent what is 'always or for the most part' true concerning human action.

Action and plot

Aristotle is emphatic that tragedy is a representation of an action, not of character. As he says at *Po.* 1450a16ff., it is 'a representation not of men, but of action and life and happiness and unhappiness: for happiness comes under the heading of action'. The action is not included for the sake of character-study in a tragedy, but *vice versa*. The unity of a tragedy is a unity of action contained in plot, not a unity of character: on the subject of unity of plot he remarks perceptively that the *Iliad* and the *Odyssey* are unities because they are about actions that form a whole, and that in neither case did Homer attempt to include the entire history of the chief character, Achilles or Odysseus.

The doctrine that tragedy represents an action 'that has a certain magnitude and is complete in itself' is explained further in ch. 7. The action represented must be a whole: it must have a beginning, a middle and an end, a beginning being something which is not a necessary consequent of anything else, but from which other things follow, and an end, conversely, being something which follows from something else but from which nothing else results. Well-constructed plots must not begin and end at random, but should form such a whole. Moreover the plot should have a certain length, and here natural organisms are used as an analogy. Each kind of living creature has a definite size, and beautiful creatures, he suggests, are those that are neither very large nor very small. So too with plots, he argues, they must be of some length, but of a length that may be easily grasped by the memory.

He goes in considerable detail into the varieties of plot and how they should be constructed. Thus he distinguishes between 'simple' and 'complex' plots, arguing that the latter are superior. These are plots that involve 'discoveries', ἀναγνωρίσεις, when one of the characters finds out something of which he had been ignorant, and 're-versals of fortune', περιπέτειαι, but these should both arise, he insists, out of the actual structure of the plot, as the necessary or probable consequences of what has already taken place. He gives examples and suggests that it is especially effective when the 'discovery' coincides with the 'reversal', as happens in the Oedipus Tyrannus.

He analyses, too, the various types of changes of fortune that might form the basis of a plot. Having considered most of the theoretical possibilities, for example that of wicked men passing from bad fortune to good or vice versa, he suggests that a tragedy will best achieve its end —to arouse pity and fear—when it represents a man who is not preeminent in virtue or justice suffering a misfortune that is brought about not by his own wickedness, but by some great mistake or imperfection, ἁμαρτία (Po. 1453a7ff.). What exactly Aristotle means by this is disputed. It is clear, first of all, that he explicitly distinguishes ἁμαρτία from vice, κακία or μοχθηρία. The person to whom the misfortune occurs should be a good man, one who is better than the average but nevertheless imperfect. We should remember that virtue and vice are, in Aristotle's view, dispositions, and he allows that brave men, for example, may and sometimes do commit cowardly acts. If we refer back to the *Ethics*, ἁμαρτία there sometimes refers to an error of judgement or a mistake due to ignorance, and sometimes to a defect of feeling or disposition, and in his account of ἀκρασία Aristotle had attempted to explain how it is that a person may know in general what is right and yet in a particular situation do what is wrong. In the ideal tragedy the misfortune does not happen purely by chance—for tragedy should represent what occurs probably or inevitably. The misfortune is, rather, one that arises directly or indirectly as the result of an imperfection in the person to whom it occurs. Yet it is not deserved, or at least not fully deserved, for it is only undeserved misfortune that arouses our pity.

Plot, according to Aristotle, is the starting-point and as it were the soul of tragedy (*Po.* 1450a38f.), so it is natural that it should receive the lion's share of his attention. But he distinguishes five other constituent parts of a tragedy which he discusses in varying detail. These are character, thought, diction, song and spectacle (1450a7ff.). Spectacle, he says, is seductive, but inartistic, and of all the parts it has the least to do with poetry. Song and diction are the means used in the representation, and diction, at least, is discussed at length in chh. 20–22. But the most important parts, after plot, are character and thought, for these are the two main sources from which action arises. Thought, διάνοια, is revealed whenever the persons in the drama try to prove or disprove anything, express their opinions, play on the emotions of others and so on. All this comes under the head of what Aristotle calls 'rhetoric', and is in fact principally dealt with in his work of that name. The other main source of action is character, and here he has a number of general recommendations to make. The doctrine that tragedy represents people who are better than the average is explained in ch. 15 where he says that the characters should be 'good of their kind' —the term is χρηστός, the primary meaning of which is 'serviceable'. In this sense even a woman or a slave may be 'good'—relative to other women or slaves—'although the one is an inferior creature and the other completely worthless' (*Po.* 1454a20ff.). And he specifies further that character should be 'appropriate', 'life-like' and 'consistent'.

The aim of tragedy

The principal aim of tragedy, in Aristotle's view, is through pity and fear to effect a 'purging' of these and similar emotions. What does he mean by 'purging', κάθαρσις, in this famous and much discussed phrase? First the term had a technical use in medical vocabulary, and Aristotle himself uses it in this context often enough in the biological works, as for example at *GA* 738a27ff. where he speaks of the need to bring about a κάθαρσις or evacuation of the residues that cause diseases in the body. Then the term was also used in a religious context, both of a return to normality from a state of 'enthusiasm' or being possessed by a god, and of ritual purification in general: it is used in this last sense at *Po.* 1455b15 of the purification of Orestes after he had murdered Clytemnestra. When Aristotle speaks of tragedy effecting a 'purging' of the emotions of pity and fear, he is no doubt influenced by these other uses of the term. Unlike diseases, the emotions or affections are not necessarily bad in themselves. In the *Ethics* it is pointed out that we are praised or blamed not for feeling anger, but for feeling it in a certain way. The emotions are natural, for we are born with a capacity for certain feelings. But Aristotle believes that excessive emotions require relief, and this relief may be procured not only by watching a tragedy but also, for example, by listening to music. In the *Politics* (1342a4ff.) he observes that the emotions that some people happen to experience very strongly, such as pity and fear, and 'enthusiasm', occur in all men to a greater or lesser extent; and in describing how those who are 'possessed' are restored by music he says that they obtain 'a cure, as it were, and a purging'. Tragedy, then, like music, has in a sense a therapeutic function, in that it procures relief from excessive emotion: and at the same time this relief, being a return to a natural state, is accompanied by its own pleasure.

Aristotle's discussion of poetry is dry and analytic, and it suffers from certain fairly obvious shortcomings. His analysis sometimes strikes one as artificial, as when he distinguishes tragedy from comedy by referring to the moral quality of the persons represented, or when he considers what type of change of fortune makes the best plot. Many of his ideas are influenced by his taking the

Oedipus Tyrannus as the chief model for his ideal, but this was in some ways an untypical play, and it leads him to take a rather narrow view on such topics as the mechanics of plot construction. Again he assumes too readily that while the various genres, tragedy, epic and so on, had evolved in the past, they had in his day reached their natural forms, and the analogy of the living organism, which he uses to suggest that there is a normal length for a tragedy or for an epic, is a dangerous one. But if his analysis is dry, it is full of common sense, and it has certain positive features. The idea that a poem should be a unity, obvious though it may seem to us, is one example. And his judgement that plot is more important than character tallies with what remains of Greek tragedy far better than the opposite view, that of the nineteenth-century romantic ideal of the tragic hero. But undoubtedly his most important contribution to literary criticism was to have rescued poetry from the denunciations of Plato. Against Plato he emphasises the seriousness and moral value of poetry, arguing that what the poet represents is the universal, even though he does so by means of the particular. And in contrast to Plato again, he insists that the pleasure that they both agree is to be derived from poetry is not an insidious and morally damaging one, but harmless and indeed positively beneficial.

CHAPTER 13

CONCLUSION

Discussing the growth of Aristotle's thought, I argued that there is an important continuity in his development. Naturally his views on many questions, including, for example, such a fundamental problem as the ultimate source of movement in the universe, changed during the course of his life, and he certainly also developed important, and engrossing, new interests. But whether any drastic revolution took place in his thought is doubtful.

Even his rejection of the teaching of Plato was not a matter of a simple, sudden and dramatic break so much as a complex, gradual and continuing process. His disagreements with his master date from early in his career and for some time after he had rejected the theory of Forms he still considered himself a member of the circle of Platonists. Conversely, long after his links with the Academy had become rather tenuous, there remained much in common between his mature philosophy and Plato's. Moreover while in zoology, for example, he pioneered a new approach to the study of the animal kingdom, his detailed investigations in that field tended to endorse certain doctrines, such as that of the final cause, that owe an obvious debt to Plato. Aristotle's work was wider-ranging and more original than that of any earlier philosopher, indeed of any philosopher of any time, but certain methodological assumptions and key ideas underlie a great deal of his thought. It is now time to consider the question of the unity and coherence of his philosophy.

Method

First a common method runs through almost all the branches of his thought. The first notable feature of this method is that he considers it important to discuss the common views and the opinions of his predecessors on a problem before attempting his own solution. His usual practice is to begin with a survey, sometimes quite an extended survey, of previous views. On the subject of 'first philosophy', for example, he devotes a whole book, *Metaphysics* A, to earlier ideas, and in the various branches of physics he regularly reviews earlier doctrines before setting out his own. He does this, for instance, in *Physics* I (on fundamental principles), *de Generatione et Corruptione* I, chh. 1 and 2 (on coming-to-be), *de Anima* I (on soul), *de Respiratione* chh. 2–7 (on respiration), *de Partibus Animalium* I, chh. 2–4 (on methods of classifying animals), *de Generatione Animalium* I, chh. 17 ff. (on sexual generation) and IV, ch. 1 (on sex differentiation). Again in the *Ethics* he surveys earlier ideas on pleasure in book VII, for instance, and at 1145 b 2 ff. he explicitly says that their aim should be 'after first discussing the difficulties, [to] go on to prove, if possible, all the common views about these affections, or, failing that, most of them and the most authoritative ones'. Equally in the *Politics* the preliminary study of the question of the ideal state in book II consists in a critique of the theories of other writers and an analysis of the actual states that were believed to enjoy good constitutions. Logic alone is an exception to the rule that he begins with a study of his predecessors' work, and the reason for this is simply that Aristotle found nothing of any value on the subject in earlier writers. As he says in the *Sophistici Elenchi* (183 b 34 ff.): 'as regards our present inquiry [into modes of argument], it is not that one part of it had been worked out before, and another not, but rather that it did not exist at all.'

Time and again Aristotle's inquiry starts with a review of what his predecessors had had to say on the subject to be discussed. This helps him to formulate the problems and to identify the difficulties. In proceeding to try to resolve these he has two main techniques, which he himself distinguishes on many occasions, (1) appeals to theoretical arguments, λόγοι, and (2) appeals to concrete evidence of one sort or another. We have met many illustrations of the first technique during our discussion of the various branches of his philosophy. Thus destructively, he frequently criticises his opponents for inconsistencies in their arguments, for example, or refutes them by forcing them on to the horns of a dilemma. A good instance of the second type is the argument used against the doctrine of pangenesis which I outlined on pp. 82–3. And constructively, his analysis of many problems includes a survey of the theoretically possible alternatives, after which he arrives at the most satisfactory solution by a process of elimination. He uses this type of argument, for instance, on such widely differing topics as the generation of bees (pp. 76–7) and the best kind of reversal of fortune for the plot of a tragedy (p. 278).

His second main argumentative technique is the appeal to concrete evidence, to what he calls the 'facts' or the 'data', ἔργα or ὑπάρχοντα or γιγνόμενα or συμβαίνοντα, or to the φαινόμενα. As we have seen (p. 57) the force of this last term varies in different contexts. Sometimes it refers to what we should call the data of observation: indeed on occasions he specifies τὰ φαινόμενα κατὰ τὴν αἴσθησιν, the 'perceived' or 'observed' phenomena, as he does, for example, when referring to what is observed to happen in eclipses of the moon during the course of his proof that the earth is spherical (*Cael.* 297 b 23 ff., p. 162). But elsewhere, for example in the passage in the *Ethics* where he comments on his method in that inquiry (*EN* 1145 b 2 ff., p. 206), τὰ φαινόμενα refers rather to the common opinions and what is usually said or thought about a subject. The term συμβαίνοντα is also used in connection with evidence of very different types. In the *Politics*, for instance, he often refers to the evidence of actual case-histories under the heading 'what takes place'. But elsewhere, when he uses the term at *GA* 750a21, for example, what he refers to is not direct evidence so much as an argument from analogy. We must allow, then, that what Aristotle takes to be relevant evidence varies a good deal in different contexts: and even when he states that he is referring to the 'facts' or to the 'phenomena', this is no guarantee that his argument is one that we should describe as empirical. Nevertheless appeals to concrete data and to particular examples are, of course, a prominent feature of his method both in natural science and in other fields, as can be seen, for instance, from his citations of actual

Greek plays in his analysis of tragedy in the *Poetics* and his references to historical examples in the *Politics*. He not only often states, but appears indeed to practise, the general principle that, whereas in demonstration the starting-point is 'what is better known absolutely' and the universal, the process of discovery and learning begins with what is closer to sense, the particulars and 'what is better known to us' (see *APo.* 71b33ff., *Ph.* 189a5ff., *Metaph.* 1018b31ff.).

When he contrasts arguments from the 'facts' with theoretical arguments his idea of what comes under the former heading is an elastic one. But his appreciation of the value of research is amply demonstrated by the extensive programmes he undertook in the biological and social sciences especially. Indeed one might say that the idea of carrying out systematic research is one that we in the West owe as much to Aristotle and to the Lyceum as to any other single man or institution. His own researches were conducted in the light of certain theoretical assumptions and with the object not merely of describing the phenomena, but also and more especially of establishing their causes. Thus his zoological researches may be said to have been carried out primarily to investigate the operations of the formal, final, efficient and material causes in animals and their parts, and his work on political constitutions was directed to such questions as the causes of the changes and stability of states, and the ends that different types of constitution serve. Under the heading of the theoretical assumptions that his investigations presuppose may be included, in the first example, the doctrine of the four causes itself, and in the second, his conception of man as a rational animal with a moral sense.

But to say that his researches were conducted in the light of certain theoretical assumptions does not mean, of course, that they were undertaken simply in order to support or confirm his preconceived opinions. An important aspect of his method is his willingness to withhold judgement where the evidence was inadequate or where he was, for one reason or another, unable to arrive at a satisfactory solution. We noted his comment on the particular problem of how bees are generated in the *de Generatione Animalium* (760b30ff., p. 79): 'the facts have not been sufficiently ascertained. And if they ever are ascertained, then we must trust the evidence of the senses rather than theories, and theories as well, so long as their results agree with what is observed.' And he adopts a similar position on other much more important problems as well. Thus he is far from being dogmatic on the question of the number of unmoved movers, where he says that 'if those who study these things come to some conclusion which conflicts with our present statements, we must love both parties, but believe those who give the more exact account' (*Metaph.* 1073b15ff., p. 152), and even on an issue as fundamental as the distinction between living and lifeless things we find him remarking that 'nature proceeds little by little from inanimate things to living creatures, in such a way that we are unable, in the continuous sequence, to determine the boundary line between them or to say on which side an intermediate kind falls' (*HA* 588b4ff., p. 88).

To review his predecessors' views and the common opinions, to attempt to resolve the difficulties by means of both dialectical arguments and appeals to concrete evidence and to particular examples, to undertake, where appropriate, detailed researches to ascertain the facts and to help determine the causes at work, these are the main recurrent features of Aristotle's method. But while a common method provides one link between his work in different fields of investigation, there are common general doctrines that also form an important bridge between different aspects of his thought. Three closely related doctrines appear to be of fundamental importance, namely (1) the antithesis between form and matter, with which may be linked the doctrines of limit and the mean, (2) the antithesis between actuality and potentiality, and (3) the doctrine of final causes.

Form/matter

The form/matter antithesis plays an impressive number of roles in different branches of Aristotle's work. Any concrete individual is a complex of form and matter. Sensation is interpreted as the reception, by the sense-organ, of the sensible form without the matter of the object perceived, and similarly reasoning is described as the reception of the intelligible forms by the so-called passive reason. These are two of the faculties of soul, and soul in general is sometimes described as the form of the living creature, the body being its matter. Change in general is represented in terms of a progression from the privation to the form or *vice versa*: this applies even to locomotion, where the motions of heavy or light objects towards their 'natural places' are said to be motions towards their forms (*Cael.* 310a31ff.). And in his account of sexual reproduction in particular he argues that the male provides only the form, the female only the matter, of the embryo. In physics the distinction between a sublunary and a celestial region may be seen as a distinction between the region where form always exists in conjunction with matter, and the region where pure form is possible. Even in logic, finally, he applies the form/matter distinction in an analogous sense: in a definition, as he suggests at *Metaph.* 1038a5ff., for example, the genus is as it were the matter, and the differentiae as it were the form, of what is defined.

The antithesis between form and matter may be connected in turn with that between limit and the unlimited, and this takes us to a further set of related doctrines, including the ethical and aesthetic doctrine of the mean. At *Ph.* 209b7ff., for instance, matter is equated with the indeterminate, ἀόριστον, form with what limits or determines it. It is form that is knowable and definable; matter as such is unknowable. But in the sphere of sensible objects, at least, what discriminates and judges the indeterminate range is the mean, and so sensation is described as a mean. And while in the *de Anima* sensation is a mean in respect of what is sensible, in the *Ethics* moral virtue is a mean in respect of feelings, and in the *Politics* the best and safest constitution is said to be the mean or intermediate one, the constitution in which those citizens who avoid the extremes of wealth and poverty are predominant. Finally Aristotle's preference for the limited rather than the unlimited comes out in a different context in his discussions of infinity, especially in *Physics* III, chh. 4–8. He allows that the idea of the infinite has some valid uses: thus magnitudes are infinitely divisible, and both time and number are infinite by addition, although only potentially so—the infinity of time consists in a process of coming-to-be and is never actual. But it is striking that Aristotle holds that mathematics does not require an infinite line, only a finite line as long as one wishes (*Ph.* 207b27ff.). And he argues at length that an infinite body cannot exist and that the universe is finite. The infinite, he concludes at *Ph.* 207b34ff., is a cause in the sense of matter, and its essence is privation.

Actuality/potentiality

Matter is identified with potentiality, form with actuality: but although these two antitheses are in a sense equivalent, to describe matter as potentiality is to draw attention to the possibility of change, whether this is brought about by an external efficient cause, as in artificial production, or by an internal source of movement, as in natural change. The wood is potentially a table or a chair, the seed of the tree potentially a mature specimen. Other natural changes too, including change of place, are the actualising of potentialities. Thus in his account of the motions of the simple bodies, 'heavy' and 'light' are defined as potentialities for falling and rising (*Cael.* 307b31ff., 311a3ff.). Then the technical definition of soul is 'the first actuality of a natural body that potentially has life', and here he uses not ἐνέργεια, the usual antonym of δύναμις, but ἐντελέχεια: this too means actuality, and it is explicitly opposed to 'potentiality' at *de An.* 412a9f. and elsewhere, but the associations of the word are different, since it is connected with and indirectly derived from τέλος, goal or end, rather than ἔργον, work or function. If ἐνέργεια is used especially of actuality *qua* activity, ἐντελέχεια is used rather to refer to actuality *qua* fulfilment. The actuality/potentiality distinction has another role to play in his psychology, in that the 'faculties' of the soul are 'potentialities'—Aristotle uses the term δύναμις in both senses—and the sense-organ actually becomes what it perceives when it perceives it. Finally the same distinction recurs in different contexts in his ethics and in his theology. Happiness is said to consist not in a mere state, nor in a mere potentiality, but in an actuality, 'the activity of soul according to virtue' (*EN* 1098a16ff., p. 213), and the prime mover is pure actuality, being described both as ἐνέργεια (*Metaph.* 1072b27) and as ἐντελέχεια (*Metaph.* 1074a36).

Final causes

Happiness is man's goal, his τέλος, and the aim of political constitutions is or should be to ensure the conditions that will permit man to attain this goal. But final causes are at work not just in the sphere of human activity, but throughout nature, even though nature does not deliberate. He claims that the animal kingdom provides evidence in abundance of 'the absence of chance and the serving of ends' (*PA* 645a23ff., p. 70). Less accessible, but more perfect, are the divine heavenly bodies themselves, concerning which he observed that 'nothing in the heavens takes place spontaneously' (*Ph.* 196b2f.) and that 'there is much clearer evidence of order and definiteness in the heavenly bodies than there is in us' (*PA* 641b 18f.). But even when we consider the lifeless sublunary elements, it is always the case that, when nothing prevents them, earth falls and fire rises, and wherever a natural process takes place 'always' or at least 'for the most part' the outcome of the process may be described as its final cause, the end towards which the process is directed. Furthermore he believes that the ultimate source of movement in the universe as a whole is a mover who brings about movement as a final cause—in the sense of the good aimed at in an action, not in the sense of the object for whose good an action is performed (pp. 142–3).

Unity of Aristotle's cosmology

A great deal of Aristotle's philosophy can be subsumed under the heading of one or other of these three major interrelated doctrines of form, actuality and final cause, and it is perhaps not merely coincidental that this applies particularly to the most difficult, obscure or speculative parts of his thought, as for example his conception of god, his doctrine of substance, his theory of the ultimate origin of movement, and his account of reason. Notwithstanding the great variety of his interests, his vision of the cosmos is a remarkably unified one. Gods, men, animals and inanimate elements all have their places on a single scale of being. Aristotle certainly did not ignore the distinctions between the various inquiries related to these different objects, for example theology and astronomy, ethics and politics, physics and its branches: indeed in many cases he was himself the first person to name and define these different subjects: yet he sees much closer links between them than we should tend to do.

Consider first the place of ethics. Man alone of the animals has moral choice and can be praised and blamed for his actions. Ethics and politics, then, are inquiries that relate to man alone. Yet Aristotle's conception of the position man occupies on the scale of being, between gods and animals, is far from being unimportant for his ethics. The highest life for man is the life of reason, the faculty that man shares with the gods and which is described as 'divine in comparison with man'. Moreover happiness is not possible unless the goods of the body are present, among which he includes health, that is the well-being of man *qua* animal. Secondly, while in normal English usage physics and biology are coordinate disciplines, Aristotle's φυσική is a general term covering both sciences—the inquiry into anything that has a source of movement in itself—and this is no mere accident of nomenclature, but reflects his tendency to bring together the study of living and that of lifeless things. Thirdly, although logic does stand apart from the other disciplines I have mentioned, as the inquiry into the tools of thought, it is characteristic that in his brief account of the difficult problem of induction, of how the mind grasps the universal, he should consider this faculty to be developed from a faculty common to both men and animals, namely sensation (p. 126).

The doctrines of form, actuality and the final cause span, in each case, both his natural and his moral philosophy. Furthermore his conception of nature itself incorporates a system of values. First, natural objects from the divine heavenly bodies down to the humblest pebble are arranged in a scale of being that is at the same time a scale of perfection, and within this scale the more perfect types provide an ideal, as it were, to which the less perfect aspire. This can be seen most clearly in the zoological treatises, where other animals are often considered from the point of view of their similarities to and differences from human beings, who provide the standard by which the less perfect animals are judged. But then more generally Aristotle identifies the final cause, in nature as elsewhere, with what is desirable and good. One passage in which this identification is explicitly made is *Metaph.* 983 a 31 f. The doctrine is true above all of the unmoved mover, who moves by being the object of desire and love, in the same way as the good moves us (p. 142): as he argues in his psychology (p. 190), the cause of local movement in both men and animals is desire, whether for the good or for what appears to be good. Throughout the sphere of natural coming-to-be, even where no conscious desire or motivation is involved, nature is said to seek or wish for 'what is better' (*GC* 336 b 27 ff. and often elsewhere). Even matter itself, at one point, is said to desire and yearn for form (*Ph.* 192 a 20 ff.). The causes of things are, then, sometimes classified not according to the regular four-fold schema of material, formal, efficient and final causes, but according to a simpler two-fold schema, where 'what happens from necessity' is contrasted with 'what happens for the sake of what is better', as for example at

GA 731 b 20 ff. We saw that the unmoved mover neither creates nor cares for the universe. But each kind of natural object, according to Aristotle, seeks or is directed towards the form and fulfilment appropriate to it, and in this sense, then, the good operates as a final cause throughout the universe.

Finally the scale of living creatures is not the only important instance of Aristotle's use of the notion of a hierarchy of being. The conception of the distinction between ruler and ruled is a prominent and pervasive feature of his thought: indeed he believes that some such distinction runs through both society and nature. So far as society is concerned, he argues in the *Politics* that the distinction between master and slave is a natural one largely on the grounds that similar distinctions can be traced in both nature and art (p. 251), and the examples he gives show how widespread his application of this idea is. Thus within the individual living creature the soul rules the body, and in animals the male is usually superior to and rules the female, and so too the elder and more mature is said to be more fitted to rule than the younger and immature (*Pol.* 1259 b 1 ff.). He says, too, that plants exist for the sake of animals, and the other animals for the sake of man, to provide him with food and clothing (1256 b 15 ff.). Then in his cosmology it is not surprising that he sometimes describes god as a ruler, although he rules as final cause, not as one who issues commands (*EE* 1249 b 13 ff.). The term ἀρχή itself, which is used to mean 'cause' or 'principle', sometimes retains some of the associations of its other Greek meaning, namely seat of authority. We see this, for instance, in the famous passage at the end of *Metaph.* Λ where having criticised those who make the ἀρχαί a plurality he quotes approvingly from Homer: 'the rule of many is not good; let one rule' (1076a4). The Homeric verse, in which Odysseus speaks of the need to obey the commander-in-chief Agamemnon, is not considered irrelevant to the question of the number of ultimate cosmic principles. Moreover while in the *Politics* he argued that the ruler/ruled distinction is natural in society because it exists in nature too, he reverses the argument in the *Metaphysics*. At 1075a11ff., when he considers the question of how the nature of the whole possesses the good, the two illustrations he uses to convey his answer are both drawn from human institutions: the first is the army, where 'the good' lies both in the ordering of the parts and in the general, and especially in the latter; and the second is the household, where free men and slaves make different contributions towards the good according to the extent to which their actions are governed by reason. Likewise in the universe everything is ordered in a single whole, but different things occupy different places in the cosmic scheme.

The above paragraphs are an attempted analysis of some of the fundamental ideas that run through Aristotle's philosophy. But we may now return to the question of his intellectual development with which we set out. If this analysis is in broad terms correct, at what stage, we might ask, and under what impulse, were the main foundations of his mature philosophy laid? Some of the possible answers to this difficult question may be confidently excluded. First, our sources for the *Eudemus* and the *Protrepticus* provide limited, but fairly definite, evidence of a period in Aristotle's life before he had developed some of what I take to be the fundamental doctrines of his mature philosophy. Thus he apparently suggested in them that the soul so far from being the actuality of the living body does not exist naturally in the body, and he described its life independent of the body in terms borrowed largely from the eschatological myths of Plato. We recognise this period, then, as being one when he was still much influenced by aspects of Plato's teaching that he was later to abandon completely.

Turning now to the other end of his career, we may be sure that the doctrines of form and matter, finality, actuality and potentiality, did not require the conditions of the Lyceum for their formulation. Nor indeed is there any reason to suppose that they were the direct product of the detailed biological work that he began during the period of the travels. On the contrary, the way in which he justifies his inquiry into the parts of animals strongly suggests that the doctrines of form and finality were not the conclusions of his biological work, so much as the motives for his detailed investigations in that field. Those doctrines were, we may repeat, fairly clearly the outcome not of any detailed research in any particular branch of inquiry, whether biology, sociology or logic, but of critical reflection on theoretical problems that he inherited from Plato and from earlier philosophy, especially the problem of change and what in the *Metaphysics*

(1028 b 2 ff.) he describes as 'the age-old and present and eternal question and difficulty, what is being?'

Dissatisfaction with Plato's ontology must be considered the chief factor that stimulated Aristotle to formulate his own doctrine of form and his conceptions of actuality and the final cause. But how far can one go towards answering the other major, and even more obscure, question that I raised concerning the predominant characteristics or pre-occupations of Aristotle's philosophy? As I noted before (p. 25), widely differing views have been taken on this issue. Some have seen Aristotle as first and foremost a biologist, whose metaphysics and ethics alike reflect his experience as a practising naturalist, while others have emphasised the influence that his logic had on other aspects of his work. This too is a question that we must now take up in the light of our suggested analysis of some of the fundamental ideas that run through his philosophy.

The three doctrines of form, finality and actuality are extremely pervasive in his thought. But in each case it seems possible to distinguish between what may be called the primary, and the secondary, uses of the theory. Both the doctrine of potentiality and actuality, and that of final causes, relate primarily to the problems of change and coming-to-be, although to different aspects of those problems. The doctrine of potentiality and actuality—however many and varied its eventual applications—seems most likely to have been originally suggested by the circumstances of the growth of living creatures. Final causes, on the other hand, apply primarily, one might suggest, to the sphere of artificial production, although again within nature living creatures and their parts supply Aristotle with many important examples.

The third doctrine, that of form, is at once a more complex and a more interesting case. The question of immanent versus transcendent form is the chief philosophical problem on which Aristotle took issue with Plato. Two aspects of Aristotle's preference for immanent form have already been emphasised. (1) In some ways the method that he recommends for the philosopher in general is particularly suited to the natural sciences: contrary to Plato's view, the philosopher should investigate form by studying the particular instances of it, but while the particulars provide the starting-point of the process of learning, they are studied not for their own sake, but for the sake of the form they embody. (2) Biological species provide good examples of forms that are both comparatively clearly delimited and self-perpetuating. In these two respects his preference for immanent form may be connected with his interest in natural science and especially in biology. Yet not all his ideas on the subject of form either derive from, or are even well suited to, the study of living creatures. Here we may refer back to the account of 'scientific knowledge' that he gave in the *Posterior Analytics*. In *APo.* 73 b 26 ff. (pp. 123–4) he suggested that 'scientific knowledge' demonstrates connections that are 'universal' in a special sense which he illustrates by referring to the relationship between the attribute 'possessing angles equal to two right angles' and the subject 'triangle'. In this passage his examples are drawn exclusively from mathematics, which clearly provides his chief model in his accounts of both demonstration and definition. Yet those accounts are intended to have a general application, and we noted that elsewhere in the *Posterior Analytics* he includes examples drawn from the biological sciences, such as for instance the syllogism that demonstrates that all broad-leaved trees are deciduous. Yet while his theory of demonstration and definition is well suited to the exact disciplines of mathematics and the mathematical sciences, it has only a very limited relevance to such a science as biology, for the chief problem that faces the biologist—as Aristotle's own practice bears out—is not how to present his knowledge in a syllogistic form that will make clear that the conclusion has been validly demonstrated, but rather to discover the causes that form the middle terms of such syllogisms. Thus in the example in the *Posterior Analytics* II, ch. 17 the conclusion that all broad-leaved trees are deciduous is established by means of a middle term that consists in the definition that sets out the cause of trees being deciduous: he suggests, for the sake of argument, that this is because the sap coagulates at the junction of the leaf-stalk and the stem. But it is just this cause, the definition that states why deciduous trees are deciduous, that the biologist has, of course, to discover. And it is perhaps significant that when he comes to discuss the reasons for deciduousness very briefly in the *de Generatione Animalium*, 783 b 18 ff., he accounts for this in terms of a lack of 'hot fluid', giving a rather more technical explanation than the one he had mentioned for the sake of supplying the middle term in his syllogism in the *Posterior Analytics*.

Aristotle's philosophy is a comprehensive and in the

main well-integrated whole, and no one part of his work dominates all the others in the sense of providing the framework into which his ideas in other inquiries are fitted. Many of his epistemological and ontological doctrines reflect his interest in the problems of change as they affect the world of natural phenomena. Against Plato, Aristotle upholds two theses especially, the immanence of form, and the gradual realisation of form in living things, and his moral philosophy too is profoundly influenced by the ideas of realisation and fulfilment. Yet important though his interests in biology are, they are sometimes subordinated to other considerations: thus the ideas he expressed on the conditions of 'scientific knowledge' in general, and on demonstration and definition in particular, derive not from biology, nor from any other branch of natural science, but from mathematics.

No Greek philosopher was gifted with greater originality than Aristotle. In logic, biology, chemistry, dynamics, psychology, ethics, sociology and literary criticism, he either founded the science or inquiry single-handed or else made a fundamental contribution to it. Yet he remained, of course, very much a product of his age and culture, as we can see when we consider some of the assumptions on which his philosophy is based and contrast them with our own ideas. Three features of his thought may be mentioned particularly in this connection.

Permanence of the cosmos

First his conception of the universe as a whole, and of both nature and society in particular, is strongly influenced by the notion of their permanence. He believes that the universe is eternal. Change certainly takes place in the sublunary region, but the major changes that affect the earth are thought of as forming a cycle that repeats itself continuously. Moreover the ideal is clearly one of complete absence of change of any sort, as we can see from his conception of the nature of the unmoved mover: Aristotle's unchanging first principle may be compared with other examples of a preference for an unchanging reality in earlier Greek philosophy, notably with Parmenides' conception of being, and Plato's theory of Forms. Then Aristotle not only declares that the heavens are completely unchanging, but also assumes that the natural species of the sublunary region are fixed and permanent. In the sphere of politics, too, while he puts forward various ideas about the developments that had taken place in human society in the past, the city-state represents his ideal, and he neither anticipates nor desires further major changes in social institutions. Even in his theory of literature, finally, he assumes that the various literary genres had, in his day, reached their natural forms. Three ideas which play a fundamental part in our own world-view are all quite foreign to Aristotle: these are (1) the cosmological idea of an expanding universe, (2) the biological idea of the evolution of natural species, and (3) the socio-economic idea of continuing material progress to be achieved by applying scientific knowledge to technological invention.

Rationality

Secondly, Aristotle's thought is dominated by the twin ideas (1) of the rationality of the universe, and (2) of the ability of the human reason to comprehend it. The world is finite and orderly—a cosmos. Both in the heavens and in the operations of nature in the sublunary region events take place 'always' or 'for the most part', not merely randomly. In this orderly universe, man's place is privileged. Although Aristotle has some appreciation of how tiny the sublunary region is in comparison with the rest of the universe (pp. 138 and 163 f.), there is no doubt in his mind about the importance of man in the scale of being, for man possesses reason, the faculty that Aristotle also attributes to the gods. The causes of things are there for the human intellect to discover: in our progress towards knowledge we proceed from what is better known to us to what is better known absolutely, and this idea of what is 'better known absolutely' is eloquent testimony to his belief in the objectivity of the intelligible structure of the universe. Here too our own ideas and expectations differ in many respects from those of Aristotle. Whatever we believe about the place of the human species in the universe, astronomy has long ago removed the earth from the centre of the solar system and established that the sun itself, so far from being unique of its kind, is one of many millions of similar stars. Again although Aristotle recognises that different degrees of precision are to be sought in different inquiries, the ideal of certainty in knowledge is still a powerful influence in his thought, especially in his analysis of the different modes of reasoning and in his theory of definition. But the demand for certain knowledge, which is such a prominent feature of Greek thought as a whole and not just of Aristotle's, has been modified or undermined from different points of view both by philosophy and by science. First Aristotle's attempt to reduce other modes of reasoning, including induction, to the syllogistic form would today be considered misconceived: moreover the assumption that pervades his logic is that the great majority of things are named 'synonymously'—or that the great majority of terms are univocal —and this assumption is questionable, to say the least. Secondly, while modern science has shown how much useful information can be obtained about the workings of the physical universe, it has also taught us a great deal about the limits that exist to what can be observed, both on the macro-cosmic scale—galaxies receding at close to the speed of light—and at the level of fundamental particles— where Heisenberg's uncertainty principle suggests that the velocity and the position of a particle cannot both be measured accurately at the same time.

Authoritarianism

Thirdly, the authoritarianism that pervades so much of Aristotle's thought contrasts sharply with twentieth-century liberal ideals. His assumption that the master/slave distinction is a natural and permanent feature of society is repugnant to us. While he believes that a good constitution should ensure the good of all the parts of the state, he believes that those parts do not all have equal rights and deserts: so it is good not only for the rulers to rule, but also for the slaves to be ruled. There is a marked contrast between our picture and Aristotle's of what the good society is like. Yet we should perhaps remark that twentieth-century society remains in many ways just as inegalitarian as the city-state of Aristotle's day. Powerful though the ideal of egalitarianism is as an ideal, it remains as far from realisation in our own society as Aristotle's conception of a state in which virtuous citizens control willing subjects did in antiquity.

Aristotle's influence

To attempt to cover the history of Aristotle's influence on subsequent thought in full would be not far short of undertaking to write the history of European philosophy and science, at least down to the sixteenth century. Some very brief notes may, however, serve as an introduction to this complex and fascinating subject. The importance of the school Aristotle founded, the Lyceum, has already been remarked. The next two heads, Theophrastus and Strato, while of course much influenced by Aristotle, were both independent thinkers of considerable calibre. Theophrastus continued Aristotle's studies in the natural sciences with extensive and valuable botanical treatises. Besides being an extremely talented naturalist, he continued Aristotle's researches in the history of ideas with works on the history of physical theories and on the history of theories of sense-perception. Moreover he brought a critical mind to bear on some of the central doctrines of Aristotle's philosophy, making penetrating criticisms of the four-element theory in his work *On Fire* and of the doctrine of final causes in his *Metaphysics*. We know much less about the work of Strato. Only fragments of his treatises remain, but to judge from their titles his interests were wide, and his independence can be judged especially from his work in physics, where he was an original experimentalist and evolved a physical theory which was far removed from that of Aristotle.

After Strato and until the edition of Andronicus in the first century B.C., Aristotle was, as I noted, mainly, if not perhaps exclusively, known from the literary works rather than from the treatises. In the third century B.C. the main centre of scientific research passed from Athens to the Museum at Alexandria. Meanwhile, however, if we look for signs of Aristotle's continuing influence in this and the following century, we may turn to the early Stoics who took over a good deal from the teaching of Aristotle even though they rejected the greater proportion of it. In physics, for instance, they adapted the doctrine of the four elements to their own theory, and while the originality of their logic should not be underestimated, they were fairly clearly building on Aristotle's work in, for example, their doctrine of categories. After Andronicus' edition Aristotle was, of course, much more accessible, at least to those interested in philosophy and science, and we can judge the value attached to his physics from Galen (second century A.D.) who knew and quoted freely from both the biological and the other physical treatises and who incorporated the doctrine of the four primary opposites into his own physical system.

Among Galen's voluminous writings, which include extensive commentaries on many of the Hippocratic treatises and on Plato's *Timaeus*, were, according to Galen himself, twenty-two books of commentaries, now lost, on the *de Interpretatione* and the *Prior* and *Posterior Analytics*, and from the second to the sixth century A.D. there is a series of writers who produced exhaustive line-by-line commentaries on Aristotle's works, concentrating mostly on the logical and physical treatises and on the *Metaphysics*: the ethics, politics and biology were largely neglected. This was the hey-day of Aristotelian scholarship and Aristotelian influence in antiquity. Alexander of Aphrodisias in the period around A.D. 200, Porphyry in the third century, Philoponus and Simplicius in the sixth, stand out as the greatest names from a host of other, lesser figures, and some of his commentators, at least, were not only highly perceptive and ingenious interpreters of Aristotle's words, but also intelligent critics of his thought. In the sixth centry, Philoponus, in particular, raised some fundamental objections to Aristotelian dynamics and attempted to arrive at more satisfactory general theories of motion. As a rule, however, both the Aristotelian and to a lesser extent the Platonic commentators of late antiquity wrote in a spirit of deference to the authority of their originals, convinced not merely that the texts they were interpreting were worth preserving for future generations, but also that they contained the truth.

In 529 Justinian closed the schools of philosophy at Athens, and although Greek Aristotelian scholarship continued for many centuries in Constantinople, it suffered a gradual decline. Aristotle's thought was eventually transmitted to the West by two quite different routes. First a small proportion of the logical works was known from the Latin translations, commentaries and paraphrases of Boethius (late fifth–early sixth century). These represented not just the core, but almost the sum total, of what survived of Aristotle in Europe from the seventh to the twelfth centuries. From Constantinople, however, knowledge of a far greater body of Aristotle's work passed by a much more devious route, through translations first into Syriac, and then into Arabic, back to the West. From the ninth to the twelfth century we find a number of Arabic scholar-philosophers who developed systems much influenced by Greek philosophy, and especially by Platonism and Aristotelianism. Indeed these Greek influences gradually grew in importance from al-Kindi in the ninth and al-Farabi in the tenth century to Avicenna (ibn Sina) at the beginning of the eleventh. And then in the twelfth the man who came to be known simply as 'the Commentator', Averroes (ibn Rushd), produced expositions of almost all the treatises of Aristotle that we possess. For Averroes Aristotle was 'an example which nature devised to demonstrate supreme human perfection' (*Commentary on de Anima* III), and he declared that Aristotle not only discovered but also carried to perfection the three main branches of knowledge, logic, natural science and metaphysics (*Preface to Physics*).

Latin translations of the Arabic texts and commentaries of Aristotle began to reach the rest of Europe from Spain from about the second or third decade of the twelfth century. The first treatises to arrive were the logical works, including those more technical parts of the *Organon*, in particular the *Prior* and *Posterior Analytics*, that had only been partially known from Boethius. But these were soon followed by translations of the physical treatises as well. Gerard of Cremona, for example, who worked at Toledo in the middle of the century, translated into Latin from the Arabic the *Physics*, the *de Caelo*, the *de Generatione et Corruptione* and the first three books of the *Meteorologica*, along with a great deal else, including the *Almagest* of Ptolemy. The *de Anima* and parts of the *Parva Naturalia*, the *Metaphysics* and the *Nicomachean Ethics* were also known in Europe by 1200. In general the reception these works had was enthusiastic. But some saw in Greek philosophy as a whole and in Aristotle in particular a threat to Christian orthodoxy, and during the thirteenth century the ecclesiastical authorities on several occasions condemned parts of Aristotle's work. First in 1210 the Council of Paris forbade the study of his natural philosophy on pain of excommunication, and other bans were promulgated in 1215, 1231, 1245 and 1263, culminating in the condemnation of 219 heretical theses—many of them Aristotelian—in the teaching of Siger of Brabant in 1277. But despite these proscriptions, or even perhaps partly because of them, knowledge of Aristotle increased very rapidly and so too did his popularity.

Most of the versions of Aristotle that became available in the West in the twelfth century were translations from the Arabic. But translations direct from the Greek original had already begun to be made by the end of the century by the still quite small band of scholars who had studied Greek. Direct contact with the East increased as the power of Constantinople declined—in 1204 the city itself was captured by the Crusaders—and scholars directed their efforts towards establishing the true teachings of Aristotle and the other Greek philosophers, which had often been obscured by the Arabic and other commentators. The greatest of the thirteenth-century translators—some have said the greatest of all Aristotle's translators—was William of Moerbeke, who was responsible for the Latin translations on which the commentaries of St Thomas Aquinas were mainly based.

By the middle of the thirteenth century Aristotle had achieved a position of extraordinary preeminence over the whole range of intellectual studies. In the universities he had more or less replaced the traditional education in the seven liberal arts—grammar, logic, rhetoric, music, geometry, arithmetic and astronomy—and often constituted the major part of the arts course. The prescribed books in the arts course in Paris in the year 1255, for example, included the *Organon*, most of the physical works—including the *Physics*, the *de Caelo*, the *de Generatione et Corruptione*, the *de Anima*, most of the *Parva Naturalia* and some of the biological treatises—the *Metaphysics* and the *Ethics*. Then with Aquinas himself (1225–74) we reach the high-water-mark of Aristotelian influence. The Arabic philosophers had already attempted to show how Aristotelian metaphysics might be reconciled with the religious faith of Islam. But Aquinas produced a far more complete, thorough-going and logically consistent synthesis of Aristotelian philosophy and Christianity, thereby both ensuring Aristotle's respectability, and enshrining a good deal of his thought in the subsequent teaching of the Church.

From this high point the relative influence and importance of Aristotle declined, as it was bound to do as science and philosophy developed. Indeed where in the thirteenth century many important thinkers had devoted a great deal of their energy to getting Aristotle understood and accepted, in later centuries the very dominance that he had achieved became a major obstacle to progress in science and philosophy. The fall of Constantinople in 1453 brought about an increase both in the number of Greek philosophical texts available in the West and in the number of scholars who were able to study them. The Renaissance was, however, more remarkable for the revival of Platonism than for Aristotelian studies, although Zabarella produced a distinguished series of commentaries in the sixteenth century. But in this and subsequent centuries Aristotle's influence is to be measured no longer by the eagerness with which scholars attempted to interpret what he said, but by the pains the leading thinkers took to refute him. Whether one turns to the chief propagandist of the new science, Francis Bacon—whose *Novum Organum* appeared in 1620—or to practising scientists such as Galileo—whose *Discorsi* appeared in 1638—or Boyle—whose *Sceptical Chymist* was published in 1661—they all produced passages of scathing invective against Aristotelianism, and although their principal opponents were contemporary Aristotelians rather than Aristotle himself, they were not always careful to discriminate between the two. In philosophy, too, attacks on Aristotle were almost equally prominent. Hobbes, in particular, complained at the extent of Aristotle's continuing influence and frequently poured scorn on his ideas as, for instance, in *Leviathan* (1651): 'I believe that scarce anything can be more absurdly said in natural philosophy, than that which now is called Aristotle's *Metaphysics*; nor more repugnant to government, than much of that he hath said in his *Politics*; nor more ignorantly, than a great part of his *Ethics*' (Part IV, ch. 46).

After the thirteenth century Aristotle no longer represented most of what was best in philosophy and science, and he came to be identified with a narrow-minded conservatism in those fields. He continued, however, to command admiration bordering on idolatry in other quarters. The strange story of the influence exercised by the *Poetics* on European literature begins in the fifteenth century in Italy, but that influence reached a peak in seventeenth-century France. Both Corneille and Racine believed that they constructed tragedies according to the principles that Aristotle had laid down, principles which Corneille, for example, declared to be valid 'for all peoples and for all time' (*Avertissement* to *Le Cid*, 1636).

In the greater part of this history it is fair to say both of those who admired and imitated Aristotle, and of those who refuted and denigrated him, that they had at best a vague and inaccurate notion of his philosophy. Often, indeed, his thought was quite distorted, but even those who deliberately set out to correct such misinterpretations and to restore the genuine doctrines of Aristotle himself were in general only partially successful. It was not, in fact, until towards the middle of the nineteenth century that a reasonably accurate and objective picture of Aristotle's philosophy was achieved. The major fruit of nineteenth-century scholarship was to establish a reliable text of the extant treatises: the great Berlin edition began to appear in 1831. But although the improvement in the understanding of Aristotle was considerable, most nineteenth-century interpreters—as I noted at the outset—still tended to misrepresent his thought in one important respect, in that they treated it as a static, monolithic, dogmatic system, and this tendency has only been counteracted in the present century.

For us today Aristotle has long ago ceased to be the major, let alone the sole, repository of human wisdom, and yet it is hardly surprising that he continues to be studied so widely and with such interest and respect. His physical treatises are no longer the point at which the student of natural science begins his course. But a knowledge of his work is, of course, a prerequisite for an understanding of the beginnings of modern science in the seventeenth century. In philosophy he is of much more than merely historical interest. Not only is he essential reading in any study of the history of western philosophy, but on many problems, in both moral philosophy and metaphysics, what he has to say also has continuing importance to practising philosophers. Moreover apart from the various attractions that the different aspects of his work continue to have, he engages our attention simply because it was one and the same man who was responsible for so many valuable contributions in so many different branches of thought. For all interested in the workings of the human intellect, Aristotle remains, for the power, range and originality of his thought, a most absorbing and rewarding subject of study.

SUGGESTIONS FOR FURTHER READING

General works

I have selected eight of the most useful books on Aristotle in English and made some brief comments on their nature and scope:

D. J. Allan, *The Philosophy of Aristotle*, 2nd edition (Oxford, 1970). A most illuminating discussion of the essentials of Aristotle's thought.

Sir David Ross, *Aristotle*, 5th edition (London, 1949) A comprehensive account, valuable as a work of reference.

W. Jaeger, *Aristotle: Fundamentals of the History of his Development*, 2nd edition, translated by R. Robinson (Oxford, 1948). The pioneer work on the development of Aristotle's thought.

A. E. Taylor, *Aristotle*, revised edition (London, 1943). A stimulating, short account.

G. R. G. Mure, *Aristotle* (London, 1932). Includes a brief account of earlier Greek philosophy and is particularly helpful on Aristotle's metaphysics and logic.

M. Grene, *A Portrait of Aristotle* (London, 1963). Includes an excellent discussion of the influence of biological interests on Aristotle's thought and ch. 1 contains an important critique of work on Aristotle's development since Jaeger.

J. H. Randall, *Aristotle* (New York, 1960). Stimulating, but open to the criticism that it makes Aristotle seem more modern than he is.

J. L. Stocks, *Aristotelianism* (London and New York, 1925). Contains the best short account of Aristotle's influence on subsequent thought.

Editions, commentaries and translations

The latest complete edition is the Berlin Academy Edition (1831–70) and the treatises are still referred to according to its pages.

Particular editions and/or commentaries that are especially valuable are:

Sir David Ross' *Physics* (Oxford, 1936), *Metaphysics*, 2 vols. (Oxford, 1924) and *de Anima* (Oxford, 1961).

R. D. Hicks' *de Anima* (Cambridge, 1907)

H. H. Joachim's *de Generatione et Corruptione* (*Aristotle On Coming-to-be and Passing-away*) (Oxford, 1922) and commentary on the *Nicomachean Ethics*, ed. D. A. Rees (Oxford, 1951).

J. Burnet's *The Ethics of Aristotle* (London, 1900)

The best complete translation is the Oxford Translation, 12 vols. (*The Works of Aristotle translated into English*) edited by Ross. Some volumes (for example *Historia Animalium*) also contain extremely valuable notes.

For most of the treatises there is also a Loeb edition with translation. Those of the *de Caelo* (W. K. C. Guthrie), *Meteorologica* (H. D. P. Lee) and the biological treatises (A. L. Peck) are particularly valuable.

The Clarendon Aristotle series (edited by J. L. Ackrill, in progress) contains several excellent translations with detailed commentaries, namely Ackrill's own *Categories* and *de Interpretatione*, R. Robinson's *Politics* III and IV, D.W. Hamlyn's *de Anima* II and III, W. Charlton's *Physics* I and II, D. M. Balme's *de Partibus Animalium* I and *de Generatione Animalium* I, C. Kirwan's *Metaphysics* Γ, Δ, E, J. Annas' *Metaphysics* M and N, and J. Barnes' *Posterior Analytics*.

J. R. Bambrough, *The Philosophy of Aristotle* (Mentor books, 1963). Contains translations of selected texts, and very useful introductions to the main branches of Aristotle's philosophy.

Further bibliography: the bibliography in the latest edition of Ross' *Aristotle* may be consulted in the first instance: this may be supplemented by referring to the extensive bibliography in I. Düring, *Aristotles: Darstellung und Interpretation seines Denkens* (Heidelberg, 1966), and to the comprehensive up-to-date bibliographies in the four volumes of *Articles on Aristotle* (edited by Jonathan Barnes, Malcolm Schofield, Richard Sorabji, London, 1975-9), where many of the most important recent articles, some translated from French or German, and some in revised versions, are reprinted.

GLOSSARY OF GREEK TERMS

I list some of the main difficult or technical Aristotelian terms, giving the translations I have used, and referring to the chief pages of the text where the meaning is explained.

ἀκρασία	lack of self-control, 233–4
δύναμις	(i) potentiality, (ii) faculty, 63–5, 187, 216, 292
εἶδος	form, species, 55, 58–60, 92
ἐνέργεια	actuality, activity, 63–5, 291–2
ἐντελέχεια	actuality, fulfilment, 185, 292
ἕξις	habit, disposition, condition, 198, 216–17
ἐπιστήμη	scientific knowledge, 122–3, 224
κάθαρσις	purging, 280–1
καθ' αὑτό and κατὰ συμβεβηκός	essential and accidental, 128
κατηγορία	(i) predicate, (ii) category, 112–16
κοινὰ αἰσθητά	common sensibles, 194
μίμησις	representation, 274–5
μῖξις	combination, 172
νοῦς	reason, rational intuition, 195–8, 224, 238
ὁμοιομερής	uniform, 171
οὐσία	being, substance, 48, 52, 113, 129–32
πολιτεία	(i) constitution, (ii) 'constitutional government', 254–5
προαίρεσις	choice, purpose, 230–1
στέρησις	privation, 58
σύνθεσις	agglomeration, 171–2
τὸ τί ἦν εἶναι	the 'what it is to be a thing', essence, 48, 129–31
ὑποκείμενον	(i) substratum, (ii) subject, 58, 114
φαινόμενα	phenomena, 'what is thought to be the case', 57, 79, 206, 286
φαντασία	imagination, 190–2
φρόνησις	practical intelligence, 224–7
φύσις, φυσική	nature, the study of nature, 133
ψυχή	soul, 181–2

GENERAL INDEX

GENERAL INDEX

324